INVISIBLE
ICEBERG

INVISIBLE ICEBERG

WHEN CLIMATE AND WEATHER SHAPED HISTORY

DR. JOEL N. MYERS

Skyhorse Publishing

Copyright © 2024 by Joel N. Myers

All rights reserved. No part of this book may be reproduced in any manner without the express written consent of the publisher, except in the case of brief excerpts in critical reviews or articles. All inquiries should be addressed to Skyhorse Publishing, 307 West 36th Street, 11th Floor, New York, NY 10018.

Skyhorse Publishing books may be purchased in bulk at special discounts for sales promotion, corporate gifts, fund-raising, or educational purposes. Special editions can also be created to specifications. For details, contact the Special Sales Department, Skyhorse Publishing, 307 West 36th Street, 11th Floor, New York, NY 10018 or info@skyhorsepublishing.com.

Skyhorse® and Skyhorse Publishing® are registered trademarks of Skyhorse Publishing, Inc.®, a Delaware corporation.

Visit our website at www.skyhorsepublishing.com.

10 9 8 7 6 5 4 3 2 1

Library of Congress Cataloging-in-Publication Data is available on file.

Cover design by Kai Texel
Cover images from Getty Images and Wikimedia Commons

Print ISBN: 978-1-5107-7663-0
Ebook ISBN: 978-1-5107-7664-7

Printed in the United States of America

Contents

Foreword

I first met Joel in 1974, as a new meteorology grad student at Pennsylvania State University. I won the department's forecasting contest and caught the attention of Professor Myers, who was teaching the department's main weather forecasting course. I became his teaching assistant and a couple of years later, after getting my master's degree, survived a grueling interview process and landed a three-year contract at his budding company, AccuWeather.

And the rest is, well, history. Forty-five years later, I am still employed at AccuWeather, and Joel is still actively managing the company as executive chairman of what has become one of the world's largest non-governmental weather forecasting entities, founded by Joel in 1962. I've had the privilege of eye-witnessing him through productive decades—his many innovations, relentless striving, and deep dedication in steering and growing AccuWeather and its forecasting victories leading to saving tens of thousands of lives and billions of dollars.

Of course, weather affects all of us nearly every day. From the rain that curtails our outdoor activities, to the blizzard that causes us to stock up on milk and toilet paper, to the drought that causes our food prices to rise, to the hurricane that causes extensive damage and increased insurance premiums, to the excess heat and poor air quality that threaten our health, weather plays a role in nearly every human activity. This book reflects Joel's great interest in both weather and history, examining the weather and climate events that changed more than just our activities, but also altered the very flow of human history. The world would be a very different place today if not for these weather and climate events.

If not for the change in climate brought about when an asteroid or comet hit the Yucatan Peninsula sixty-six million years ago, dinosaurs might still be Earth's dominant lifeform.

If not for dense fog and later, a sudden turn to colder weather, George Washington would have almost certainly been defeated and likely hung for treason.

If not for cold Russian winters, Napoleon might have conquered the world and Germany might have won World War II.

And if rain had only lasted an hour longer in Dallas on November 22, 1963, the presidential limousine would have had its glass top on, John F. Kennedy would have likely been reelected as president, and the United States might never have escalated its war in Vietnam.

So sit back and enjoy your reading—Joel is about to take you on a magical journey through the history of what was and even suggestions of how history might have been—if only the weather was different.

—**Michael Steinberg**

Introduction

"Snow! Snow! Snow!"

I grew up in the northern part of Philadelphia within a couple of miles of the border with Cheltenham. My mother tells me that when I was three years old I fell in love with snow. When the flakes began to fall and made the world outside a beautiful, clean landscape, I would stand at the window, pointing, full of excitement.

Weather, I saw, can transform the world. I do not point at the window and say "snow" anymore, but I still find storms thrilling.

One of my most vivid early memories is of a snowstorm that happened when I was seven years old. My aunt was marooned in our house because the streets were impassable and everything was shut down. I kept coming downstairs during the night to look out the window at the snow that kept accumulating. It filled me with the same sense of awe and beauty, but now I was old enough to understand what an impact the snow had on the entire community. There were no cars on the road. It didn't matter what plans my aunt or anyone else had made for the evening, we all had to stay inside and wait.

It was my first inkling of how not only the landscape, but also people's lives can be transformed by the weather. If my family could be sidelined, so could generals, kings, presidents, even entire civilizations.

As fortune would have it, that same year my grandmother gave me a diary. I used it to record daily weather conditions, and I started to recognize patterns. I started getting up early to listen to the weather reports on the radio to see if I could figure out when the next snow was going to come. This began a life-long passion to try to understand and predict the weather.

The snowstorm that hit the Philadelphia area on November 6, 1953 did not go down in history as a great turning point in the nation, but it did have a major impact on my life. That morning, of course, I listened to the forecast before I set off to school on my bicycle.

The radio said it would be cloudy with a high of 50 degrees and a chance of a shower. By the time the school day had finished, it was 33 degrees and snow was accumulating on the ground, falling at a rate of two inches per hour. It took me forty-five minutes to push my bike the one mile back to my house. I went to an open grass area and measured the accumulation and came up with thirteen inches even though the official total was only 8.8 inches. That measurement was taken at the airport, next to a river with lots of paved surfaces. What is true at the airport is not necessarily true in a neighborhood several miles away, which has a slightly higher elevation.

I started to think that maybe I could do better than the people I listened to on the radio, and this led me on the path that eventually became AccuWeather.

In its first years of operation, AccuWeather quickly became known for the accuracy of our forecasts (hence the name). When I first began gathering radio and television clients, I needed a brand name that would properly identify and represent the forecasts we were providing. After much consideration, I chose AccuWeather. It represented the most important distinguishing character of our forecasts, that we would be more accurate, more precise, more detailed than any other source. That was our goal, that was our mission, and that was the charge to all our early team members. That continues to be the case today.

It was important that we work hard to defend that brand and our first major test came in June 1972. Government forecasters, whose forecasts were available for free, were predicting that most of the heavy rains from Tropical Storm Agnes would occur in the western part of Pennsylvania, but would spare Eastern Pennsylvania. They were slow to recognize that Tropical Storm Agnes would produce serious flooding in Eastern Pennsylvania and particularly the Pocono Mountains, where ultimately about fifty people would die. AccuWeather predicted, well ahead of any other source, that there would be widespread flooding in those areas. The storm eventually came to be known as "Hurricane Agony." It caused the waters of the Susquehanna River to rise to a record height, and the flooding caused extensive property damage along the river and its tributaries. But even though it is counted among one of the state's worst natural disasters, thanks to our warnings and advice, several people avoided this fate. This was when the responsibility of my chosen profession really hit home. Early warnings are critical. Accurate weather forecasts can save lives. Over the years, thanks to our dedication to Superior Accuracy, AccuWeather's forecasts have probably saved over ten thousand lives and prevented injury to tens of thousands more, and saved tens of billions of dollars in property damage.

In that sense, maybe you could say that the snowstorm in 1953 did change the course of history. That is how it is with the weather. The atmospheric phenomena are so vast that their impacts can be felt miles away or years down the line. Throughout the course of this book you will learn about the hurricanes, the snowstorms, the droughts, and even the sunny days that changed the course of history and even the path of civilization. I hope you will find these stories as fascinating as I have and come to fully appreciate the important role that weather events and climate have played in shaping humanity and civilization.

And of course, with climate change continuing, undoubtedly with a significant portion of it due to human activity, the story continues. A sequel to this book to be written in decades hence will hopefully include many more chapters showing that, through innovation, science, technology, creativity, and common purpose, humans will prevent the disasters that might occur if global warming exceeds a tipping point.

Chapter

1

The Comet That Ended the Age of the Dinosaur

It is my firm belief that human history is, at its core, the story of how our species adapted to weather and climate and its changes through the course of time. Climate change has been with us since long before industrialization brought smokestacks and car fumes. Modern climate change, exacerbated by human activity, and how to respond to it is one of the major challenges of our time. But it's only one chapter in a long history of humans' relationship to climate. Variations in the earth's tilt and orbit, solar cycles, continental drifts, and dramatic events such as volcanic eruptions and meteorite strikes have all caused shifts in the environment we inhabit, sometimes very dramatic ones.

Climate colors every aspect of the world's various cultures from the clothes we wear (or don't wear), to the foods we eat, to the holidays we celebrate, to the wars we fight and the gods we worship. Every great empire in history has risen or fallen, in part, because of changes in climate. Climate change causes droughts and booms in insect populations that cause crops to fail, livestock to die, and has triggered pandemics that have decimated whole populations. Changes in the temperature of the seas can alter coastlines and access to food from the waters. When these changes cause widespread famine, as they are especially prone to do in agrarian societies, it leads to political instability. Hungry nations are vulnerable nations. Mass migrations when one area becomes inhospitable lead to clashes over territory and spark wars. No society is immune.

In order to set the scene to tell this complex story, we must go back, way back, before recorded history to the most important climate event for humankind: a comet or meteorite strike that led to the mass extinction of the dinosaurs. This paved the way for our ancient ancestors to emerge as the dominant life form on the planet.

Sixty-six million years ago the earth was teeming with dinosaur life. These were not only the tyrannosaurus rex and brontosaurus that have fascinated generations of school children. Dinosaur remains have been found on every continent, as they adapted to various climates, producing great variety. There were carnivores and herbivores. Some were feathered, some had plates and horns, and some were warm-blooded. There were dinosaurs the size of small rodents and others up to 77 tons (70 tonnes) and 125 ft (38 m), ten times bigger than any land animal today. (But not bigger than the blue whale, which can get up to 198 tons/180 tonnes.) There were even dinosaurs who roamed verdant polar forests.

Then, in an instant, everything changed. A massive asteroid or comet, traveling at about 12 miles/20 km per second, hit the ground at an angle of around 60 degrees from horizontal in what are now the Yucatan Peninsula and the Gulf of Mexico. It struck sulfur-rich rocks with such force that it left a crater 90 miles/145 km in diameter. The 60-degree angle was perhaps the death knell for the dinosaurs. It was just the right angle to hurtle the maximum quantity of vaporized rock into the air. If it had come in from directly overhead it would have left a deeper crater, but not thrown up as much debris. If it had come in at a steeper angle, it would have skipped across the surface. A heat pulse, with the force of 100,000,000 atomic bombs, traveled 900 miles/1,448 km in all directions, and fires caused by frictional heating rained down upon the earth. Trees around the world burst into flame. Vaporized sulfur mixed with water created a thick aerosol haze and acid rain. The impact also set off a series of earthquakes, which triggered a 650-ft/198-m tsunami in what is now the Caribbean. This is similar to a sixty-story building. These events further spread the thick dust and debris. Between the vaporized rock in the atmosphere and smoke from the widespread fires, much of the sunlight was blocked.

Any plants that had been spared by the fire were soon killed by the continual darkness and cooling that followed. Photosynthesis was arrested even as the oceans were acidified by the rain. This caused a die-off of marine life. The food chain was entirely disrupted. (According to the United Nations Intergovernmental Panel on Climate Change, something similar, but on a much slower scale, is happening today. As our carbon dioxide emissions cause the earth to warm, they are also acidifying the oceans.) It was virtually impossible to distinguish day from night. Instead of blue skies or gray clouds that brought rain, the daytime sky was almost black with virtually no daylight and a constant thick precipitation of dirt and toxic acid. Temperatures did not climb much during the daytime as they do now, and since the entire world was significantly colder due to the debris in the atmosphere reflecting much of the sunlight back into space and thereby preventing the sun's rays from warming the earth, it was a cold, dark, foreboding, other-worldly place. Almost no life survived. For a while, the earth was almost a dead planet, yet this toxic stew, as amazing as it is improbable, led to the eventual rise of humans as the dominant life form of the world of today.

Between 70 to 75 percent of all known species were wiped out. No animal larger than 55 lb/25 kg survived. Fortunately for humans, one such small creature, the cynodont, lived and became the ancestor of modern mammals.[1]

Even a slight alteration in the meteor's trajectory might have been enough to spare some of the dinosaurs. Imagine what the world would be like today if that asteroid had missed the earth. A lot of time has passed since then, enough time for dinosaurs to evolve. In 1982, Dale Russell of the Canadian Museum of Nature in Ottawa published a paper that speculated the carnivorous dinosaur, Troodon, which had a large brain, could have evolved into a line of intelligent "dinosauroids."

If intelligent mammals and intelligent dinosaurs developed side by side, climate events could have wiped out human life instead. In fact, some seventy to seventy-five thousand years ago it almost did. This was thirty-five times further back in time than when Jesus walked the earth. Since the advent of DNA studies, scientists have discovered that human beings have much less genetic variation than other primates. A single group of chimpanzees or gorillas has more genetic variation than our entire human population of 7.8 billion people.

Some scientists believe this is because of an event that wiped out a significant portion of the human population. Some estimates put the number of survivors at as few as five hundred procreating pairs of humans, while others suggest there were somewhere between one and ten thousand.

One of the main theories as to the cause of the die-off was the massive eruption of the Toba volcano on what is now the Indonesian island of Sumatra, which occurred around seventy-four thousand years ago. Its explosion sent a plume of gasses, rock, and ash 19 miles/30 km high. The debris was scattered as far away as Greenland and the volcano blasted enough molten rock (about 684 cu mi/2,800 cu km) into the atmosphere to build more than a million Egyptian pyramids.

Historic climate models suggest that the Toba eruption may have caused temperatures to plummet by as much as 30°F/-1.1°C. Such dramatic cooling could have allowed glaciers to dramatically advance, sea levels to drop signficantly, rainfall to slow, and plants to stop growing.

In the reduced sunlight and blanket of ash, nearly all broad leaf evergreen trees and tropical deciduous trees disappeared for several years.

There were, of course, no contemporary measurements of temperatures in those days. Archaeologists and geologists calculate, however, that in the wake of the Toba volcano, global mean temperatures dropped by an average of 22° F/12° C over the next five to six years, ushering in a thousand-year ice age. Homo sapiens were in danger of disappearing as other human species like the Neanderthals had, but a few survived in small groups in Africa, Europe, and Asia. It took twenty thousand years before our human population got back to its pre-volcano levels.

Not all scientists are convinced that the Toba volcano was responsible for the population bottleneck. Archaeologists have discovered evidence of settlements in India and Eastern Africa from the period that do not seem to have been greatly affected by the eruption. East Africa may also have escaped relatively unscathed. Do these settlements contradict the volcano theory or could survivors in these regions have thrived as people with other genetic traits were wiped out, accounting for the lowered genetic variation?

If it was not the volcano, what caused the prehistoric human population to contract seventy thousand years ago? Scientists can only speculate. Perhaps changes in climate unleashed a pandemic (we will read about a number of times in history when this happened throughout the course of this book).

Toba was not the first eruption of a super volcano, and it will not be the last. The next great ice age could start in Yellowstone National Park. The enchanting scenery of hot springs and geysers is caused by a giant underground magma chamber that extends halfway to the center of the earth. The Yellowstone volcano erupts on average every six hundred thousand years, and its seismic activity is constantly monitored. There are other super-volcanoes in the world, but few would be as lethal to so many millions. Scientists speculate that a volcanic winter caused by the eruption of Yellowstone is one thing that could reverse our current trend of global warming, but such a dramatic and sudden shift could be as devastating as the eruption of Toba.

So if the dinosaurs had survived and developed intelligence, and then lived through the subsequent extinction events that decimated the Homo sapiens population, maybe a descendant of the dinosaurs would be writing a book today about how climate favored their kind over us.

Many archaeologists, however, believe that the more adaptable mammals would likely have emerged dominant in any case, and the dinosaurs would have gone extinct one way or another because of the many climate shifts and ice ages that have happened in the intervening years. Any of these might have tipped the scales in favor of humans. As humans became more intelligent and dominant, they might have hunted dinosaurs to extinction.

John Pickrell, the author of a book on dinosaurs, believes that it is likely human hunting would have reduced dinosaur populations, but he likes to imagine a world in which some of the dinosaurs—maybe even the great tyrannosaurus rex—survived to the present day. "Though in our own past, large mammals were mostly wiped out, a few, such as elephants and rhinos hang on," he wrote, "so perhaps it's not too much of stretch to imagine a parallel world where today you could hop on a dinosaur safari, Jurassic Park-style, and enjoy spotting some of them, cameras and binoculars at the ready."[2]

The Volcano Effect

Throughout the course of this book, we'll learn of many instances in which climate change, brought about by volcanoes, affected the course of history. Volcanoes can affect the climate in a number of ways, depending on how they erupt. In some cases, they belch gas but relatively few dust particles reach the upper atmosphere. In a dramatic explosion, the volcanic particles can be launched well into the stratosphere. If the particles are small enough, they can remain in the stratosphere for several years and sometimes even for decades, reflecting solar radiation back into space, causing temperatures throughout the atmosphere to drop significantly. Temperatures then remain well below the historical average for many several years and, in some cases, even for decades. The particles reduce sunlight, which significantly reduces photosynthesis, thereby decreasing the number of plants that are available for food. In other volcanic eruptions, gases rather than particles are the main emission. The gases burst out of the volcano, and in those cases, the greenhouse effect exceeds the cooling effect from the reflectivity of the particles, resulting in the warming of the entire planet. Gases could also remain in the atmosphere for decades, so the global warming has a significant impact on the distribution of plant and animal life on the planet.

When the particles prevail and cooling occurs, over time snow naturally covers a larger fraction of the continents and for a greater percentage of the year. This then causes a feedback mechanism because the amount of energy that a surface reflects is determined by a property known as its albedo. The higher the albedo, the more solar radiation it reflects back into space and is not available to heat the surface of the atmosphere. In general, light surfaces have a high albedo while dark surfaces have a low albedo, and more heat is absorbed. The urban heat islands is one example where a low albedo causes higher temperatures in and around cities. The earth has an average albedo of 0.30, meaning it reflects about 30 percent of the sun's energy. Water has a low albedo of 0.10, meaning that most of the sunlight reaching the ocean

(Continued on next page)

surface is absorbed and not reflected back into space. Snow, on the other hand, has an extremely high albedo of as high as 0.95, meaning clean, white snow reflects about 95 percent of incoming radiation back into space instead of being absorbed as heat. Even though the cooling effect from dust particles in the atmosphere (by reflecting solar radiation back out into space) is important for cooling after a volcanic eruption that produces a lot of particles, the snow cover that results from the cooling actually can be more important in cooling the earth than the reflectivity from the dust particles. In the Arctic and sub-Arctic regions of both the northern and southern hemisphere, once snow and ice turn into glaciers, they may survive for decades and centuries, continuing to keep those areas and ultimately the entire earth colder than it would have been without the volcanic eruption.

This creates a powerful positive feedback effect. The colder it is, the more snow there will be. There is an old expression I used to use—"snow begets snow"—because snow cover keeps the atmosphere colder and the next storm along the rain-snow boundary is more likely to have snow than rain, whereas without that snow cover a storm might have been more likely to bring rain. Some climatologists have theorized that a warmer planet actually means more snow in the Arctic regions, because more moisture is available—and that brings on the snow blitz theory of an ice age developing quickly, completely reversing the initial warming that triggered.

Think of this on a global scale and the impact can be significant. Even though the dust particles may fall out of the atmosphere from a volcanic eruption, most of them within three to five years, the lingering effect of the snow reflectivity can last for decades, literally changing the climate. Dramatic cooling can follow a series of volcanic eruptions, or one that erupts several times within a five-to-ten-year period and can cause cooling for up to a century. In the extreme, this (forgive the pun) snowball effect can lead to an ice age. In the last two million years, we've had four major advances and retreats of glaciers. The last of those reached its peak about fifteen to eighteen thousand years ago, and we're still warming from the retreat and melting of that ice age today. At its peak the ice was 2 ½ miles thick over Montreal, Canada and the southern extent of the ice is marked by the rocks in Central Park. The impact of a "nuclear winter" brought about by nuclear explosions might be similar in some ways to the events that exterminated the dinosaurs and much of life that existed on planet Earth at that time.

Chapter

2

The Flood That Decimated Humanity

The best known Biblical weather narrative is a story of weather forecasting. Thanks to a message from God, Noah was able to prepare for a coming flood that none of his neighbors believed was coming. When, as the Bible describes, all the world (or at least the area known as the world) was covered in flood waters, Noah, his family, and one pair each of all earthly animals were able to ride out the storm for forty days and forty nights in the ark he had built.

The Old Testament story is similar to other flood tales told throughout the Mediterranean region by the Greeks, Egyptians, Babylonians, and Sumerians. While the stories that emerged in the cradle of Western civilization are most familiar to us, flood narratives exist in almost every culture. They are so ubiquitous that a Hungarian psychoanalyst once speculated that they are a biological phenomenon, caused by the dreams that come when people sleep with full bladders. It is interesting that there are flood stories of lore in virtually every part of the world. These flood stories are not limited to the Mediterranean region.

But most scholars believe the ancient stories record actual world events. There's even a word for folk tales that explain earthquakes, floods, fires, and so on: geomythology. Geologist David Montgomery, after studying flood myths of many cultures, concluded ". . . while flood myths share common elements—catastrophic inundation; a harrowing escape, usually by boat—the nature of the deluge varies from region to region. And the differences are telling. Often, the features of a fabled flood bear a striking resemblance to local geological processes, suggesting that many myths record real catastrophes witnessed in antiquity."[1] Humans have feared floods and moving water as long as they have been on

Earth. What we characterize as floods may include rapid melting from the glaciers, storm surges from major hurricanes and storms, tidal tsunamis, giant waves caused by meteors, or a combination of rapid snow melt combined with heavy rain, particularly when water is funneled into narrow valleys. Even over the last few hundred years, millions of people on Earth have died in floods.

Montgomery found that many flood tales from coastal regions in Asia and in the North American Pacific Northwest sound a lot like they are referring to tsunamis, whereas the myths of arctic and alpine cultures sound more like glacial dam breaks. Montgomery finds Noah's story similar to those told by people who live in areas that are dependent on rivers. They tend to tell stories of long periods of rain and slowly rising water.

The world's oldest surviving written literature was a flood narrative found in what is present-day Iraq. Recorded on twelve stone tablets, the Sumerian *Epic of Gilgamesh* is an epic poem about a great king. One of the figures the king encounters is Utnapishtim, a man who was granted immortality after building a ship to save his family and samples of all species of animals. After surviving many long days of storms, Utnapishtim, like Noah, released a bird to search for dry land where the travelers could re-start humanity.

Irving Finkel, a curator at the British Museum and author of a book on flood narratives, told *Time* magazine, "There must have been a heritage memory of the destructive power of flood water, based on various terrible floods."[2]

What many of these narratives have in common is great specificity about how the lifesaving ship was constructed. In the case of the Noah narrative, the ark is reported to be 300 cubits long, 50 cubits wide, and 30 cubits high. With a cubit being the distance from a man's elbow to the tip of his middle finger (roughly 18–21 in/46–53 cm), this would be an ark of about 1.5 million cu ft/42,475 cu m, or about a third of the volume of the *Titanic*.

As author Avi Steinberg noted, "In its detailed measurements, the text seems to be an invitation to real-life reconstruction, as though the workability of the ship is presented in order to prove the reality of the rest of the story. The details for the construction of the ship represent the first time in the Bible that the narrator—or, if you will, the Lord himself—insists that the story is literally true."[3]

The similarity in stories across cultures in the area known as the "cradle of civilization," and the detail of the accounts, suggests that they might be different interpretations of the same real historic event.

What is now the Black Sea was once a mere lake. It was divided from the Sea of Marmara by a ridge. Around the lake were a variety of settlements in what are now Turkey, Bulgaria, Moldova, Ukraine, Russia, and Georgia. Suddenly, about 7,500 years ago, as the ice age drew to a close, glaciers began to melt. The water levels in the oceans and seas rose and the forces on the ridge dividing the lake from the sea could not handle the pressure and collapsed. We don't know how fast this might have unfolded. If it occurred in a matter of days or weeks, it might have taken most people by surprise and they would have drowned. If it occurred over decades and centuries, it still would have had a huge disruptive impact on life, but some tribes and groups of people might have been able to adjust, migrate, and survive.

The fossil record shows that at this time freshwater mollusks were replaced with the saltwater variety. An ancient shoreline was found near the current coast of Turkey, and around it were buried stone tools and shards of pottery.

It is estimated that the collapse would have released 10 cu miles/42 cu km of seawater each day. As it flowed in, villages were inundated. When the flooding subsided, the lake, as well as the villages that surrounded it, was gone.

Around the time of the flood, archaeologists have observed that new people and cultures started to appear in such diverse places as Egypt, Prague, Paris, and the foothills of the Himalayas.

It is easy to imagine the protagonists of the flood narratives as the world's first meteorologists, people who were keen observers of natural phenomenon and who took action on the basis of what they saw. Perhaps Noah (or Utnapishtim) realized that the glaciers were melting around him. Seeing the waters rising, he knew it was only a matter of time before all the cities he knew would be inundated. If a glacier melted at a constant rate it could have taken months or even years, giving the forward-thinking Noah ample time to build a large boat.

In 2014, filmmaker Darren Aronofsky earned both critical praise and religious protest for his depiction of Noah as "the first environmentalist." Some Christian groups were offended by how the Hollywood version departed from scripture and many Muslim countries banned the film outright.

Whether Noah was, himself, an early scientist, his story has indisputably impacted the natural sciences.

Belief in the Biblical narrative colored how some of the progenitors of geology viewed the world. When Saint Augustine, in the fourth century, discovered seashells in mountain rock in a Roman province of Africa, he saw the fossils as proof of the great flood. The rising waters, he reasoned, were the only thing that could have raised sea life up to the tops of mountains.

In seventeenth-century Italy, a Danish philosopher, Hicolaus Steno, also referred back to Noah to explain his discovery of fossilized shark teeth inside rocks. He theorized that the earth must have risen out of a primeval sea. In his view, this involved six stages, one of which was Noah's flood. Of course, geologists have taught us that as the earth's crust moves and the continents create different forces, areas that were below sea level have been thrust up into a mountain a mile or higher, so geologists understand that fossils and seashells can be found on the tops of mountains, but when they were deposited they were at the bottom of a sea.

His explanation of how the sedimentary layers worked is known as the "law of superposition." Steno explained that the oldest in a series of rock layers is found at the bottom, with layers becoming progressively younger as they work their way up. This is still one of the foundational principles of geology.

As for the theological significance of the story of Noah and the flood, that is something religious scholars will no doubt debate for centuries to come.

Chapter

3

The Tempest That Ushered in Egypt's New Kingdom

When Ahmose became king of Egypt upon the death of his older brother, sometime between 1500 and 1550 BC, he was only a boy. The kingdom of Egypt itself was at a low point. There was a real chance that the great civilization, already 1,500 years old, was on the verge of being wiped out. Egypt was occupied in the north, and the Hyksos, a Philistine dynasty, had been in discussion with the Nubians to the south with a plan to join forces and take over what was left of the once-thriving empire. By the time Ahmose died, Egypt had defeated both of these rivals, expanded its borders, and begun a massive construction program that laid the groundwork for the most prosperous and powerful era in Egypt's history. In this period, the power structure of Bronze Age empires was entirely realigned.

A new translation of an ancient weather report sheds light on how this happened and explains the important role the weather and climate played. The report is in the form of a forty-line inscription in a block called the Tempest Stela, which was found in pieces in what is now Luxor. In Ahmose's time, it was Thebes, the center of his rule. The text describes a great storm "without cessation, louder than the cries of the masses." It was so fierce that it damaged the pyramids.

Two scholars at the University of Chicago believe that the storm was the result of a massive volcanic explosion at Thera, now known as the island of Santorini, in the Mediterranean Sea, which changed weather patterns in the region.[1] (If this is the case, they argue that the reign of Ahmose, generally dated to about 1550 BC, was actually thirty to fifty years earlier than previously believed.)

The dominant weather pattern in this part of the world is known as the "Red Sea Trough." It ushers in hot, dry air from East Africa. The aftermath of a volcanic explosion could have modified the atmospheric circulation enough to cause the heavy rains and flooding described on the Tempest Stela. The scholars speculate that the weather disruptions weakened the Hyksos by destroying their ports.

Another artifact dating to the reign of Ahmose is the Rhind Mathematical Papyrus. The best known example of a mathematical papyrus to have survived from Ancient Egypt, it was preserved in the tomb of its highly-educated owner. The papyrus shows that the Egyptian scholars had developed advanced mathematical skills including arithmetic, first-order linear equations, second-order algebraic equations, and geometric series. In addition to its mathematical prowess, the papyrus makes a special mention of thunder and rain, which Dr. Robert Ritner, one of the lead scholars of the Chicago study, cites as further proof that Ahmose paid close attention to the weather. In fact, Egypt's particular climate most likely spurred the advances in mathematics itself.

Archaeologists believe Egypt's climate was wetter in Ahmose's time than it is today. Evidence for this can be found in a cave in the southwestern part of Egypt. Although it is surrounded by desert today, it is known as "the cave of swimmers" for its prehistoric rock art containing what appear to be depictions of people swimming. Yet its agriculture was, as it is to a large extent today, dependent on the regular flooding of the Nile River.

The Nile's waters would rise and fall in a predictable pattern. There was an inundation period, which started around July, in which the water would rise and spill out into a series of canals built to supply water to nearby farms. Then, usually around the end of October, came a period of relinquishment. The waters receded, leaving rich deposits of silt behind. Close attention to these patterns ensured the Egyptians' survival. In order to track the pattern, Egyptians developed one of the first writing systems in the world, as well as ink and papyrus on which to preserve it, and they developed a sophisticated calendar. The rhythm of life along the Nile inspired Egyptians to understand life as a cycle of death and rebirth, a view that helped shape their religion as well as those of their neighboring cultures, as we shall see in the next chapter.

This close attention to the weather put Ahmose in a strong position when the Hyksos were weakened by the storm. Ten years after his brother's death, Ahmose launched a marine attack on the Hysksos capital of Arvaris, and followed this with a land campaign. Ahmose thus defeated the Hyskos and became pharaoh of an Egypt that stretched all the way to the Mediterranean. He then marched south and defeated the Nubians, taking over a territory rich in gold mines. Now prosperous, Egypt resumed trade with the cities of the Syrian coast. Thebes became the cultural and religious center of the country. The damaged pyramids were rebuilt and work began on Ahmose's own pyramid. The era that was ushered in with Ahmose's victory over the Hyskos is known as the Eighteenth Dynasty. It was the height of the empire's power.

Egypt's fortunes, with its dependence on the annual cycle of Nile flooding, would continue to be tied to climate fluctuations. A team of researchers studied the well-documented period known as Ptolemaic Egypt, which ran from the years 305–30 BC. They found that there was a strong correlation between revolts, political instability, and decreased expansion when Nile flooding was low and food production was important.[2] But these hardships also spurred innovation.

Ptolemaic Egyptians created technology to get them through extended periods of dryness. By the third century BC, Egyptians had invented a rotary-wheel water-lifting machine and new methods of grain storage. Farming communities also created land sharing agreements so if the Nile did not flood as usual it was less likely that any one family would have all its fields in a drought area. These innovations helped maintain the stable society that produced such cultural gems as the Great Library of Alexandria, where scholars including Pythagoras, Euclid, and Archimedes pursued their studies.

While many ancient civilizations have made marks on the world that are still felt to this day, few have had the impact of Egypt. There are, certainly, no civilizations from that time that have captured the imagination of modern artists, poets, architects, and scholars as Egypt has. Some of Egypt's stories and religious myths were passed on to Greece and Rome and had a direct impact on the development of modern religious belief.

Thanks to Egypt's funereal practices, preserving the bodies of the departed as mummies, Egyptians knew how to dissect corpses, and the medical knowledge they gained was likewise passed on to the Greek and Roman doctors who followed. Many of the magnificent temples and pyramids that were preserved and rebuilt in Ahmose's time stand to inspire artists and architects to the present day. Those tombs contained a wealth of information about the people who built them. Because we know so much about the daily life of ancient Egyptians, they hold a special fascination. Students continue to fill classrooms for courses that study the Egyptians, and museums continue to draw crowds with exhibits dedicated to them, even as the study of other ancient cultures declines. Both the Egyptians and the Mayan culture you will read about later reached their most prosperous times and scientific and cultural peaks during periods of favorable climate conditions for food production. However, it was the uncertainty of the weather and climate from year to year, and the great dependence of the success of their food supply and their society on favorable weather that caused them to excel in their knowledge of the calendar, science, and mathematics. Throughout history, societies that faced challenges that were able to be overcome have become the most advanced. At the other extreme, there are those societies where people could literally walk outside of their hut or cave and find sufficient food, requiring less innovation in order to survive. At the other extreme are the extremely harsh climates, where for example, extreme cold is such a constant threat that they have no time to innovate because they are simply trying to survive the elements. In between these extremes is where much of the innovation and scientific progress has typically occurred throughout history. Over the last hundred years, with the advent of air conditioning and more reliable heating of buildings, we have seen this restriction on innovation lifted.

In today's world with trade and where wealthy countries are able to afford food wherever it is produced, we find the most innovation and scientific progress occurring in places where the seasons occur and where the weather is changeable. Changing weather from day to day and season to season tends to be more stimulative to the mind.

Restoration experts warn that many of these cultural treasures are now at risk as high temperatures and humidity associated with our era's climate change batter the prehistoric stonework of temples and pyramids.

Chapter

Climate Disruption That Caused the Ten Plagues of Egypt

I n the Biblical story of the Exodus, God commands Moses to go to Pharaoh Ramses II and demand the release of the enslaved Israelites. When Pharaoh refused, God unleashed a series of ten plagues on Egypt: a plague of blood—in which the Nile ran red—plagues of frogs, lice, flies, livestock disease, boils, hail, locusts, darkness, and the killing of firstborn male children. The evening before the final plague, Moses instructed his people to sacrifice a lamb and paint their doors with its blood so the angel of death would know which homes were Hebrew and should be passed over, sparing their firstborn sons while non-Hebrew infants perished. This is the origin of the Jewish Passover, which celebrates the Hebrews' liberation from slavery. Biblical stories are, of course, matters of faith, but they have continued to fascinate scholars who search for historic events that might underpin them.

Modern archaeologists widely believe that the series of plagues really happened in the ancient city of Pi-Ramses on the Nile Delta. It was the capital during the reign of Pharaoh Ramses II, who ruled between 1279 BC and 1213 BC. Then, around three thousand years ago, the great city was abandoned. What happened?

According to climatologists, the abandonment of the city corresponds with a dramatic climate shift. For most of Ramses' rule, the climate had been warm and there was plenty of rain leading to bountiful crops, but this was followed by a prolonged drought, which was the catalyst for a series of disruptions.

Periods of low precipitation cause the soil to dry, creating a drought. Warmer temperatures can also lead to drought because they increase evaporation from the soil, thereby making it drier. When dry soil causes plants to die, the amount of moisture in the air is reduced even further, as the plants are unable to release water vapor into the air through the process called transpiration. Normally, some surface heat is removed as moisture evaporates, but when the land is parched, that heat remains trapped in the soil which in turn heats the lower atmosphere. Without water in the soil, it has less ability to conduct heat down into the ground, so the top layer of the land can become extremely hot. The result is a vicious cycle, where droughts increase heat, which makes the land drier, which increases the heat, and so on. When droughts and heatwaves happen together, the effect can be catastrophic. Even today, droughts are, according to the World Meteorological Organization, "the most detrimental of all the natural disasters," responsible for about one-fifth of the damage caused by natural disasters each year.

One theory on the Exodus plagues is that the rising temperatures and drought caused the Nile to dry into a warm sludge. Such conditions are ideal for the growth of red algae. As the algae sucked the oxygen out of the water, it would kill any remaining fish and the water itself would turn the color of blood. This, in turn, could explain the abundance of frogs, which left their habitats near the river in search of food and subsequently died. Without frogs to eat the insects, flies and lice would proliferate.

Dr. John Marr, an epidemiologist who studied the ten plagues, argues that the "lice" referred to in the Bible could be another bug because the plagues happened about a thousand years before Aristotle classified insects. Marr believes that the culprits were culicoides, insects that lay eggs in dust.[1] The larva that the eggs produce feed on decomposing animals such as rotting fish and frogs. Culicoides have been known to transmit two types of infections that affect cattle, horses, and sheep. This could explain the livestock deaths. The rotting livestock could then spread an airborne bacterial disease called glanders, which can cause boils.

Insidiously, recovery from the drought could be what triggered the plague of locusts. All locusts are grasshoppers, although not all grasshoppers are locusts. When weather conditions are favorable to them over a long period of time, they spread out and we call them locusts. They dine on plants, but in large numbers they can cause significant damage to crops.

The worst problems occur when there is a dry spell followed by rain. During the drought, grasshoppers are forced together in the few areas that still contain vegetation. The crowding releases chemicals in the insects' nervous systems that make them more sociable and energetic. Scientists call this their "gregarious phase." Gregarious locusts have more endurance and their brains get larger. They can even change color and shape. When the rains return, the gregarious locusts reproduce at a rapid pace creating large, dense swarms.

Thus as the Egyptian locusts swarmed, they made meals of any crops that had started to recover from the drought. (A .39 square mi/one square km swarm of locusts can eat as much food in one day as thirty-five thousand people.) Widespread starvation followed. One ancient Egyptian account speaks of the children of aristocrats lying dead in public.

In ancient times, in the face of such widespread devastation and pain, it is easy to imagine desperate Egyptians resorting to human sacrifice to appease their gods, hence the killing of the firstborn. It could also have led to social unrest and slaves rising up to demand their release against a weakened regime. As Moses said to the Pharaoh Ramses, "let my people go."

While the series of plagues can be explained by science, it is a bit harder to explain why the Hebrews would have been spared while the Egyptians suffered. Marr suggests that culicoides cannot fly well, and perhaps this prevented the vermin from reaching the Hebrew land of Goshen, which is about 100 mi/161 km north of the ancient Egyptian capital of Memphis.

According to the Bible, when the pharaoh's son died, he told Moses to take his people and go, but after a short time he changed his mind and sent his army to chase down the Jews and bring them back to bondage. In the account, Moses called on God to part the Red Sea. In the Hebrew Bible, the body of water is called "Yom Suf" or "Sea of Reeds," which has led some scholars to suggest it might have been a swamp rather than the huge body of water like the one divided by Charlton Heston in the movie *The Ten Commandments*. If this is the case, perhaps the parting of the sea can be explained by the drought and climate shifts as well.

Exodus is the foundational narrative of Judaism and is at the heart of how Jews understand their relationship to God. "I am the Lord your God who took you out of the land of Egypt, out of the house of bondage," is the opening of the Ten Commandments. Both Christianity and Islam adopted the Exodus as part of their sacred canon, which means more than half the world's religions have been fundamentally shaped by droughts and disruption caused by a climate shift that occurred more than three thousand years ago.

Modern Plagues of Locusts

Swarms of locusts are not only a crisis of ancient times. In early 2020, an infestation began on the Arabian Peninsula and soon spread to Saudi Arabia and Northern and Eastern Africa with some swarms as large as major cities. In this case, it was warm, wet weather and a series of rare cyclones that created the perfect conditions for

(Continued on next page)

desert locusts to proliferate. The infestation ravaged crops, killing between 30–100 percent of harvests, depending on the region. In some areas, starving people turned to eating the insects themselves. (Locusts were commonly eaten in Biblical times, and they are considered kosher. The Bible specifies that four types of desert locust can be eaten. Specifically the red, yellow, spotted grey, and white. John the Baptist was described as subsisting on a diet of locusts and honey. Locusts are an excellent source of protein that contain a variety of fatty acids and are an important food source in many parts of the world.) We will hear about a plague of locusts that ravaged the US Midwest as our story continues.

Chapter

5

The Wind That Created the Greek Empire

I n 480 BC, superior weather forecasting at a pivotal moment ensured the survival of Greek culture. The various peoples who called the Mediterranean their home were dependent on sea routes for trade, security, and power. The Trojans, Spartans, Phoenicians, Carthaginians, and Etruscans all paid close attention to the direction of the wind and sea currents, but the Greeks paid the most attention to the weather. Ancient Greek literature makes more numerous references to the wind than does the literature of any of its neighbors.

The first book that attempted to categorize weather in a systemic way was written in Greek. In fact, the Greeks were the first to coin the term "meteorology," and the Greek word "klima," which means "inclination," gives us the word "climate." This derives from the way Greek scholars studied the sun's angle to predict the movement of air.

During the Greco-Persian Wars, this knowledge, it turned out, would be paramount. The Greeks, as advanced as they were, had no navy. They leased ships from the Corinthians. The Persian Empire, meanwhile, was at the peak of its strength and had one of the largest naval fleets in the world. The Greek naval commander Themistocles was able to literally turn the tides of war at the battle of Salamis in 480 BC by utilizing his knowledge of the winds.

In the spring of 480 BC, the Persian king Xerxes made it his mission to claim Athens for Persia. He assembled a massive naval force estimated at about a thousand ships and 250,000 men made up of Persians, Ionians, Cilicians, and Phoenicia fighters.

With such overwhelming power, Xerxes believed that the Athenians might surrender without a fight to avoid the inevitable destruction and loss of life. He used intimidation instead of surprise and sent heralds in advance of the attack force to demand each city in his path provide provisions for the soldiers. Thus the Athenians knew exactly how many were coming and where they planned to travel. They evacuated the city in advance of the attack.

In September, the Persians burned the empty city and prepared to face down Greece's tiny fleet consisting of only 380 ships and sixty thousand men. It was clear that the Persians would beat them if it came down to force alone. So the Greek General Themistocles used the one advantage he had: his knowledge of the winds. The Greeks had observed that there were specific times at which land and sea breezes started and stopped blowing in the Aegean. The land breeze, which blew off shore at night, gave way to a sea breeze that started to blow on shore beginning in late morning because of the differential heating of the land, making it much warmer than the water in the late morning and afternoon. Warm air, being lighter, rises, pulling in the cooler air from off the sea. Themistocles used subterfuge to lure the enemy into a channel between Piraeus and the island of Salamis when he predicted a brisk wind would blow from the open sea, making it more difficult for the Persian fleet to navigate.

He let the Persians intercept a message that falsely said the Greeks were going to retreat. Xerxes sent his ships to block the narrow Megara channel where he thought the Greek ships would try to escape under cover of darkness.

The Greek ships began moving, as Xerxes expected, but they did not retreat to the south. Instead, they sailed around the north end of Salamis. As Plutarch, an ancient Greek historian, recounted, their galleys' bows became weapons:

> Themistocles is thought to have divined the best time for fighting with no less success than the best place, inasmuch as he took care not to send his triremes bow on against the barbarian vessels until the hour of day had come which always brought the breeze fresh from the sea and a swell rolling through the strait. This breeze wrought no harm to the Hellenic ships, since they lay low in the water and were rather small; but for the barbarian ships, with their towering sterns and lofty decks and sluggish movements in getting under way, it was fatal, since it smote them and slewed them round broadside to the Hellenes, who set upon them sharply.[1]

Themistocles drew the Persians to a spot where the channel was only 1,500 yds/1200 m across. This created a bottleneck. The Greeks sailed straight for it and rammed the ship. By mid-morning, the Persians had the wind to their backs and could not maintain course, while the Greeks met the wind head on, giving them greater stability. The Persians soon lost their formation entirely. As the ships in the front were damaged, those in the rear, unaware of the danger ahead, kept sailing, which caused a bottleneck. It was a disaster for Xerxes. The Persians lost one-third of their force, and, in chaos and confusion, they retreated. It took a decade for Persia to recover from the blow to its naval power.

Had Xerxes been victorious at Salamis, he undoubtedly would have been emboldened to attack the other coastal Greek city-states. Ancient Greece, and its cultural treasures, might have foundered and most importantly, the democratic traditions of Greece would not have survived, and the United States and other modern democratic republics may not have come into being. Instead, an emboldened Greece amassed its own great naval empire ensuring its survival for three hundred years to come.

Chapter

6

The Volcano That Launched the Roman Empire

On March 15, 44 BC, the "Ides of March," Julius Caesar was assassinated in Rome by members of the Roman Senate. Caesar was a popular and successful military leader who had expanded the Roman Republic. After conquering Gaul, he was named "dictator for life." Prior to that Rome had been a republic, governed by an appointed (not elected) senate. The title "dictator" up to then had been given to leaders for a limited time during states of emergency. Many members of the senate feared that their own power might be usurped. A group of as many as sixty conspirators met at the senate on March 15 and agreed to kill Caesar. They attacked the Roman leader and stabbed him twenty-three times.

The death of Caesar created a struggle for power that would end with Egypt under Roman rule and the Roman Republic transformed into the Roman Empire. Climate change caused by a faraway volcano played a major role in these events.

In the wake of Caesar's death, the most likely figure to assume leadership was Mark Antony, Caesar's close friend and right-hand man. Speaking at Caesar's funeral, Antony was able to turn popular opinion against the conspirators and force them to flee Rome. Antony was surprised, as were many in Rome, when Julius Caesar's will was read. Caesar, who had a daughter but no sons, had named his eighteen-year-old nephew Gaius Octavius as his heir.

Octavius adopted the name Caesar (later Caesar Augustus) and argued that he was entitled not only to Julius's wealth, but also to his high office as well. This was not the way succession was supposed to work in a republic, but after years of intrigue and periodic civil wars the old system was under strain. Antony resented the young upstart and referred to him as "the boy."

Octavius had no intention of compromising his ambitions. He used his inherited wealth to raise his own army to challenge Antony. The famous orator Cicero, who had opposed Julius Caesar, feared that Antony and the pro-Caesar faction might become tyrants and end democracy in Rome. So in order to protect the Republic, he backed Octavius. Antony fled with his legions to Gaul and was pursued and defeated by Octavius's self-funded army.

Unbeknownst to any of them, halfway around the world, in what is now Umnak Island, Alaska, a volcano was erupting and leaving a crater 6.2 mi/10 km wide.

Because the volcano was so far north, particles from the blast were able to rise into the Arctic stratosphere and easily spread. Based on the evidence in ice cores and tree rings, a team of researchers published a study in which they determined that the fallout from the eruption lowered temperatures in the Northern Hemisphere by up to 13°F/7°C for two to three years, and the below normal temperatures lasted years longer.[1] The climate impact from the volcanic eruption also changed the pattern of rainfall, with some areas being inundated by 400 percent more precipitation than normal, flooding farms.

"In the Mediterranean region, these wet and extremely cold conditions during the agriculturally important spring through autumn seasons probably reduced crop yields and compounded supply problems during the ongoing political upheavals of the period," wrote Andrew Wilson, one of the study's co-authors.[2]

"This is the second coldest year in the last 2,500 years," lead author Joe McConnell said, "And when you're talking about an agrarian society that's living close to the edge as it is, it had to have had a big impact."[3]

The disaster created what the study's authors called a "state of exception in which business as usual becomes unfeasible and political and cultural norms are suspended, thereby providing room for rapid social and political change."[4] This quote understates the upheaval and social turbulence that resulted from crop failures. There is no question that wars and violence often quickly develop when the economy becomes unstable, a result of crop failures and a hungry and sometimes desperate population. When people are hungry and their children are too, their first and only thought is to find food. One of the points of this book that may be understated is if the weather and climate turn so unfavorable that there is an insufficient food supply, little else matters and humanity will face great turmoil.

As Europe became colder and crops failed, Antony allied with another Caesar supporter, Marcus Aemilius Lepidus. With most of Julius's loyalists backing the slain dictator's old allies, Octavius, now known as Augustus, decided it would be prudent to join the consolidating pro-Caesar power base. They formed a triumvirate (a board of three rulers) and divided up their spheres of influence. Lepidus would rule in Africa, Antony in the east, and Augustus in the west.

Their first act as a triumvirate was to address the social unrest with a bloody show of force. They ordered all of Caesar's remaining opponents, as well as other political enemies, killed. Instead of using their own military to do this dirty work, they posted lists of the condemned and offered a share of the victim's property to anyone who brought the authorities the severed head of someone on the kill list. Among the enemies to meet this gory end was Cicero. And his death on December 7, 43 BC is generally considered to mark the end of Rome's days as a republic.

Another martyr to the cause of the republic was Marcus Porcius Cato Uticensis, more commonly known as Cato the Younger. Cato had been one of the most vocal opponents of Julius Caesar's power grab. After the pro-republic faction had been quelled, Caesar Augustus sought to glorify his victory with a show of mercy. He offered clemency to any of his opponents who would recant their previous views. Cato was so dedicated to his principles that he killed himself rather than compromise.

The April following Cicero's death, famine descended on the Mediterranean. Rome, Greece, and Egypt all suffered food shortages because of the cooling and rain caused by the volcano. When Antony and Augustus sent their forces to Greece to track down and kill two of Caesar's assassins, Brutus and Cassius, in 42 BC, Plutarch wrote of the clash at Philippi that the Roman army was forced to scavenge on wild plants, bark, and small animals "never tasted before by men." In recognition of their victory, however, the soldiers had been promised a share of farms confiscated from the regime's political enemies.

The estates were not producing enough to give the troops what they had been promised, and so Augustus and Antony started imposing arbitrary confiscations, which created even more unrest. Augustus's solution was to rile the people up against a foreign threat. He demonized the queen of Egypt, Cleopatra, who just happened to be Antony's lover. This, needless to say, did nothing to improve relations between Augustus and Antony. Ultimately, the two faced off against each other in the Battle of Actium in Greece in 31 BC. Antony was defeated and committed suicide the following year.

With Antony out of the picture, Augustus, now thirty-three years old, had no serious rivals. This put an end to a long era of civil wars in Rome and brought increased food and stability to its citizens. And, of course, the weather returned to more normal conditions, bringing greater economic stability. In 63 BC, Augustus became Rome's first emperor. Under his rule, power was centralized. Augustus had the power to write or veto laws and commanded the army. The formerly representative assembly and senate were marginalized in importance. The senate still had the power to remove an emperor, but as the emperor had to give consent for anyone to hold public office, the body was made up of people unlikely to pose any great challenge to his leadership. The assembly became, according to National Geographic, "virtually ceremonial."[5]

Augustus continued to reign until his death in 14 AD. He expanded the empire by annexing Egypt, parts of Spain, central Europe, and the Middle East. When Augustus died, he was proclaimed to be a god by the senate. Historian Jurgen Deiniger has said the end of the Roman Republic was "certainly among the most significant political events in the history of 'classical' antiquity . . . it may be said that the crisis of the Roman republic and its transition to monarchy was a profound and irreversible long-term change of the political system for which there is hardly any real parallel in ancient history."[6]

During the Enlightenment, which lasted approximately from 1637 to 1804, the history of ancient Rome was a cornerstone of a classical education. References to Rome provided common points of reference to educated elites throughout the western world. America's founders were no exception. When they wanted to make a case for their new system of government, they instinctively turned to Roman references to give their arguments substance and historical precedence in much the same way modern Americans evoke the Founding Fathers.

In England, which was on a path to becoming the largest empire the world had ever known, discourse on Rome tended to focus on what caused the Empire to fall and how England could avoid the same fate. The American revolutionaries held a less favorable view of empire. When they looked to Rome, they identified with the defenders of the republic. Josiah Quincy, a spokesman for the Sons of Liberty, best summarized this view when, in the years leading up to the American Revolution, he compared the tyrannical Caesar to King George, asking, "Is not Britain to America what Caesar was to Rome?"[7]

Cicero and Cato became heroes of the American revolutionary movement. Cato's martyrdom, in particular, became a rallying point thanks to a play by Joseph Addison, who was an essayist and editor of *The Spectator*. *Cato, A Tragedy*, while rarely performed today, was the most popular theatrical production of the eighteenth century. It was George Washington's favorite play, and when his soldiers were exhausted and hungry at Valley Forge, Washington had the troops crowd into a small building to boost their morale by watching a performance by a group of traveling players.

Patrick Henry's famous cry of "Give me liberty or give me death!" may have been inspired by a scene from the play in which Cato says, "It is not now a time to talk of aught / But chains or conquest, liberty or death."[8]

The famous quote attributed to Nathan Hale before his execution, "I only regret that I have but one life to lose for my country," has echoes of a line from Act IV when Cato declares:

How beautiful is death when earned by virtue?
Who would not be that youth? What pity is it
That we can die but once to serve our country![9]

Thus we have an example of how weather and climate can subtly bend the long arc of history: A volcano that erupted in 43 BC in what is now a part of the United States helped lay the foundations for that nation thanks to its effects on the weather in ancient Rome.

Chapter
7

Volcanic Disruptions That Caused the Justinian Plague

I t has been called the world's first pandemic. It originated near what is now Port Said, Egypt, in the year 541 AD. A historian of the era, Procopius, said the "pestilence" spread in all directions "as if fearing lest some corner of the earth might escape it."[1] It killed wherever it went, but its biggest impact was in Constantinople (now Istanbul)—the capital of the Eastern Roman, or Byzantine, Empire. Modern historians think that five thousand people per day were dying in the city at the height of the outbreak, wiping out as many as 40 percent of the population. In the rest of the empire, a quarter of the residents were killed. The infection traveled so quickly that the emperor Justinian had to appoint a special officer to deal with all of the corpses. It was so catastrophic that it hastened the final end of the Roman Empire.

Rome, in its heyday, benefited from mainly favorable climate conditions. The weather was warm and stable with the right amount of rain to support a thriving agrarian society. But in AD 536–537 a literal veil of dust fell upon them. Scholars do not agree on what caused the sky to darken. Some say it was a volcanic eruption or even a series of eruptions. Others suggest it was the result of an impact from a comet.

A team of Oxford University researchers reviewing the scientific literature in 2004 concluded that comets are more likely than asteroids to spark fires.[2] Because comets dissipate their energy higher in the atmosphere than asteroids, their shock waves do not reach the ground where they might actually blow out a fire.

Normally, dust from a forest fire settles out from rain and other causes in a matter of days or weeks. In 2023, a series of Canadian wildfires sent smoke into the atmosphere almost continuously for several months. In order for particles to make their way all the way up to the stratosphere, where fine particles might remain for years, you would need a widespread fire with such heat that it would send a plume 60–80,000 ft/18,288–24,384 m into the atmosphere. A comet, if it burst over a wooded section of Northern Europe, could have sparked widespread fires that would have sent sufficient soot height into the atmosphere to cause far-reaching effects.

The team estimated that it would only take a comet less than a kilometer in diameter to start a fire that would create a dust veil capable of disrupting sunlight and causing cooling and crop failures for several years in a row. They further argued against the super-volcano theory, noting that ice-core studies in Greenland and Antarctica failed to find evidence of significant acidity in the atmosphere, as might be expected after a volcanic event.

Whatever it was, written records, and the work of ice core and tree ring experts, confirm that something blocked out solar energy and caused temperatures to fall in the area between Europe and Asia Minor. The chill of what is known as the "Late Antique Little Ice Age," lasted for at least 150 years.

During the Late Antique Little Ice Age (approximately AD 550–700), there were climate disruptions throughout the world, which caused widespread famine and social upheaval. In China, famine entirely wiped out villages in a number of regions. Parts of Sweden and Norway were abandoned entirely. Norse mythology started to tell stories of a "great winter"—Fimbulwinter—which was a prelude to Ragnarok, or the end of the world. The disaster is believed to have been the catalyst that set the Vikings sailing, seeking new worlds to live in and conquer. Vikings spread across Europe, founded Russia, and occupied North Africa.

In East Africa, climate change brought severe drought which was followed by heavy rain. During the drought so many of the rodents that fed on grain died that their predators died as well. When the rain came back, the rodents were able to spring back before their predators did. Egypt became infested by gerbils and mice. The rodents had been living with a bacterium called *Yersinia pestis* for some time. It did no harm to them. The pathogen had to make a few jumps before it made its way into human beings. First, the abundant rodents stowed away on ships where they were bitten by fleas. The fleas were not immune to *Yersinia pestis*. It caused them to become engorged with clotted blood. So even though they were full, they were starving. They bit any creature they could find. Each bite transferred some of the bacteria. In this way it moved to ship rats who off loaded at ports in dense trading cities. All roads led to the capital of the empire, which meant all germs eventually got there as well.

In 542, death came to Constantinople, which was, like New York City in modern times, an international hub, making it an especially vulnerable target for pathogens. The disease started with a fever; as Procopius observed, it was so mild it did not "afford any suspicion of danger."[3] But soon the lymph nodes became engorged and lumps, or buboes, appeared in the groin and under the arms, giving the name to the Bubonic Plague. People vomited blood. Some fell into comas or delirium. Procopius noted that those who cared for the sick "were in a state of constant exhaustion. For this reason everybody pitied them no less than the sufferers."[4] The illness came to rich and poor alike. Even Emperor Justinian caught it, although he recovered.

So many men died that it became difficult to maintain enough military force to defend against a series of emboldened enemies. The followers of the new major religion, Islam, took territory from the empire in the east, while much of the Western empire was annexed by the Franks. The plague continued to reappear in waves for another 250 years before it finally burned itself out. By then the geographically-connected Roman Empire had dropped drastically from its peak of seventy million people to a mere thirty thousand or so.

This caused a massive shift in the balance of power throughout the region. William Rosen, author of *Justinian's Flea and the Birth of Europe*, has argued that were there no plague, Rome might have continued to exert control over Western Europe.[5] Instead, the centers of power were dispersed. Power was drawn away from the Mediterranean and toward what would become France, Germany, and England, setting the stage for the world we know today.

Chapter

8

Drought Destroys the Mayans

Mayan Civilization flourished from 200–900 AD as a system of interconnected city-states, some of which numbered as many as one hundred thousand residents. They created advanced art, pottery, architecture, agriculture, and advanced knowledge of astronomy. They developed the only fully formed writing system of the pre-Columbian Americas, built complicated weaving looms, made glittery paints from the mineral mica, and developed rubber thousands of years before Charles Goodyear stamped his name on anything. They left behind inspiring architecture including pyramids. One of the most famous is the El Castillo at Chichen Itza. Mayan pyramids were smaller than their Egyptian counterparts, but they were more ornate, and served more functions. They were constructed to note important points on the calendar. While some Mayan pyramids were decorative landmarks or tombs, many were centers of religious ritual with steps leading up to temples. They were built in large complexes that included courtyards, ball courts, and plazas.

While most of the indigenous populations of Mesoamerica were scattered, the Maya were centered in one area covering the Yucatan Peninsula and parts of what are now Guatemala, Belize, Mexico, Honduras, and El Salvador. This geographic concentration kept them relatively protected from invasion, but it came with its own challenges. Their territory was on the northern edge of a belt of low pressure where the trade winds of the Northern and Southern Hemispheres meet. This area, where the northeast winds of the Northern Hemisphere converge with the southeast winds of the Southern Hemisphere, is known as the Inter Tropical Convergence Zone, or ITCZ. This convergence leads to upward motion, condensation, and rain. The ITCZ moves north and south seasonally with the sun, in an area that varies as weather and climate shift. It would normally get as far north as the Mayan civilization, bringing plentiful rains to feed the crops, but in some years, and even some series of years, the ITCZ didn't reach that far north. Most years the Mayans had the seasonal rains they needed to grow their crops, but other years the rains did not come, and the crops failed.

Dependent as they were on the seasonal rains for their survival, the Mayans developed astronomy and one of the most advanced calendars in the world to track the climate. The calendar was based on a 365-day year, which contained a ritual cycle of 260 named days. Together, they formed a "Calendar Round," which tracked a longer cycle of 18,980 days, or fifty-two years. The Mayan calendar was the basis of all other Mesoamerican calendars.

They were skillful in their use of the environment, creating a huge system of canals to increase the amount of farm land to serve their ever-growing population. Some scholars believe that these efforts may have partially contributed to their downfall, as deforestation left the land vulnerable to erosion.

Along with their scientific advances, the Mayans, like other ancient Mesoamericans, practiced ritual sacrifice of both animals and human beings to appease the rain god Chaac. Most of the victims were boys. "It was thought that the gods preferred small things and especially the rain god had four helpers that were represented as tiny people," said archaeologist Guillermo de Anda. "So the children were offered as a way to directly communicate with Chaac."[1]

At Chichen Itza, tour guides who grew up in the area tell a centuries old tale passed down through generations of the descendants of the Mayans. They describe a highly ritualized game played annually on an I-shaped field known as a playing alley. Players on horseback tried to pass a ball through a narrow stone hoop high above the stands on what would be the north and south end zone of a football stadium.

The one who got it through the hoop was the victor and received the great honor of being sacrificed to the rain god by being tied to a specially chosen woman and weighted down and thrown into a pit of water where they drowned. [2]

At its peak, Mayan civilization included nineteen million people, but then around the year 800 AD, and then increasingly in 1000 AD, it began to dramatically contract. The cause was a drought, or more accurately, a series of droughts caused by a climactic shift in the ITCZ.

The trouble began in the south in what are now Guatemala and Belize. In the ninth century, Mayan cities began to fail. The north fared better, but it too, was affected by what a joint UK/US team of archaeologists called a period of waning creative activity.

Yet many cities continued to thrive, including one of the world's "New Seven Wonders," the pyramid at Chichen Itza.

In the late tenth century, the rains returned and the Mayans enjoyed a short resurgence before their art and building dropped to half of what it was between 1000 and 1075 AD. In the eleventh century, the region experienced the most severe drought it had seen in two thousand years. The previous drought had destroyed Mayan civilization in the south, and this one finished it off in the north. Most Mayans migrated toward the Caribbean coast in search of water.

While Mayan civilization never again claimed the dominance it had before the drought, the Mayans hardly went gently into the night. In fact, the last unconquered New World kingdom was that of the Itza Maya. The Itza's battled the Spanish 150 years after the Europeans had colonized most of the Yucatan Peninsula. The Itzan capital was taken by the Spanish on March 13, 1697. Even after that, the descendants of the once mighty empire continued to fight against their European colonizers. When Mexico achieved its independence from Spanish rule, the Yucatan Peninsula remained largely autonomous due to its remoteness from Mexico City. The Mayan community, made up mostly of subsistence farmers, lived there in a community called Chan Santa Cruz. The Chan Santa Cruz community continued to employ advanced agricultural techniques and was responsible for developments in sugar, banana, and citrus production. The community even briefly established its own trading relationship with the British as a separate Mayan state.

In 1847, after Mexico achieved independence from Spain, the Mexican government began to expropriate what the Mexicans considered to be public land and what the Mayans considered to be theirs. The Mayans revolted, leading to what is now known as the Caste War of Yucatan, one of the longest-running wars of the nineteenth century and Mexico's bloodiest conflict. Mayan chief Manuel Antonio Ay was assassinated on July 26, 1847, and Mexican forces seized the last autonomous Mayan community on July 1, 1901. The war officially ended at this point, but skirmishes with Mayan settlements continued until 1933.

It is easy to imagine that, had weather and climate change not brought down the advanced and powerful civilization centuries before, the Mayans might have resisted Spanish rule entirely and much of what is now Mexico and Central America might today be an independent Mayan state. With their great scientific achievement, they might be a major player on the world stage today. Fascinatingly, the knowledge of the weather that was so critical to their achievements ultimately became their undoing because the rains became less reliable due to climate change. This shows how sensitive our civilization, scientific progress, democratic processes, and ultimately our survival depend on the stability of our climate.

Anasazi's Quick Decline

The Ancient Pueblo Indians (Anasazi), renowned for their extensive cliff-side dwellings in the American Southwest, met an even more precipitous decline. After existing for a thousand years, the Anasazi rather suddenly deserted their sites (1275–1300). Within a single generation their culture faded, and surviving peoples headed south as refugees to escape severe drought. Drought brought malnutrition, strife, and dramatic displacement. Some households look frozen in time, pots seemingly left mid-meal as though total abandonment was not intended. Only traces of this culture remain. If such a dry climate resulted in arid conditions like the present in this parched region, as scholars suggest, the bleak conditions were understandably insurmountable, decimating the long-established Anasazi culture.

History of Weather Forecasting

At one time, most people believed that weather was caused by their gods and some believed that they could bring about more beneficial weather by praying or offering sacrifices to their gods. Most early weather forecasting methods going back a thousand years were based on the hypothesis that weather is caused by the movement of planets and mediated by regional and seasonal climate conditions. However, the results were of little or no value. The central question that such calculations did not answer was how can weather vary so much from one year to the next when the seasons are caused by regular repeating patterns produced by Earth's spherical shape and its interactions with the sun? Geoffrey of Anjou, father of King Henry II of England, posed that question to the twelfth-century philosopher William of Conches. Rulers and religious leaders were always looking for forecasts with some kind of skill so they would be able to better address practical societal concerns such as military strategy and food supply, both of which were heavily affected by the weather. Bankers and traders were willing to pay for such valuable information.

Of course, there have always been people willing to provide forecasts for money. The problem is that many of the forecasts provided were not based on science, and proved to be worthless because they were generally not accurate. The flaw was that too much emphasis was given to the movement of the planets rather than understanding the physics of the atmosphere. Of course, it was known that the sun and the moon were the most significant astronomical bodies. The sun's effect on

(Continued on next page)

the weather and climate through its light and heat was long established, and the moon's influence over ocean tides, bodily fluids, and plant growth was also widely recognized, at least by the educated.

You probably know the legend of Benjamin Franklin's kite-flying experiment in which he showed that lightning was electricity. But Franklin was also the first to observe that storms in the Northeast generally approach from the southwest; he proposed models to describe the movement of storm systems and published some of the first weather forecasts in the United States. Franklin's enhancements with meteorology ran from shifting air pressure, to tornadoes, to even climate change, all of which make the eighteenth-century polymath all the more astounding.

As America expanded westward in the nineteenth century, railroads and agriculture brought about a dramatic increase in the monitoring of weather conditions, and the first official government weather forecasts.

Skipping ahead to World War I, we find the English mathematician and pacifist Lewis Fry Richardson doing equations on his hand calculator while serving with a Quaker ambulance unit. His postulation: that the equations of fluid dynamics and thermodynamics could be used to forecast the future state of the atmosphere. He spent weeks calculating a six-hour forecast by hand, but his results made no sense due to errors in his calculations.

Yet, with the invention of computers around 1950, Richardson's mathematical approach was vindicated. The early computerized weather forecasts were limited by the speed and memory of these early computers, but in the ensuing decades they have gained in sophistication and accuracy to reach a point today where it is difficult for even the best meteorologist to consistently improve on computer-generated forecasts.

Chapter

9

The Rain That Built the Mongol Empire

The Roman Empire looms large in our cultural imagination, but it was not the biggest contiguous empire on earth. In fact, it was dwarfed by the Mongol Empire, which, at its height, controlled an area of nine million square miles—about five times the size of the Roman Empire. (In comparison to some other great powers: it was slightly larger than the Soviet Union and about three times the size of the modern United States. In terms of history's greatest empires, the Mongol Empire was second only to the British Empire, which, at its peak, controlled 13.7 million square miles.) Imagine the feat of controlling such a vast territory in an era when the fastest mode of travel was the horse!

Under Genghis Khan, and then his successors, the Mongols ruled Eurasia from China to the Middle East and Russia. This domination had a profound impact on the world. Adjusted for global population levels, Mongol invasions ended the lives of more people than any other war; as much as 5 percent of the world's population at the time may have been killed. The viciousness of the conquest, paradoxically, ushered in a period of relative peace and stability. While they were dominated by the Mongols, nations and tribes that would otherwise war with one another were united under the umbrella of the empire. Still, they lived under a dictatorship. The empire connected nations from east and west, introducing Chinese inventions such as gunpowder to Europe. Modern climate scientists believe the Mongol Empire might never have been ascendant were it not for a wave of fortuitously mild weather.

In the late 1100s, the Mongols were a group of tribes who were divided and often at war with one another. Then, in the 1200s, a new leader, Genghis Kahn, emerged from an obscure background. The first account of his early life, written contemporaneously, was a fanciful affair. He was believed to be of aristocratic stock. Thanks to his excellence as a soldier and undoubtedly great natural ability to rally his troops, he was able to make himself the ruler of a highly disciplined military. Within decades, Kahn had united bands of nomadic horsemen into an unparalleled fighting force that expanded in all directions.

By studying the rings of trees, researchers from West Virginia University found that the turbulent period prior to Genghis Kahn's rule was marked by an intense drought.[1] Then, in the exact period that Kahn rose to prominence, there was unusual rainfall and warmth, which stimulated the growth of the grasslands. Horses were central to the Mongols' military that relied on chariots and mounted warriors, and additional grass allowed the warriors to support more horses. Grass for the Mongols was like oil today— wars were fought over it. The Mongols' equine advantage would be analogous to a modern nation possessing the resources to build and fuel more tanks, drones, missiles, and airplanes than its neighbors.

Each Mongol warrior was able to maintain a team of five or more horses. The Mongols were able to build the greatest cavalry the world had seen at a time when many other nations were suffering from devastating drought.

"The transition from extreme drought to extreme moisture right then strongly suggests that climate played a role in human events," said Amy Hessl, who led the study. "It wasn't the only thing, but it must have created the ideal conditions for a charismatic leader to emerge out of the chaos, develop an army and concentrate power. Where it's arid, unusual moisture creates unusual plant productivity, and that translates into horsepower. Genghis was literally able to ride that wave."[2]

Starting in 1236, Genghis Khan's third son, Ögedei, set out to conquer as much of Europe as he could. His troops were ruthless to any group that resisted, but generous to those that surrendered and one tribe after another fell to its rule. By 1240, they commanded what is now Russia and Ukraine and then seized Romania, Bulgaria, and Hungary.

And then everything changed. In December 1241, Ögedei Khan died unexpectedly. The following year, the Mongol forces suddenly retreated and the major war campaign in the west was over. Ultimately, warm temperatures (which had allowed the Mongols to become an empire) combined with drier conditions, lowered the yield and productivity of the Mayan crops, which reduced their food supply, thereby preventing their further westward expansion. A decade later, Genghis Khan's grandson, Kublai Khan, would set his sights on Asia.

Mongol rule brought in a century of peace between neighbors who would otherwise have warred with one another. This era, from 1280–1360, became known as the Pax Mongolica. This allowed for a reopening of trading routes between China and

Europe. So while the Mongol warriors are mostly remembered for violence, their reign saw growth of population and fewer people lost to war. Mongolian rule also transformed Russia, which until then had been a series of self-governing city-states. The various Russian-speaking people united in their opposition to the Mongols.

The united Russians, led by the Grand Duchy of Moscow, finally threw off the Mongols in 1480 and started on the path that would ultimately make them a world power. Meanwhile, the introduction of gun powder from China allowed the Russians to develop superior firepower and to conquer much of the territory once controlled by the Mongols, including Outer Mongolia where Genghis Khan was born. From then on, almost everyone who tried to invade Russia, as we shall see, was thwarted by a combination of Russian determination and climactic and weather challenges.

Chapter

10

Tropical "Kamikaze" Storms Save Japan

When Kublai Khan became ruler of the Mongol Empire in 1260, his ambition was to take over all of Asia. He was largely successful, taking over Northern China and creating a new capital city there called Xanadu. He then added Korea to the empire and set his sights on Japan. In 1273, he sent a message to Japanese Emperor Kameyama asking him to give up his rule peacefully or face a disastrous war. Kameyama refused and Mongol forces with their Chinese and Korean vassals prepared an armada to attack mainland Japan. The combined forces set out in October 1274 with a force of forty thousand men and nine hundred ships. The Japanese, with only ten thousand fighters, should have been no match for them.

But what the Mongol/Chinese force lacked was knowledge of the seasonal nature of tropical storms. Atlantic hurricanes almost always happen between June 1 and November 30, with the most intense storms usually between mid-August and mid-October. Typhoons have a lengthier season and, while it is possible for typhoons to form year round, most happen between May and November. Thus, by setting sail in October, the force had picked the worst time of year, climatologically, to sail to capture Japan. After making short work of the occupied islands of Tsushima and Iki, the force quickly advanced to Hakata Bay in the northwestern part of Fukuoka city on Kyūshu, the southwesternmost major island of Japan.

The invaders rested in their ships, prepared to launch an attack of the mainland the next day. Unfortunately for the Mongols, a major typhoon was in their path. The storm reduced their armada to wooden beams and splinters and destroyed most of the army. The Shinto priests called the meteorological intervention a "divine wind" or "kamikaze."

Kublai, who had never lost a battle before, was more determined than ever to take over the island. He continued to send threats to Japan, which only helped the Japanese prepare for the invasion. Having annexed the South China Empire in 1279, he now had even greater resources and, in June 1281, a force of 140,000 soldiers set out in 4,400 ships, the largest army and armada ever assembled by any nation up to that point.

After securing the outer islands, the Mongol force set sail for the mainland of Japan. When the invaders reached Hakata Bay, they were met not by a small band of samurai warriors but by an army fighting as a team from behind a wall. The Mongols and their vassal soldiers withdrew to prepare for a fresh assault only to sail straight into another typhoon on August 15. The fleet, as impressive as it was, could not endure winds of such magnitude. In fact, the sheer number of ships worked against them as the hulls of damaged ships careened into other ships, thus trapping them in the harbor. Having his army twice destroyed by divine winds, Kublai Kahn gave up on his plans, and Japan remained an independent nation. The story of the "divine wind" was passed down for centuries, giving Japanese warriors a sense of inspiration and strength. Soldiers continued to invoke the kamikaze into World War II and it influences Japanese culture to this day.

Hurricanes and Typhoons

Mid-latitude storms, the kind that we are most familiar with as bringing rain and snow in winter and rain and thunderstorms in summer, are fueled primarily by the contrasts between air masses. In contrast, tropical storms are fueled primarily by the latent heat of condensation, which is the energy released when water vapor condenses into liquid water droplets. Warm tropical bodies of water act as a source of that water vapor, and the warmer the air is, the more likely it is to rise. When air rises, it cools, which means it can no longer hold as much water vapor. If it rises and cools sufficiently to become saturated, the water vapor condenses into clouds of water droplets, releasing energy, thereby heating the air, causing it to rise further and faster. The higher the ocean temperature, the more latent heat of condensation is released when water vapor condenses, and the more powerful the updraft. Of course, more air has to circulate in to fill in for the air that's rising.

Over tropical bodies of water, there is sometimes sufficient water vapor in the air to cause this cycle to accelerate and, as the air rises, the barometric pressure also drops, which causes surface winds funneling toward the center to pick

(Continued on next page)

up speed. Unless there are certain processes in the atmosphere to cap this process, once it begins it can accelerate, causing the formation of a tropical cyclone. Many climatologists speculate that global warming, which leads to the rising ocean temperatures, will lead to more frequent and more powerful hurricanes. The evidence for this is that surface water temperatures need to have a threshold of 81 degrees for hurricanes to form, and we know that the most intense hurricanes and typhoons tend to form over the warmest parts of the ocean and at the time of year when water temperatures are highest.

These tropical cyclones are known by a number of names depending on their strength and geographic location. The weakest are called tropical depressions. When the winds reach 39 miles per hour, depressions become tropical storms. Once a system reaches a sustained wind of 74 miles per hour, depending on where it is in the world, it will be called a hurricane, typhoon, or tropical cyclone. Hurricanes are found in the North Atlantic (which includes the Gulf of Mexico and Caribbean), central North Pacific, and eastern North Pacific. In the South Pacific and Indian Ocean, it is called a tropical cyclone. In the Northwest Pacific, such a storm is a typhoon. Hurricanes and typhoons are some of the most dramatic, violent, and sometimes history-changing storms on the planet. In the case of Japan, typhoons have killed tens of thousands of people from high winds, inland flooding resulting from heavy rain, and from storm surges; yet as we have seen, two typhoons saved this island nation from capture. During WWII, before Hiroshima, the Japanese Navy was greatly weakened by a powerful typhoon that sank and disabled dozens of their ships. Their meteorologists apparently did not do a good job of forecasting this typhoon because by that time in the war, the Americans had controlled most of the Pacific, especially the area from where the typhoon was coming.

Chapter

11

Climate Change Brings the Black Death and the First Biological Warfare

istorians know the exact date when the pandemic that came to be called "the Black Death" arrived on British shores. It was May 8, 1348 at Melcombe Regis when a ship that had left Bordeaux a few weeks before landed. By August, the plague had reached London, and by the end of September it was a nationwide disaster. The Black Death was a variant of the same bacteria that had ravaged Rome in Justinian's day. It moved fast, killing a person infected within days of the first symptoms. Victims developed a high fever, a rash, and horrible pus-filled boils that turned black and burst. Before it ended, the epidemic had killed between 75 and 200 million people, about 30 to 50 percent of Europe's population. (To put this in context, Europe's current population is around 742 million. If 30–50 percent were killed, it would be 223 million to 371 million dead.) So many died in England that genetic diversity is lower to this day than it was in the eleventh century despite immigration from other lands.

The European plague was caused by climate change, but not by changes in the local climate. It was the weather in Asia that led to devastation in another part of the globe. In a tree ring study of more than seven thousand historical plague outbreaks, researchers saw that climate changes in the Karakorum Mountains in northern Pakistan between 1250 and 1850 correlated to plague outbreaks in European port cities. It was not easy to miss, because the events happened only fifteen years apart. This time gap was due to the much slower speed of travel and commerce in those ancient times.

In areas where the bacterium that causes the plague is found, it is common in rodents such as gerbils. When climate conditions become warmer, the gerbils have a harder time finding food, and many of them die off. When this happens, their fleas start looking for other animals to bite, including humans. The bacteria then spreads, as poet John Donne observed, "It sucked me first, and now sucks thee,/And in this flea our two bloods mingled be."[1] This cycle of transmission, from rodent to flea to human, causes outbreaks of the plague to this day in parts of Asia.

Inevitably, travelers carried blood-gorged fleas and lice onto caravans and ships. But even at their top speed, it would take a year or two to make their way from rural Pakistan to the population centers of Asia. The 2,500 mile/4,023 km journey to Europe was traversed at a rate of 200 to 250 miles/322–402 km per year.

The Pax Mongolica increased international trade and sped transport. Thriving Mongol trade routes—like the Silk Road—were the historic equivalent of busy airline routes. Where the Mongol army went, the plague followed.

Things took a dramatic turn for the worse in 1349. Following the death of Genghis Khan, the empire had fractured into a series of rival Khanates. One of these had made it as far as Crimea and laid siege on the trade city of Caffa. The residents of the walled city were not as vulnerable as the Mongols hoped. The invaders remained outside the city in crowded camps and suffered a deadly outbreak of the plague. As the weakened army succumbed, the leader of the Mongol force resorted to a desperate and deadly plan. He ordered the bodies of the dead gathered up. He catapulted them over the city walls. The putrid corpses spread the disease and leaked toxins into the ground, poisoning the drinking water.

This was considered to be the world's first biological attack. Those who made it out of Caffa alive got on ships to Italy, and from there it began its route to other parts of Europe.

As the plague took hold in Italy, the government took measures to prevent its spread. Ships that arrived in Venice had to wait in port for forty days before passengers were allowed to debark. It is from the translation of the Italian "forty days"—*una quarantina di giorni*—that we get the word "quarantine."

So many died that it took two centuries for world-population levels to return to pre-plague levels. The nineteenth-century theologian and historian Bishop William Stubbs wrote that the Black Death was responsible for "nearly all the social changes which take place in England down to the Reformation."[2] This may be an exaggeration, but the experience was certainly transformative.

Bearing witness to so much death also created a profound cultural shift that had ramifications into the next century. It ushered in a new era of art marked by images of death. Two of the most enduring are the Grim Reaper and the Danse Macabre, or Dance of Death, both of which were created in this period.

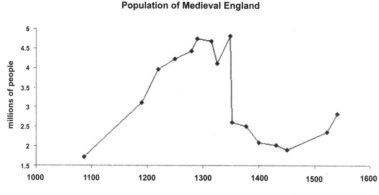

Population of Medieval England

data from Broadberry et al 2010, English Medieval Population

It also shook up the social structures that had previously reigned. The fact that the plague cut down peasant and priest alike caused many to question the existing religious hierarchies and set the stage for the "Great Schism," which ultimately led to the Protestant Reformation.

The Flagellant Movement, led by a self-proclaimed master with no formal religious background, emerged at this time. Its followers went from town to town whipping themselves to atone for their sins. Flagellants were one of many groups fueling a frenzy of attacks on supposed outsiders, including Romani gypsies and especially Jews. A Papal Bull issued by Pope Clement was not enough to stem the tide of violence against Jewish communities. Many in Germany, Austria, and France were completely destroyed, leading to mass migrations of Jews to Poland and Eastern Europe.

Feudal systems of labor also came into question. With a smaller healthy population, labor became more valuable. In England, Parliament responded to this assault on the social order by passing a law keeping wages from rising. This backfired and led to the Peasants Revolt of 1381 and many smaller local uprisings. The Peasants Revolt itself was unsuccessful, but, as historian Barbara Tuchman noted, "In an age when social conditions were regarded as fixed, such action was revolutionary."[3] Economic historian Şevket Pamuk, in a 2007 paper, suggests that these revolts laid the foundation for the labor disputes of the Industrial Revolution.[4]

Historian and theologian F. A. Gasquet suggested that property inherited in the wake of so many deaths led to the creation of the middle class. "The most striking and immediate effect of the mortality was to bring about nothing less than a complete social revolution," he wrote.[5]

The Black Death, wrote Tuchman, "may have been the unrecognized beginning of modern man."[6]

Chapter

12

The Little Ice Age's Witch Trials

Beginning around the start of the fourteenth century, the average global climate cooled, with temperatures dropping as much as 3.6°F /2°C, and the cool period lasted about five centuries, into the 1800s. The era is known as the Little Ice Age.

Archaeologists have various theories as to what caused the cooling. Some blame sun spots or an increase of volcanic eruptions. Some scientists believe the underlying cause of the volcanism was changes in the ocean currents that altered pressure on the continental shelves, leading to more seismic activity. This means more volcanic eruptions, which threw more dust and debris into the atmosphere and reduced the sunlight. Whatever its cause, it ushered in a period of cooling known as the Little Ice Age. Meteorologists probably do not pay enough attention to the role of ocean currents and how changes in ocean currents brought on by climate change would impact weather patterns. Sometimes changes in ocean currents could intensify global warming or could counter it. These are not nearly as well understood as other weather and climate impacts.

The term "Little Ice Age" was coined in 1939 by a Dutch-born American geologist named F.E. Matthes. It is most commonly applied to a broad period of cooling which occurred between 1300 and 1850, but some scientists use it specifically for the later part of the era from 1500–1850. Temperatures across the Northern Hemisphere fell by an average of 1.1°F/.6°C. This may not sound like much, but it shows how sensitive the weather is to what may seem like minor temperature variations. Keep in mind, an average drop of 1.1 degrees over hundreds of years means that some years might have been as much 4–10 degrees colder than normal in some places, which is like having NYC experience the climate of Montreal, Canada. These are averages, so in certain years, temperatures would have been much more extreme, as much as 10–15°F below normal. That can cause all the crops to be wiped out. It was enough to cause glaciers to expand and weather to be more volatile throughout the Northern Hemisphere.

Severe winters were followed by cool, wet summers. The River Thames and the Po River froze over for months on end. Charles Dickens novels spoke much about cold weather and snow. It was colder in England then. There were violent storms throughout Northern Europe and the Baltic seas. Norway suffered widespread crop failures, which made it dependent on grain imported from the North German plains. Without modern storage, refrigeration, communications, and commerce, crop failures resulted in widespread famine. Starving cows failed to produce milk, and in general, cows produce less milk when it is cold. The effects were not felt equally in every city and village: some thriving areas were hit hard, while others remained relatively unscathed.

Frightened populations in these areas knew nothing about the large-scale climatic shift behind their troubles. In these less enlightened periods, demonic forces were suspected. While a belief in magic and witchcraft was not new, the Little Ice Age fostered a new idea: witches could control the weather. As Tad Baker, who wrote a book on the Salem witch trials, put it, "the higher the misery quotient, the more likely you are to be seeing witches."[1]

But misery was only one ingredient. While disruptions because of the shifting climate were widespread, accusations of witchcraft tended to emerge in specific sorts of communities, and it was not necessarily in those that had suffered the most. If an agrarian village saw its crops fail, but the loss was suffered across the entire community, people were less likely to attribute their woes to personal malevolence. In areas where certain groups were harmed more than others, especially where there were already social divisions and resentments, the citizens were more likely to blame their misfortunes on a personal enemy and to appeal to authorities for retribution.

According to *Scientific American*, "In regions with a strong government and legislation such trials were rare or nonexistent, even during climatic unfavorable phases."[2] Witch trials occurred where the religious authorities felt their grip on power was more tenuous. Such leaders were most likely to be swayed by a populace demanding action against forces that were, in reality, beyond anyone's control. And supporting such activity helped deflect blame away from the church for not doing something to end the misery.

Witch panics, and systematic witch hunts, rose alongside climate-induced suffering, reaching their peak as the cooling did. Witch fever began in Switzerland in the 1430s and quickly spread. It was not until the 1480s that the notion that evil women could change the weather had become widespread enough to be officially accepted by the Catholic Church. In 1484, Pope Innocent VIII issued a Papal Bull officially endorsing the concept.

Shortly thereafter, Dominicans Johann Sprenger, dean of the University of Cologne, and Henrich Krämer, a teacher of theology at the University of Salzburg and the Inquisitor of Tirol, Germany, published the definitive guide to witch hunting. It described how to identify witches and how to interrogate and punish them for doing things like raising hailstones and tempests and causing lightning blasts. The book guided inquisitors for centuries.

Witch trials flared up from Spain to Russia as communities suffered crop failures and disruption. Between 1580 and 1620 in the Bern, Switzerland region alone, more than a thousand suspected witches were burned, drowned, or hanged. In Treves, France between 1581 and 1595, an estimated 2,700 people were executed.

Historic diaries and sermons from Massachusetts show that the Salem Witch Trials in 1691–1692 occurred during an especially harsh winter. Local records show that Rev. Samuel Parris, whose daughter was the first to accuse a witch of making her fall ill, had been arguing with his parish over short supplies of wood.

As the global temperatures started to become warmer and more stable, the number of witch trials diminished. By the 1770s, there were only a few isolated witch panics in Central Europe. The last European to be executed as a witch died in 1782. The warming has continued to this day. Make no mistake, carbon dioxide is a greenhouse gas and the amount of carbon dioxide in the atmosphere has increased by nearly 50 percent over the last seventy-five years. Much, but not all of the warming is due to the burning of fossil fuels. Furthermore, as the earth has warmed, methane has escaped from the permafrost in Northern Canada and Siberia, further exacerbating the greenhouse effect. On top of that, as temperatures rise the atmosphere can hold more water vapor and water vapor is still another greenhouse gas. The feedback mechanism to warming all seems to be in the same direction, toward higher temperatures.

The Milankovitch Cycle and Climate Change

About a century ago Milutin Milankovitch, a Serbian scientist, theorized that long-term changes in the relationship between the Earth and the Sun are a strong driver of changes in the Earth's climate, and are responsible for triggering the beginning and end of the Ice Ages.

He examined three specific variations in the Earth's orbital movements that affect the amount and distribution of solar radiation that the Earth receives, and these are now known as Milankovitch cycles.

These Milankovitch cycles include:

1. Eccentricity, which is the shape of Earth's orbit,
2. Obliquity, which is the angle Earth's axis is tilted with respect to its orbital plane, currently 23.5 degrees, and
3. Precession, which is the direction Earth's axis of rotation, North and South Poles, is pointed.

Eccentricity: The Earth's orbit around the sun is not perfectly circular but rather slightly elliptical, due primarily to the gravity pull from Jupiter and Saturn. This means that the distance between the Earth and Sun is not constant, but varies from about 91.4 million miles (147.1 million km) in its closest approach about January 3 (known as perihelion) to 94.5 million miles (152.1 million km) at its farthest about July 4 (known as aphelion).

Eccentricity is the measure of this variation and is why our seasons are slightly different lengths, with summers in the Northern Hemisphere currently about 4.5 days longer than winters, and springs about three days longer than autumns. If the Earth's orbit were perfectly circular, the lengths of the four seasons would be equal.

The difference in the distance between Earth's closest approach to the Sun (known as perihelion), which occurs on or about January 3 each year, and its farthest departure from the Sun (known as aphelion) on or about July 4, is currently about 5.1 million kilometers (about 3.2 million miles), a variation of 3.4 percent. That means on each January day, about 6.8 percent more incoming solar radiation reaches Earth than it does on each July day. Counterintuitively, this means that the Earth actually currently receives slightly less heating from solar radiation in Northern Hemisphere summer than in winter.

The Earth's eccentricity varies in cycles of about one hundred thousand years and is currently approaching its minimum, when the amount of solar radiation reaching the earth is about 23 percent lower than at the maximum eccentricity.

These cycles are believed to be one of the primary causes of the earth's Ice Ages but because each cycle takes one thousand centuries, they have minimal impact on the kind of climate change we are currently experiencing.

(Continued on next page)

Obliquity: This is the angle Earth's axis of rotation is tilted as it travels around the Sun and is the cause of seasons. The greater this tilt angle the more extreme our seasons are, as each hemisphere receives more energy when tilted toward the Sun in summer and less when tilted away in winter.

When the tilt angle is larger, glaciers tend to melt and retreat, especially in higher latitudes, while glaciers tend to grow when this angle is smaller.

The tilt angle varies from about 22.1 to 24.5 degrees and is currently 23.4 degrees and decreasing in a cycle that lasts about forty-one thousand years.

As the tilt angle decreases, it results in increasingly warmer winters and cooler summers. The warmer winters allow for more moisture to be held in the atmosphere, resulting in more snowfall, and the cooler summers means that not all of the snow melts each summer so that over years and centuries the snow builds up into glaciers and ice sheets at higher latitudes. As this ice cover increases, it reflects more of the Sun's energy back into space promoting additional cooling, which enables the ice sheets to grow even faster and to spread toward the tropics, radically changing the climate of the Earth.

Precession: This is a slight wobbling of the Earth upon its rotational axis, like a slightly off-center spinning toy top, that is caused by the tidal forces from the gravity of the Sun and Moon making the Earth bulge at the equator.

The trend in the direction of this wobble relative to the fixed positions of stars has a cycle that lasts a little more than twenty-five thousand years.

This axial precession makes seasonal contrasts more extreme. While the Earth is basically 70 percent water and 30 percent land, the distribution is very uneven between the hemispheres—the Northern Hemisphere has about twice the land mass as the Southern Hemisphere. So the variations from day to night over the land and from winter to summer in the Northern Hemisphere tend to be much more dramatic. Given that there is more heat in the winter, when we are closest to the sun, and less in the summer, the extremes are less than they will be in thirteen thousand years. But in approximately thirteen thousand years it will be the opposite. Starting in eight thousand to ten thousand years, ice will be favored to grow and glaciers might form in one hemisphere, currently the Southern Hemisphere, while making them less extreme in the other, currently the Northern Hemisphere.

Axial precession does affect seasonal timing relative to Earth's closest/farthest points around the Sun. However, the modern calendar system ties itself to the seasons, and so, for example, the Northern Hemisphere winter will never occur in July. Today Earth's North Stars are Polaris and Polaris Australis, but a couple of thousand years ago, they were Kochab and Pherkad.

There is also a second kind of precession, known as apsidal, in which the oval-shaped path the Earth follows around the Sun also wobbles due to the gravity of Jupiter and Saturn, with one cycle lasting about 112,000 years.

The combined effects of axial and apsidal precession result in an overall precession cycle spanning about twenty-three thousand years on average.

The variations in the three Milankovitch cycles can be combined to generate a picture of the changes in Earth's climate over the past few million years.

Milankovitch calculated that Ice Ages occur approximately every forty-one thousand years, and researchers examining ice cores confirmed that this was the case from about one to three million years ago. But about eight hundred thousand years ago, the cycle of Ice Ages lengthened to one hundred thousand years, matching the Earth's eccentricity cycle, though scientists do not yet have a clear answer why this transition occurred.

Scientific research to better understand the mechanisms that cause changes in Earth's rotation and how specifically the Milankovitch cycles combine to affect climate is ongoing, although most scientists do agree that they drive the timing of glacial-interglacial cycles. Earth is currently in an interglacial period, a period of milder climate between Ice Ages. If there were no human influences on climate, scientists say Earth's current orbital positions within the Milankovitch cycles predict our planet should be cooling, not warming, continuing a long-term cooling trend that began six thousand years ago.

Milankovitch cycles provide a strong framework for understanding long-term changes in Earth's climate, including the beginning and end of Ice Ages throughout Earth's history. But Milankovitch cycles can't explain all climate change that's occurred over the past 2.5 million years or so. And more importantly, they cannot account for the current period of rapid warming Earth has experienced since the pre-Industrial period (the period between 1850 and 1900), and particularly since the latter part of the twentieth century.

While the Milankovitch cycles have become well-accepted in recent decades as a driver of long-term climate change, nearly all meteorologists have historically been skeptical that there is any possibility that changes in solar output have any

(Continued on next page)

significant effect on the Earth's weather. After all, there is a reason that the solar output is called the solar constant. And while it is not actually constant, the solar output varies on a scale that has been believed to be much smaller than weather and climate variation.

However, over the past ten to fifteen years new research has suggested mechanisms by which relatively small changes in solar output can be substantially amplified in the upper atmosphere and translated at much greater magnitude into lower layers of the atmosphere where humans live. If this concept is correct, this would enable solar activity to have a much larger effect on weather and climate than was previously believed.

So, while some meteorologists still believe that any relationship between solar activity and weather is at best pseudoscience, attitudes are perhaps beginning to change.

There do seem to be at least two correlations between solar activity and weather that are related to sunspot cycles, which average about eleven years. One is a direct correlation between sunspot activity and temperature—higher sunspot activity seems to be reasonably correlated with higher temperatures averaged across the Earth. The second is an inverse correlation between the length of sunspot cycles and Earth's average temperatures, where shorter sunspot cycles are correlated with higher global (or at least Northern Hemisphere) temperatures.

These correlations do fit well with the Maunder Minimum, of the late seventeenth and early eighteenth centuries, which seems to be reasonably well coordinated with the cold weather of the Little Ice Age. During the Maunder Minimum, sunspots were rare, with many years reporting totals in the single digits. Over the two-and-a-half centuries since, most years have had more than one hundred sunspots, with more than two hundred annually in most years from the 1940s to early 2000s, known as the Modern Maximum.

One can speculate on what this means going forward. Even though some recent years have been the warmest on record, much of which is generally attributed to human activity, the correlations with solar activity, if they are real, suggest that the twenty-first century thus far should have been a cool period, as sunspot numbers have dropped significantly over the past two decades. Of course, since these are not well understood, there could be a lag between the drop in sunspot activity and the cooling, possibly offsetting some of the human induced warming, although this is pure speculation.

If in fact solar activity has been keeping the Earth cooler than it would have otherwise been in recent years, once the solar activity moves into a more neutral pattern, which current solar forecasts suggest it seems likely to do in about twenty years, the Earth's average temperature will jump by an additional 2–4°F beyond where it would otherwise be, raising temperatures to what are generally considered to be catastrophic levels for parts of the Earth.

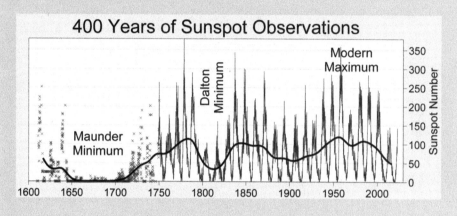

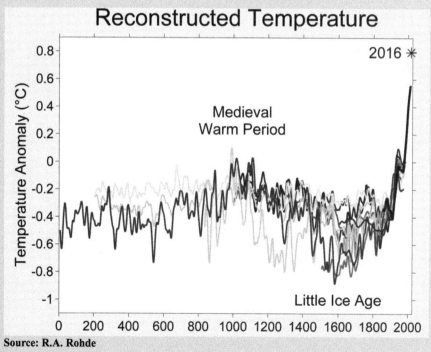

Source: R.A. Rohde

(Continued on next page)

However, scientists have not yet determined the reason for the solar cycles, nor have they determined how to successfully forecast them beyond the next cycle. So, any forecast of solar activity beyond about 2035 should be considered highly speculative. Despite these forecasts for increasing activity, it is even possible that the recent weak cycles are the start of another century comparable to the Maunder Minimum and, if that were the case, we might expect the Earth's temperatures to cool significantly, perhaps offsetting some of the human-induced warming.

Of course, as you see in this book, there are other factors that can greatly impact our climate. These include major volcanic eruptions, changes in the albedo of the Earth caused by human activities, planned or unplanned, changes in vegetation coverage, and of course, significant changes in ocean currents and flow, and cloud cover. But the important role of greenhouse gases, such as CO_2, Methane, and water vapor is best understood.

Chapter

13

A Storm Ends French Florida

oday Spanish influence can be seen throughout Florida. Had a Huguenot adventurer been more successful, however, Florida, Georgia, and South Carolina would have been colonized in the name of France. A hurricane intervened in these plans.

Ponce de Leon had claimed Florida for Spain forty-nine years earlier, but the great Spanish explorers, Juan Ponce de León, Hernando De Soto, and Pánfilo de Narváez, were all gone. The dream of unlimited treasure and finding the Fountain of Youth in America had died with them. On September 23, 1561, King Philip II of Spain called off any future exploratory missions.

This created an opportunity for France, which was then embroiled in religious conflict. Admiral Gaspard de Coligny, a leader of the persecuted Protestants, known as Huguenots, appointed a charismatic young captain, Jean Ribault, to sail to the New World and find a place for them to practice their religion, establish a French military outpost, and, if possible, make a fortune.

Ribault set sail on February 18, 1562 and, on May 1, arrived at what is today the mouth of the St. Johns River in Jacksonville. He named it "the River of May." Ribault built a monument with the French coat of arms and declared it French territory. He then sailed north and established a colony at what is now Parris Island, South Carolina. He called it Fort Caroline. From here, he hoped to establish a base of operations to attack treasure-filled Spanish merchant ships on their arrival. The French built a fortress, and Ribault returned home to stock up with fresh supplies.

He arrived to find his people at war with the Catholics. So he fled to England, hoping he might be able to get some new ships and supplies there. Instead he was imprisoned in the Tower of London. Because of this misunderstanding, he was not available for the return journey to the colony. His lieutenant, Rene Goulaine de Laudonnière, was chosen to lead the expedition instead. He and three hundred colonists set to work building a second fort in Florida near the River May.

This did not go unnoticed by the Spanish. Philip II sent Captain Pedro Menéndez de Avilés and a fleet of eleven ships with orders to find any foreign settlers and "cast them out by the best means that seems to you possible."[1]

Back in Florida, things were not going well. Laudonnière did not inspire the same sense of mission as Ribault had. The colonists, who had been attracted by the promise of riches, became restless as their supplies dwindled. Laudonnière narrowly avoided being poisoned by a team of angry conspirators.

Meanwhile, Ribault was finally released from the Tower of London and made his way back to the colonies with a fleet of seven ships in late August. Ribault's presence, as well as an infusion of six hundred fresh colonists—including soldiers, workers, and families—brought new hope to the struggling colonies.

A week later, however, the colonists spotted the Spanish fleet. The French mariners quickly put out to sea and, with their smaller, faster vessels, were able to chase the Spanish away. The Spanish retreated to St. Augustine, about thirty-five miles south.

Laudonnière and Ribault disagreed on what to do next. Laudonnière thought his side would have the advantage if the Spanish launched the offensive, which the French could defend from their fort. Ribault, however, was a man of action. He wanted to make short work of the Spanish by overwhelming them with their superior force before they could land. Had they gone with Laudonnière's plan, Florida might have stayed in French hands. Instead, Ribault had his men load four ships and set sail for St. Augustine on September 10, right in the center of the hurricane season.

The storm blew them right past the Spanish outpost all the way to Cape Canaveral, where the ships foundered. Remarkably, there were few casualties. But Ribault's soldiers were stranded on shore with no shelter and no supplies.

The storm that capsized the French emboldened the Spanish. Menéndez saw the tempest as a divine judgment on the heretics. And with the soldiers out of the way, Menéndez ordered his men to set sail for Fort Caroline. The colonists were defenseless, and 132 were killed. The Spanish needed only one hour to secure the fort. The few survivors, mostly women and children, were allowed to return to France in a small ship captained by Ribault's son. The Spanish later built a fort on the site and called it Fort Matanzas—Spanish for "massacre."

A STORM ENDS FRENCH FLORIDA

Meanwhile, facing starvation, the hurricane survivors began to surrender. The Spanish asked them to convert to Catholicism and take confession as a price for their lives. Most did not, and were executed as Huguenots.

That was the last French attempt to colonize the area. Thanks to a hurricane, Spain was able to retain control of Florida until ceding the territory to the United States in 1821, leaving an indelible mark on its history and culture.

Chapter

14

A Storm Inspires Shakespeare's *The Tempest*

William Shakespeare was a master of language. His originality was such that he added about 1,700 words and word combinations to English. He was not, however, highly original when it came to his plots. All but two were adapted from familiar stories from literature, history, or mythology. One of the two wholly original plays was *Love's Labour's Lost*. The other, the last one he ever wrote, was inspired by the weather. It was called *The Tempest*.

The "tempest" in question was probably a hurricane, which battered a fleet of nine English ships somewhere near the mid-Atlantic archipelago of the Azores as they made their way to resupply and repopulate the Jamestown Colony. Witnesses described the storm as a "cruel tempest" and a "most terrible and vehement storm."[1]

Hurricanes are unusual in the Azores. When they do occur, such storms usually start in the tropics and generally move east to west and sometimes approach the East Coast of the United States. At some point, they encounter the westerly winds at mid-latitude, causing the storm to recurve heading north and then northeast and race east across the Atlantic, sometimes bringing gale force winds to parts of Europe and sometimes as far south as the Azores. The strongest Azores hurricane during the era in which such things were measured was hurricane number eight of 1926. (This was before hurricanes were given names.) It made landfall on São Miguel Island near Ponta Delgada at peak Category 2 strength (105 mph/169 kph winds). Winds of such magnitude cause waves up to forty feet high with an eighty-foot total amplitude from trough to crest. Obviously, the Shakespearean play occurred long before there were official measurements or a historical record of such storms.

A STORM INSPIRES SHAKESPEARE'S *THE TEMPEST*

The fleet in question had departed on June 2, 1609, and the journey was uneventful with favorable winds until the morning of July 24, 1609, when the sailors encountered a storm. The furious winds and choppy seas made it impossible to keep the fleet together. The deputy governor of Virginia, William Strachey, was on board one of the ships, the *Sea Venture*, and witnessed

> the clouds gathering thick upon us, and the winds singing, and whistling most unusually . . . a dreadful storm and hideous began to blow from out the Northeast, which swelling, and roaring as it were by fits, some hours with more violence than others, at length did beat all light from heaven; which like a hell of darkness turned black upon us, so much the more fuller our horror . . . For four-and-twenty hours the storm in a restless tumult had blown so exceedingly as we could not apprehend in our imaginations any possibility of greater violence . . . The Sea swelled above the clouds, and gave battle unto heaven. It could not be said to rain; the waters like whole rivers did flood the air . . . winds and seas were as mad as fury and rage could make them.[2]

One ship was destroyed. Strachey's ship, the flagship *Sea Venture*, got separated from the rest of the fleet and was presumed lost. The *Sea Venture* had actually run aground far off course on the archipelago now known as Bermuda. (Shakespeare and his contemporaries called it Bermoothes.)

William Strachey wrote an eyewitness account of his adventure full of descriptive passages and vivid imagery. Shakespeare knew members of the company, maybe even Strachey himself, and he likely had an opportunity to read Strachey's letter before the wider public. Some of Strachey's phrases found their way into Shakespeare's play.

Strachey described Bermuda as "*Devils Ilands* . . . feared and avoyded . . . above any other place in the world" but they became a land of "deliverance" for the survivors who huddled in whatever broken piece of the ship would shield them. It was a wonder to all that everyone survived.

After that trauma, Strachey described a mystical experience, "An apparition of a little round light, like a faint star, trembling and streaming along with a sparkling blaze . . . shooting sometimes from shroud to shroud, tempting to settle as it were on any of the four shrouds . . . half the night it kept with us, running sometimes along the mainyard to the very end, and then returning."[3]

What the survivors actually saw was a glowing plasma created by an electric field caused by the storm, a phenomenon known as "St. Elmo's Fire." St. Elmo's Fire is seen when high electrical voltage, such as lightning, affects a gas and causes a "glow discharge."

It is a naturally occurring version of what happens inside the tube of a fluorescent light bulb. St. Elmo is the patron saint of sailors. His name is etymologically related to the Greek word for torch, *elene*. Because the effect tends to occur toward the end of a thunderstorm, mariners have traditionally considered St. Elmo's Fire a good omen.

Shakespeare personified the phenomenon in the character of the sprite Ariel who ran about Prospero's wrecked ship:

> I flamed amazement: sometime I'd divide,
> And burn in many places; on the topmast,
> The yards and bowsprit, would I flame distinctly,
> Then meet and join.

The same month that Strachey's letter reached England, another ship and another bit of bad weather may have given the Bard the inspiration to finish his script. What has apparently gone unnoticed is that a royal ship was not only launched much closer to home the same month that the Strachey letter arrived in London, but that its launch was also nearly thwarted by bad weather.

The *Prince Royal,* dedicated to Prince Henry, the son of James I, was scheduled to launch on September 25, 1610 to great fanfare. Large crowds turned out to witness the event, but a sudden storm on the Thames nearly destroyed the ship before the launch. In the aftermath, the ship's builder, Phineas Pett, wrote a journal describing his suspicions that his enemies had summoned the storm in order to wreck his ship and humiliate him.

The following summer Shakespeare's new play made its debut. In it, the character Prospero uses magic to attack a king's ship as it passes the enchanted island where he was stranded. Weather influences fate prominently in other Shakespeare plays—"wise" flashes of lightning in *King Lear*, a cold forest of mixed blessings in *As You Like It*, and a hot July heralding the passions of lovers in *Romeo and Juliet*.

Why did these reports of these storms have such an impact on Shakespeare? The reason is, it is likely that storms of such magnitude and severity were highly unusual in and around London. The impact and life-threatening effects of a hurricane had such an impression on Shakespeare that he decided to create a play based on the theme since it would also be dramatic for most Londoners who would see the play because they were also unaccustomed to such severe weather.

Perhaps, people in Europe had rising curiosity about hurricanes as stories of their severity in the Caribbean islands and the colonies became more widespread.

Hurricane Names

Before 1953, tropical storms and hurricanes did not have human names. The one exception was in the West Indies where hurricanes were given the name of the saint's day on which the storm hit. For example, Puerto Rico was struck on July 26, 1825 by Hurricane Santa Ana. July 26 is the feast day of Saint Anne.

In the United States, as we saw with the number eight Azores hurricane of 1926, they were identified by year and numbered sequentially as they were spotted. The system caused some confusion when two or more tropical storms were active at once. It was not always easy to remember whether your town was in the potential path of tropical storm five or six. In the late 1940s and early '50s, to try and rectify this situation, military names were given such as Abel, Baker, Charlie, etc. That meant the same names were used year after year. Before that, names were given based on where the storm hit or came from.

In 1953, the United States tried to rectify this by giving the storms female names. In 1978, some storms in the Northern Pacific started to be given male names. A year later, storms in the Atlantic were given alternating male and female names as well.

Atlantic hurricanes now have a list of names that repeat on a six-year cycle. If a name becomes associated with a particularly deadly storm (for example, 2005's Hurricane Katrina) it is retired and at the next meeting of the international committee of the World Meteorological Organization a new name is selected to replace it on the list.

Chapter

15

Lack of Rain Sparks the Great Fire of London

A t the center of London stands one of the most recognizable monuments in the city. St. Paul's Cathedral, designed by Christopher Wren in an English baroque style, is the spiritual heart of Anglican London. The architectural marvel boasts one of the world's largest domes. Winston Churchill's funeral was held here, as was the wedding of Prince Charles and Princess Diana. In addition to its regular worshipers, the cathedral is visited by two million tourists each year. And it owes its existence to a dry summer and a strong easterly wind. The prevailing wind in London comes from the west.

The entire look that we now associate with London emerged from the ashes of the Great Fire, which blazed through the wooden walls of the medieval city, reducing more than thirteen thousand houses and buildings, including the old St. Paul's Cathedral, to ashes.

The early months of 1666 saw decreased precipitation throughout Europe. In England, there was so little rainfall from November 1665 on that, by summer 1666, the River Thames at Oxford was reduced to a trickle. The great diarist Samuel Pepys recorded that the year was one of the hottest and driest on record and June 7 was "the hottest day that I have ever felt in my life."[1] As a result, there were major fires in cities throughout the continent. None, however, was as dramatic as the Great Fire of London, which began on the hot, dry, windy evening of Sunday, Sept. 2, 1666. Conditions were perfect for the rapid spread of a fire that started in a bakery belonging to the king's baker, Thomas Farriner. London saw 436 acres destroyed, including 13,200 homes and eighty-seven churches.

London was a congested city, still surrounded by Roman walls. Many of the houses on its narrow alleys were "jettied," which meant that the buildings on either side of the road jutted out on the upper levels so they nearly touched at the roof line. Homes were lit by candles and heated by fireplaces. In this environment, fires were common, and, in its first day, the people were not overly alarmed. Neighbors came out to throw whatever liquids they had on hand on the flames, believing this fire, like many others, would burn itself out. Yet it soon became clear that this was no ordinary fire.

The timbers of the houses, dry from the parched summer, went up like so much kindling. As London was the manufacturing center of the nation, the fire spread to buildings full of flammable products like wool, rope, flour, and pitch. There were even warehouses full of barrels of gunpowder. A strong easterly wind carried embers far from their original source, setting buildings that were hundreds of yards away ablaze. When buildings caught fire without any major fires nearby, a panicked public suspected arson and looked for scapegoats.

On the fourth day of the fire, Samuel Pepys climbed a church steeple to survey the damage and described it as "the saddest sight of desolation that I ever saw; everywhere great fires, oyle-cellars, and brimstone and other things burning."[2] Parts of the city continued to burn for months. There were flare ups in cellars as late as the following March. In the end, the old St. Paul's Cathedral could not be saved, and seventy thousand of the city's eighty thousand people were left homeless; this was nearly 90 percent of the cities' residents. Officially, there were only six deaths from the fire, but historians now believe that many more perished in the fire than recorded.

It took fifty years to rebuild. The London Building Act of 1667, designed to prevent another great fire, changed the look of the city. The London that re-emerged was one of flat-fronted houses made of brick. The result was an elegant, restrained form of architecture with Wren's St. Paul's Cathedral as its center. Some roads were widened, two new streets were created, and the quayside was improved. It was, said one Londoner, "not only the finest, but the healthiest city in the world."[3]

St. Paul's Cathedral was completed in 1711. The circumstances of its creation are memorialized in the south portico, which features a carving of a phoenix rising from the ashes with the Latin word *Resugam* ("I shall rise again") inscribed underneath. London did rise again. In the next centuries, it would become the center of the largest empire the world had ever seen.

London was not the only great city to burn and be rebuilt after a drought set the stage for a conflagration. We will hear about another famous fire as we continue, along with a nearly forgotten fire that was more deadly than either one.

Chapter
16

Climate Yields the Sweet Stradivarius

Violins crafted by the luthier Antonio Stradivari are among the most valuable instruments in the world. In 2011, a single violin that was once owned by the granddaughter of Lord Byron sold for $16 million (£9.5 million) at a charity auction. The most expensive cello ever sold was a Duport Stradivarius made in 1711. Stradivarii are rare. Only 602 of the 1,116 instruments made by the master are known to have survived. But rarity alone does not account for their value. Though a lot depends on who does the playing, the instruments can produce elegant tones and a clean quality known as "brilliance." This character may be a product of dense wood from trees that grew slower during the Little Ice Age.

Stradivari was born in 1646, during the Maunder Minimum, the coldest part of the Little Ice Age. The cooling trend continued until 1715. As he grew, so did the spruce trees in the Southern Alps that would one day provide the wood for his instruments. This wood was already the material of choice for instrument makers. In difficult growing conditions, trees reserve their energy by growing more slowly. During the cold period, trees showed the slowest growth rates of the past five centuries.

Before the lumber made its way to the luthier, however, it was processed by lumberjacks. They soaked the wood in a mineral bath to ward off worms and fungus. A study published in 2016 suggests that these minerals hardened to the wood through chemical bonds and also contribute to the instruments' special sound.[1]

Stradivari was trained in his craft by Nicola Amati, the grandson of the inventor of the modern violin. By the time he was ready to open his own shop, the trees had produced an especially dense, strong wood owing to its narrow growth rings. From 1666 to

1684, Stradivari used this raw material to make instruments in the style of his teacher. Twenty years on, however, he began to experiment and started to produce what would be his most valuable creations. They were larger than his first instruments, with innovative proportions and a special method of treating the wood. He used deep varnish that soaked into the pores of the wood and preserved it. This layer was covered with a glossy coat of egg whites and honey and finally another layer, with a secret combination of ingredients. Some argue that it was this gloss that gave his instruments their special qualities.

Another reason is their age itself. In 2016, a study by Hwan-Ching Tai, a professor of chemistry at National Taiwan University, found that a wood component known as hemicellulose had eroded over time. About one-third had decomposed in Stradivarii and other instruments of the period. Hemicellulose is absorbent. When there is less of it, the wood holds less moisture. The less moisture there is, the more "brilliant" an instrument sounds. Tai also found that over time there was a detachment in the wood fibers, probably from years of the vibrations of being played. "Top violinists often feel like these old violins vibrate more freely," said Tai, "which allows them to express a wider set of emotions."[2]

It is this particular set of circumstances, unique in history, that makes the instruments so special and so highly sought after. If it had not been so cold, humanity would never have been exposed to the sounds of the Stradivarius.

Chapter

17

A Chill
Freezes Birds and
Transforms Europe

All over Europe on January 6, 1709, people woke up shivering. Some found their nightcaps frozen to their headboards. They would continue to suffer for months to come in the coldest weather the continent had seen in five hundred years. It has not been as cold again since. Across large parts of Europe the average temperature for months was as much as 12°F/7°C below the average for twentieth-century Europe.

William Derham was the rector of Upminster, 16.5 m/26.6 km northeast of Charing Cross in London. He was a keen amateur meteorologist who took notes on barometric pressure and temperatures several times a day. Derham records that on the night of January 5 the temperature fell dramatically and kept on falling. It reached its lowest point, 10.4°F/-12°C, on January 10. In Paris it was even colder, with temperatures descending to 5°F/-15°C on January 14. They remained at that level for eleven days. At the end of the month there was a brief respite and then the frigid temperatures returned and remained until mid-March.

It was so cold that trees were said to explode. In Scandinavia, the Baltic Sea was solid enough for people to walk across it as late as April. Livestock froze to death in their barns, sailors froze to their bunks, and the soil was frozen to the depth of a meter. Author and student of the time, Virginia Woolf, wrote that "birds froze in mid air and fell like stones to the ground." In England, it was called the Great Frost. France dubbed it *Le Grand Hiver*.

It was the climax of the Little Ice Age, but why this particular winter was so harsh has never been fully explained. Climatologist Dennis Wheeler notes that there were some major volcanic eruptions in 1707 and 1708, including Mount Fuji in Japan and Santorini and Vesuvius in Europe.[1] As we have seen, these could have created dust veils that depressed temperatures.

Whatever the cause was of the climate disruption, its effects are beyond doubt. If the people of Europe had known what was coming, they could have planned ahead, but with no weather forecasting in the eighteenth century, the population was taken by complete surprise as the Thames froze over, roads were blocked by snow and ice, and river barges were stopped in place, halting commerce. Paris was essentially cut off from the rest of France for three months.

When transportation did get going again, there was little for merchants to sell. The winter had killed livestock, and the late frost had decimated the harvests.

In France, starving citizens tried to make meals of ground ferns, nettles, and thistles. Over the next two years, the French birth rate plummeted and 630,000 people died as a consequence of what happened in the winter of 1709.

England and France each experienced deep recessions. In England, there was a 14 percent drop in economic activity, and in France a 15 percent drop.

As one observer recalled, "Nobody could pay any more, because nobody was paid. The people of the country in consequence of extractions had become insolvent; commerce dried up and brought no returns. Good faith and confidence were abolished. Chaos, ruin and universal suffering prevailed."[2]

While most commerce eventually returned, one French industry was wiped out entirely—walnut cabinetry. Walnut furniture, sourced from French trees, had been the fashionable furnishing of the well-to-do in the early eighteenth century. But France's walnut trees were so damaged by the Great Frost that exports were banned in order to allow the stocks of timber to be renewed. It was almost a century before a new generation of trees could grow to maturity. In the short term, France's loss was Virginia's gain, as the colony was home to abundant walnut trees. It wasn't long, however, before aristocrats developed a taste for a different exotic rich brown wood from the colonies—mahogany. Plantations in Jamaica, Cuba, Honduras, and Belize supplied the material. Harvested by the work of enslaved people, it took ten to fifty slaves working in teams to extract. As the sources became scarcer, more enslaved people were needed in order to meet the demand, and large areas of the Caribbean were deforested.

The European freeze also set off a wave of emigration from the area that is now Germany. Many people arrived starving and destitute in England. Initially the nation responded with sympathy and charity, but as the numbers of immigrants increased, anti-immigrant sentiment started to grow. By the end of 1709, England had banned all German immigration. This had an impact on Pennsylvania, as Quaker William Penn was working to develop the colony and encouraged displaced Germans to find a new home across the Atlantic.

Author Derek Wilson has pointed out that in spite of the wide-ranging effects of the frigid winter of 1709, most history books focus their attention on the exploits of monarchs and soldiers:

> What you will almost certainly find no reference to is the 1709 Great Freeze. And this, despite the fact that it changed Europe more profoundly than all the activities of kings, parliaments and armies put together. It transformed the political balance in the East and North. It gave a new impetus to colonial settlement. It changed the shape of economic activity. It shifted large masses of Europe's population. It created new fashions. And it killed more people than all the wars that had raged for half a century or more. And that puts us human beings in our place. It reminds us that all our endeavors—good and bad—may at any time be swept into the dustbin of history. No one knows what caused the Great Freeze, but the fact is that for a mere three months out of the last half-millennium Europe was subjected to arctic conditions the like of which it had never before experienced and which it has never since experienced. We need to be humble enough to allot the Great Freeze its appropriate place in our story.[3]

Nowhere were the extremely cold effects of the winter of 1709 more profoundly felt than for the Swedish soldiers battling in Russia, and that will be our next story.

Chapter

18

A Winter Elevates Peter the Great

Long before the era of modern weather forecasting, battles and wars have hinged on the superior ability of one side or another to predict the weather. Throughout their history, Russians have turned their familiarity with, and their adaptability to, their nation's harsh climate into a pillar of defense. Invader after invader underestimated the challenges of the Russian winter. The first time this came into play on a grand scale was in 1709 when a young Swedish King Charles XII set his sights on the Russian territory.

Of course Sweden is no stranger to frigid temperatures itself, but Charles had chosen just about the worst time to launch a northern war. Europe was deep in the throes of one of the most extreme periods of the Little Ice Age. Places that were usually relatively mild, like Paris and Venice, were frozen over from one of the coldest winters ever seen. Russia was doubly cold.

In all fairness to King Charles, Russia had started what would one day be called the Great Northern War. It began when an ambitious Peter I declared war on its neighbor in an attempt to drive Sweden out of the Baltics. Peter understood that the main barrier to both trade and power was that the vast nation lacked decent warm water ports. As French historian Fernand Braudel noted, "Russia could not really exist unless it filled the whole isthmus between the Baltic and the southern seas, and controlled any links between them."[1]

Gaining a foothold in the Baltics would not be easy for Peter. Sweden was the much bigger player on the world stage. It controlled an area that included what are now Finland, Estonia, and parts of Latvia, as well as eastern Russia all the way to St. Petersburg.

King Charles had every reason to believe he could make short work of the Russian attack. In the first battles, it seemed as though it was going to go that way. The Russian army was easily defeated in the battle of Narva by a much smaller Swedish force. Charles, assuming he had nothing more to fear from the Russians, decided to invade places like Denmark and Poland before finally getting back to Peter eight years later.

Peter had been using the time to build up his military. It seemed, however, that it would not be enough. They were trounced by the Swedes again in the battle of Holowczyn in July 1708. In order to prevent Charles from taking Moscow, the Russians set fire to their own territory as they withdrew, leaving no shelter or food for the advancing enemy. With no amenable place to make camp, the Swedes changed course, heading south toward Ukraine. Unfortunately for them, they finally got to a place with a building or two left standing, so they decided to stay there. It was November and Ukraine in November is never a good place to camp. That year it was especially challenging. It was one of the coldest winters the people of the region had experienced.

One by one, Charles's men, with little shelter and dwindling provisions, succumbed to frostbite. Their cattle and horses fell dead, and the forces abandoned heavy cannons they could no longer pull. Their snow-soaked gun powder was ineffective.

The Swedish forces, once fifty-one thousand strong, had been cut down to a ragtag assemblage of disfigured, weary men dressed in whatever coats they were able to scavenge from fallen soldiers. More than a third were sick. Even so, they took the offensive at the battle of Poltava as the Russians also suffered from the cold—but it was their territory.

In early January, they achieved a small victory by taking the fortress of Veprik. The offensive cost them a thousand lives. Charles's forces, such as they were, managed to survive to spring but they found no relief from the elements. As the heavy ice and snow melted, the ground could not absorb it quickly enough, and the territory became an impassable muck. It was not until May 1709 that the Swedes could get their carts moving again.

Learning that Russian reinforcements were on the way, Charles decided to make a last ditch charge against the main Russian defensive position. His army, now down to just seventeen thousand sickly soldiers, was no match against forty thousand Russians. Only 1,500 of the Swedes survived to retreat into Turkey.

"The victory in the decisive Battle of Poltava in 1709 became a sensation in Europe," wrote Russian historian Boris Egorov. "The wild Russian bear had managed to defeat the powerful Swedish lion. An obscure duchy of Muscovy, located on the outskirts of Europe, suddenly became the center of attention for leading European powers. Despite the fact Peter I only took the title of emperor after the end of the Great Northern War in 1721, Europeans started calling Russia an empire after the victory at Poltava."[2]

The victory gave Peter the breathing room to build up his naval strength in the Baltic Sea and eventually—twelve years later—to win the war. By the end of the conflict, Sweden had lost its position as a major European power. Russia was ascendant.

From that day forward, Henry Kissinger described Russia's global ambitions as having "a special rhythm of its own over the centuries, expanding over land mass . . . interrupted occasionally over time . . . only to return again, like a tide crossing the beach."[3]

Chapter

19

A Fog Creates Independent America

The war between England and its American colonies did not begin with the signing of the Declaration of Independence on July 4, 1776, but the act of defiance raised the stakes and set the stage for the largest battle of the war. England, determined to isolate New England from the rest of the colonies, assembled a huge force of thirty-two thousand men who set sail in five hundred ships. Led by General Sir William Howe, they established a base on Staten Island.

In contrast with the British, George Washington's militia was a ragtag assemblage of loosely organized men, almost a third of whom had no weapons. What is more, they had no naval support. If New York was to be defended, Washington would have to hold Brooklyn, on the southwest portion of Long Island. Defending an island surrounded by navigable water and with the east and west sides of New York also surrounded by water was just about the worst possible situation for anyone trying to fend off the greatest navy in the world.

George Washington was forced to split his troops, sending one-third, about twenty thousand men, to Long Island, and leaving the rest to defend New York proper. On August 22, 1776, the British landed a force of about fifteen thousand men on the western tip of Long Island and set up camp. Fighting began a week later and in short order the British had the Americans nearly surrounded. As a group of four hundred soldiers from Maryland held off the British, Washington and his forces retreated to Brooklyn Heights, on the western edge of Long Island. (The battle that followed is sometimes known as the Battle of Long Island and sometimes as the Battle of Brooklyn or Brooklyn Heights.)

A FOG CREATES INDEPENDENT AMERICA

There was only one possible route of escape for the American soldiers: across the East River. A steady north wind kept the British warships from moving into New York Bay and the East River to completely cut the retreat off, but this was a minor concern for the British. As they waited in the comfort of their ships and well-appointed camps, Washington's men were suffering in the rain with no tents and few provisions. If the weakened army made any moves, they would be easily taken and the uprising would be thwarted. General Washington finally gave the order to retreat across the East River at 11:00 p.m. on August 29 as a northeastern storm subsided, shifting winds to the southeast, which allowed the Continental boats to cross the East River. Had the British noticed the retreat, they could easily have sent their warships to meet the overloaded rowboats and massacre the weakened Continental troops.

But the British did not notice the escape. The retreat was carried out in silence and secrecy. "We were strictly enjoined not to speak, or even cough. All orders were given from officer to officer, and communicated to men in whispers," recalled one soldier.[1] And most fortuitously of all, at about two in the morning a thick fog rolled in, blanketing the region.

A major in the Continental army reported that the fog "seemed to settle in a peculiar manner over both encampments. I recollect this peculiar providential occurrence perfectly well; and so very dense was the atmosphere that I could scarcely discern a man at six yards' distance . . . In the history of warfare I do not recollect a more fortunate retreat."[2]

Incidentally, if the battle happened today, Washington's troops would likely have been visible. Thanks to the "heat island effect," the New York City area is rarely blanketed in such a thick fog anymore, especially not in August. To form that kind of fog, you not only need high relative humidity near the ground, but also strong radiational cooling at night, which is heat leaving the Earth, usually under cloudless skies. However cities trap heat more effectively than greener pastures because concrete stores heat. Cities heat up in the day and take longer to cool down at night; therefore fog is less likely to form in modern cities than it was before the age of concrete, brick, and cement.

The Battle of Long Island was a decisive victory for the British, with four hundred Continental soldiers lost and another 1,200 Americans taken prisoner. Washington's army was forced to retreat all the way to Pennsylvania and control of New York City remained in British hands for the remainder of the war. But thanks to the intervention of the fog, only three of Washington's men were lost that night, and another ten thousand lived on to keep fighting. They had lost the battle, but would win the war, and with it American independence.

Chapter

20

Hail Sparks the French Revolution

When small water droplets get lifted by the updraft of a thunderstorm and they are carried high enough, they rise into cold air and form into ice. A bit of ice then gets heavy enough that it starts to fall and gather a coating of liquid moisture. Depending on the strength of the updraft, the hailstone might get pulled up to the freezing level again and again. The coating of liquid freezes each time, making the stone larger and larger. Once it becomes heavy enough to overcome the strength of the updraft, it falls out of the cloud to the ground. Most hailstones are too small to do much damage—around 1 inch (25 mm) or less. In the right conditions, however, this process can continue until the stone is as big as a golf ball or even a baseball. Hail does not loom as large in the popular imagination as tornadoes and tsunamis, but it is consistently one of the most costly weather phenomena.

Large hail can damage property and can be deadly to people and animals that are outside when it falls. Hail can also damage crops. There is hail insurance, which many farmers buy. Many insurance companies use AccuWeather to warn car dealers to get cars under cover in advance of a hail storm. Even an hour's notice of severe hail pinpointed can save millions of dollars for a dealership.

But can it change the course of history? In the right circumstances, yes.

In 1788, the Kingdom of France had the largest population in Europe, but was facing an escalating economic crisis, caused by a major drought. The drought was a double whammy because it caused great suffering among small farmers, which made up a significant percentage of the population, and also caused the price of wheat to rise substantially. Simultaneously, the nation was dealing with the heavy debt it had racked up helping the

American Colonies in their war against England. France was just beginning to recover from the first drought when another hit.

The majority of the French had a diet that consisted largely of bread, and bread accounted for 60–80 percent of the budget of a wage-earner. As crops failed a second time, the cost of bread rose beyond what many people, including tenant farmers, could afford. This did not stop their landlords from demanding the same amount of tax and the powerful church from demanding tithes.

Just when it seemed things could not get any more precarious for the peasant farmers, the sky dealt one last injury. A great storm raining deadly hail pummeled the Versailles region. The British ambassador to France, Lord Dorset, sent a diplomatic report to his foreign secretary. He described hail stones 16 in/40.64 cm in diameter. This was undoubtedly an exaggeration. If the stones were that large, they would be bigger than anything ever scientifically documented. (The largest hailstone on record was 9.3 in/23.62 cm in diameter, recorded in 2018 in Cordoba, Argentina. The largest recorded hailstone in the United States was slightly smaller. It was 8 in/20.32 cm in diameter and weighed almost two pounds/.91 kg. It fell on July 23, 2010, in Vivian, South Dakota.)

Dorset described the effects:

> [I]t is impossible to give description in detail of the damage that has been done: Some of the largest Trees were torn up by the Roots; all the corn and vines destroyed, windows broken and even some houses beaten down. No computation has yet been made of the losses that have been sustained, but it is certain that a Country of at least thirty Leagues (which is 90 miles/145 km) in circumference is entirely laid waste, and it is confidently said that from four to five hundred Villages are reduced to such great distress the inhabitants must unavoidably perish without the immediate assistance of Government; the unfortunate Sufferers not only lose the crops of the present year but of three or four years to come, the vines being entirely cut up.[1]

With the cumulative effects of the drought and the violent hail storm, the French were headed into the winter without the usual stores of food. This would have been deadly enough in normal times, but in 1788 they were about to face an especially cold winter. Thomas Jefferson, then the US minister to the Court of Versailles, recorded that the mercury there dipped to -50°F/-45.6°C. If Jefferson's readings were accurate, the temperature was lower than anything recorded in modern times. The lowest temperature documented in France was -42°F/-41°C in Mouthe in the Bourgogne region of Eastern France on January 17, 1985.

In those conditions, rivers froze to the point that grain mills could not operate, and vintners lost what they had been able to produce when their wine froze and barrels shattered. Forced to stay inside or risk freezing to death, the poor, who now had neither sufficient reserves nor income-producing work, began to starve. Sporadic, unfocused acts of violence started to erupt in late winter and early spring.

The economic causes of the French Revolution were complex, ranging from treaties that allowed English goods to flood the French market, to reduced demand for French cloth in the Mediterranean. "But," as economic historian Lillian Knowles noted, "in 1789 unemployment, lack of food and bitter weather gave point to the other grievances."[2]

In 1789, the vast majority of the French, twenty million out of twenty-six million inhabitants, earned a living through agriculture. Whether they owned or leased their land, they were required to pay, in addition to taxes to the king and tithes to the church, a feudal fee due to lords known as seigneurs. These lords may or may not have been the owners of the fields in question, but they had rights to collect money or the output of the farms they controlled. The peasants who worked the land resented having to pay these dues in the best of times.

As food became scarce, the demand for productive land increased and prices shot up, sometimes doubling. The seigneurs tried to compensate for the higher cost of land by raising feudal dues. Further, while many lords had previously accepted a percentage of the output of the fields as payment, most were now demanding money payments. This forced some farmers to take out high interest loans on the value of their future crops in order to satisfy the obligation to the lords. Meanwhile, a new class of middleman started to arise. These were essentially collection agents. They sought out obsolete feudal claims and started to press for payments on arrears, some going back decades. To make matters worse for the farmers, they priced the dues not on the past prices, but on the inflated prices of the famine year. For peasants who were already being squeezed beyond what they could bear, that was the last straw.

It was not until the middle class "bourgeoisie" got involved, however, that a political movement began to foment. Educated doctors, bankers, and lawyers, who resented the aristocracy, began circulating pamphlets drumming up resentment of a king and queen who lived in ostentatious luxury as their citizens starved.

One phrase that was not in these pamphlets was Marie Antoinette's supposed utterance "Let them eat cake"—or in a more accurate translation, "let them eat brioche." Not only did the French queen never say this, but the first time any publication claimed that she did was fifty years after the French Revolution. The idea was, because of the high prices, most people could not afford to buy bread, so when Marie Antoinette asked what the people wanted, the supposed answer she gave was "if there is no bread to eat, let them eat cake instead."

HAIL SPARKS THE FRENCH REVOLUTION

"Where the middle classes pinned their faith to a constitution and financial reform," wrote Knowles, "the agricultural classes, by far the most numerous, looked to the abolition of seigniorial rights and more land as the remedies for their troubles."[3]

In May 1789, there was a meeting of representatives of the Estates-General, which consisted of clergy and aristocracy, and the Third Estate, which was everyone else. The purpose of the meeting was to solve the economic crisis, but the meeting broke down when the electors could not agree on a system for voting. This proved to be the final straw. Angry members of the Third Estate decided to form their own governing body. King Louis XVI realized he was losing control of the situation, and so he allowed a new National Assembly to be formed. It would allow for the direct representation of all social classes. The plan was to let the body endure during the crisis, and then to disband it.

By July, the situation was dire. New crops had been planted, but they were still weeks from the harvest. The little bread that remained was being sold at exorbitant prices. The social unrest was about to boil over. On July 14, 1789, a crowd gathered around the Bastille Prison, which had become a symbol of the tyranny of the Bourbon monarchs, a dynasty that had ruled France, sometimes harshly, since 1589, because it was believed political prisoners were being held there. After some intense negotiation, the revolutionaries stormed the fortress. They were able to take the prison when some of the guards changed loyalties and joined the invaders. The fall of the Bastille was the beginning of the French Revolution. Soon the drafting of the Declarations of the Rights of Men and the overthrow of the king and queen would send shockwaves throughout Europe. None of it might have happened were it not for an ill-timed hail storm a few weeks before.

I have one of the largest collections of antique barometers in the world, about three hundred of all sorts and they go back as far as 1692. The barometer was invented by Torricelli, a student of Galileo, in 1644. Most of my barometers were made in the late 1700s and the 1800s and were manufactured in Italy, France, the United States, and England.

When I was recently in France, I purchased an antique barometer that was owned by Marie Antoinette and which hung in the Palace of Versailles. I have it hanging in my dining room with about a dozen other French barometers.

Most of my barometers that were manufactured in the United States were made in New England, where the weather can be very stormy. I have found barometers in antique stores all across the United States, with many coming from antique stores in New Orleans, New York City, and also London, Italy, and France. I bought my first one in 1977. The idea of collecting them was inspired by one of my former employees, Dr. Joe Sobel, who had an antique barometer in his house that I saw and admired a few years before I bought my first one.

Chapter

21

Russian Winter Thwarts Napoleon

In 1806, Napoleon Bonaparte seemed invincible. He had annexed what are now Belgium and Holland, as well as parts of Germany, Italy, and Croatia. His reach extended into Poland and Spain, and that worried several neighboring countries. On the other hand, England and Russia deferred to the French leader to avoid disastrous conflict. Napoleon had achieved effective control over most of Europe.

But that year Alexander I, czar of Russia, decided to stand up to him. He stopped complying with a French embargo of English goods, imposed a heavy tax on French luxury goods, and, as a final straw, refused to let Napoleon marry one of his sisters.

Napoleon could not let such open defiance stand, and he spent the next six years preparing one of the greatest fighting forces Europe had ever seen. As many as 650,000 men from all over Europe were put into service to "finish off these barbarians to the north."[1]

He expected to make short work of it. Russia's forces numbered only 180,000. Napoleon planned to be out before the harsh Russian winter set in. But what the Russians knew and Napoleon did not (and, as we shall see in a later chapter, neither did Hitler 135 years later) was that Russia's climate is one of extremes in every season.

Napoleon's troops marched into Russia on June 24. The Russians retreated, allowing Napoleon to take Vilna with little effort three days later. They quickly wondered if it was worth having, as a severe thunderstorm pounded them with cold rain and hail that killed a number of the soldiers and horses that had been untouched by the battle. The next day they found that their heavy carts loaded with provisions were stuck in deep mud. Many had to be abandoned.

RUSSIAN WINTER THWARTS NAPOLEON

It was, of course, still summer. The very chilly rain and hail were followed by abnormally high temperatures as Napoleon's army, less its supplies, marched toward Moscow. The soldiers, who slept out in the open, became dangerously dehydrated. Some were desperate enough to drink horse's urine to stay alive.

The Russians were content to let *La Grande Armée* wear itself out fighting the elements rather than Russian soldiers. The French advanced and the Russians refused to engage them. After two months, heat, exhaustion, illness, and dehydration had killed one hundred thousand of Napoleon's troops.

It was September before there was a full-scale battle, the Battle of Borodino, a bloody conflict that ended without a decisive victory on either side. The Russians withdrew again, leaving the French to battle with nature.

A few weeks later, Napoleon's men limped into Moscow. This was supposed to be *La Grande Armée's* great victory, but they discovered the city had been abandoned and set ablaze. The Muscovites had left behind little food, but there was ample alcohol, and as the French soldiers awaited the expected Russian surrender, they drank and pillaged, loading up on whatever they could take from the empty houses and shops. They filled sacks with valuables such as jewelry, candle sticks, and picture frames, prizes that would come to seem less than worthless in the coming months. Alexander, with the vast reaches of Russia to retreat into, and winter approaching, had no intention of surrendering.

By that point it was October, the infamous Russian winter was on the way, and Napoleon knew his men could not survive it. He was forced to abandon the Moscow campaign and regroup. The French were given a false sense of hope throughout October, which was relatively mild. In November, everything changed. The snow began to fall. The Russians were well prepared to survive their landscape of ice and snow. The French, however, expecting a quick victory, had not prepared for cold temperatures. They were dressed in uniforms designed for summer fighting with light fabrics and no coats. The ragtag force wrapped up in whatever they could scavenge from abandoned buildings: furs, liturgical vestments, women's dresses.

The wheels of the remaining carts were removed and makeshift skis were fitted to them. But the ground would freeze and thaw. What was solid and slippery one day was a mud pit the next. The runners did no good and more carts with provisions were left along the way. All eight hundred of *La Grande Armée's* cannons were eventually left behind. The horses that fell dead were the soldiers' main source of sustenance.

By November 25, they reached the Berezina River, a tributary of the Dnieper River in Belarus, to find that the bridge had been destroyed and the weather conditions were the worst possible for crossing. Were it a bit colder, the river might have been frozen, thus allowing them to march across. It was, however, flowing with chunks of ice and cold enough to be deadly to already weakened soldiers and horses.

Napoleon's army was forced to stop and build two bridges. They worked throughout the night and, on November 26, were able to cross. When they were safely on the other side, they burned the bridges so the Russians could not follow. On December 6, temperatures dropped to -36°F/ -38°C. The extreme cold killed an estimated forty thousand French soldiers in just four days.

Of the seemingly unbeatable French force, only thirty thousand survived. This is less than 5 percent of the initial force. The Russian campaign during extremes in weather is seen as the beginning of the end of Napoleon's reign, culminating in his ultimate downfall at the Battle of Waterloo. If extreme weather had not saved Russia on so many different occasions, one might speculate how different the face of Europe and even the whole world might have evolved. Since the history of the second half of the twentieth century was mostly defined by the Cold War era conflicts between the Soviet Union and the West, one can imagine so many different plausible scenarios. It might have been a very different society not only in Europe, but even in the United States with perhaps less focus on the powerful military industrial complex. Without the Soviet threat, the United States would have had less reason to build up its military to unprecedented levels.

Chapter

22

Tornado Saves Washington, DC

The War of 1812, fought mostly along the US/Canadian border, is not well known in Europe, which had its hands full dealing with Napoleon. In the United States, it is remembered mostly for producing the national anthem, *The Star Spangled Banner*. For Canadians, it was a conflict that shaped their national identity as they stood their ground against an American invasion.

Politicians in the United States saw themselves as liberating Canada from British rule, and thought that it would require little effort. "We can take Canada without soldiers," said US Secretary of War William Eustis, "We have only to send officers into the provinces and the people, disaffected toward their own government, will rally around our standard."[1]

The Canadians were less grateful to be invaded than their neighbors had anticipated. After two years of fighting, the war was still basically a draw. The British-Canadian forces had taken the city of Detroit and then the Americans took it back. In April 1813, US forces captured the city now known as Toronto (then called York) and burned it to the ground. The British could not let this stand, and they sent a well-equipped army of four thousand from England, fresh from battle with Napoleon, to do the same to the American capital. President James Madison knew of the plan, and he and his wife planned to leave Washington, DC when the invasion began. (Famously, First Lady Dolly Madison rescued Gilbert Stuart's portrait of George Washington as the couple fled.)

When they marched in on August 24, the British Army found the city almost abandoned, and they made short work of Washington's small, volunteer force. Only one British soldier died in the conflagration and three were wounded.

It was a hot day, around 100°F/38°C, and it was soon to be made hotter as the British set fire to everything in sight, stopping only to gloat by sitting on the seats of American government, rummaging for souvenirs in the White House drawers, and having a meal in the White House dining room before setting the whole thing ablaze.

The following day they continued their path of destruction. They managed to blow up thirty of their own men in an attempt to destroy the American reserve of gunpowder, but they met little resistance from the Americans. What they did not know was that nature was about to intervene. The hot summer air was rising and swirling beneath the cold air and wind shear of a thunderstorm. A tornado was created. The storm may have produced as many as three tornadoes. It is possible that the fires themselves contributed. Small tornadoes sometimes develop above forest fires. With the conditions already ripe for the development of a tornado, the British might just have sealed their own fates with the fires they had set.

They were not prepared for what followed. Tornadoes are not unheard of in Britain, but they are rare and almost never reach the force of those in the United States. Tornadoes, although relatively uncommon in Washington, DC as well, have been known to kill people in and around the Capitol. After a deluge of rain quenched the fires, the tornado smashed through the city, ripping off roofs, flinging cannons, and trapping soldiers under toppling walls.

The storms battered and demoralized the British, causing them to abandon their occupation of Washington. President Madison returned to the city a few days later on August 27, and the war ended the next year. It was the last armed conflict between the United States and the United Kingdom, including British Canada. The treaty that ended it clarified the border between the United States and Canada, which is today the longest demilitarized border in the world.

With Washington, DC in ruins, the US Congress, meeting in makeshift quarters, debated whether to move the capitol. If it were not for the votes of just five congressmen, the United States capitol would be in Philadelphia today.

Chapter

23

A Rainstorm Ends Napoleon's Reign

At the start of the nineteenth century, one man dominated Europe: Napoleon Bonaparte. His expansionist zeal was matched by his military prowess. In 1804, in a lavish ceremony, he crowned himself emperor and set out to expand his sphere of influence. For fifteen years, his attacks on his neighbors were unrelenting. In all, he went to battle with six different coalitions. The Battle of Waterloo put an end to the Napoleonic Wars. Napoleon's downfall was so significant that the expression "to meet his Waterloo" is still used to refer to a final defeat.

The Battle of Waterloo came soon after Napoleon returned to power. In March 1814, a coalition of troops from Austria, Prussia, Russia, and Sweden seized Paris and Napoleon was forced to abdicate. He was banished to the island of Elba. The French Senate reinstated the Bourbon dynasty. Those who had fought to remove the monarch remained loyal to Napoleon. A little less than a year later, Napoleon escaped his exile with the help of his supporters. He, and a group of more than a thousand, entered Paris on March 20, 1815 to cheering crowds. The new king, Louis XVIII, remembering what had happened to his brother, decided not to wait for an appointment with the guillotine and fled. Thus began what came to be known as Napoleon's "One Hundred Days Rule."

An army of Prussians under the command of Field Marshal Gebhard Leberecht von Blücher—116,000 men—and a ninety-three thousand-strong coalition of Belgians, Dutch, Germans, and British, led by the Duke of Wellington, moved into France's neighbor to the north, Belgium. They were to be joined by an army made up of six hundred thousand Russians and Austrians in July where the massive force would march on France.

Napoleon got word of the planned invasion. He built up a force of 125,000 men and marched on Belgium. He first encountered two Prussian corps. As the French forces started their attack, there was a downpour. This interfered with the effectiveness of their muskets; perhaps it made their powder wet. Instead, they engaged in a bloody battle with bayonets. Although the French were victorious, they had lost eleven thousand soldiers. It was a weakened French force that prepared to meet Wellington's force. On the morning of June 17, thunder clouds still hung over the field, which meant Napoleon would have to wait to engage Wellington until at least the afternoon. The delay allowed the duke to get word of the Prussian defeat. Knowing that he would not have their support, he decided to withdraw to a better position. Napoleon sent a unit to hunt down the remaining Prussians and keep them from joining forces with Wellington, but the team was so slowed by the muck that it never reached their camp.

Napoleon's soldiers spent a soggy night camped in the mud. The next morning the rain had stopped, but the ground was still muddy. Napoleon's commander, General Antoine Drouot, worried about the effects on the cavalry, and they waited for the soil to harden. It was not until noon that the attack finally began. At first they seemed to be winning, but then the Prussians arrived and the combined forces defeated Napoleon once and for all. This marked the end of the period of French dominance and paved the way for the British Empire. Lord Byron celebrated the teamwork that ended Napoleon's reign in a passage of his poem *Childe Harold's Pilgrimage*. He described the forces as the "united nations." The phrase resonated with Winston Churchill who used it as the name of the global organization created after World War II, but actually, Franklin Delano Roosevelt, the US president, had first used the name for the organization in 1942, three years before. The first Napoleon defeat of Russia was partially because of the weather, and weather helped Arthur Wellesley, the Duke of Wellington, as well.

"If it had not rained on the night of June 17, 1815, the future of Europe would have been changed," wrote Victor Hugo in *Les Misérables*. "A few drops of rain mastered Napoleon. Because Waterloo was the finale of Austerlitz, Providence needed only a cloud crossing the sky out of season to cause the collapse of a world."[1]

So if it hadn't been for the weather in two separate major battles, France might have ruled much of Europe for decades beyond Napoleon's rule, and the rise of the English empire might have been delayed or perhaps never even occurred.

Chapter 24

A Summer-Less Year Brings Frankenstein and Vampires and More

T hroughout history there have been many famous impactful volcanic eruptions. There was Mount Vesuvius in Pompeii; and in recent memory Washington's Mount Saint Helens. Yet neither had the power or world-wide impact of the April 9, 1815 eruption of Mount Tambora. Its ash blotted out the sun and caused climate disruptions, droughts, and a global pandemic. Scholars estimate that Tambora erupted with a similar force to Alaska's Okmok volcano, which played a role in transforming the Roman Republic into the Roman Empire. Unlike Okmok's eruption in 43 BC, we can describe the Tambora eruption with some detail, because there were people around to witness the event and record what they saw.

Tambora is located on the island of Sumbawa in what is now Indonesia, but that was then the Dutch East Indies. On April 9, its population of 170,000 had no idea what was about to occur. On that evening, there were a series of small tremors. Things remained fairly stable until about 7 p.m. the following evening. According to an eyewitness account, "three distinct columns of lava burst forth near the top . . . all of them apparently within the verge of the crater, and after ascending separately to a very great height, their tops united in the air in a troubled confused manner. In a short time the whole mountain next to Sanggar appeared like a body of liquid fire extending itself in every direction."[1]

The fire continued to shoot up in plumes until there was so much debris in the air that it could no longer be seen. Around 8 p.m., stones "some of them as large as two fists"[2] started to fly through the air. Then ashes began to rain down and a violent whirlwind followed. The mountain's height was reduced by a third. Billions of tons of sulfate gas and ash were belched into the air. The darkness, according to geologist Charles Lyell, was "so profound, that nothing equal to it was ever witnessed in the darkest night."[3] The ash on the ground was up to a meter (3.28 ft) high in places. An estimated ten thousand people perished from a variety of horrible factors. Some were killed directly by burning lava, others were asphyxiated by the venting gas that resulted from breathing in from a protoplastic cloud, and still more were drowned by the tsunami it triggered. Some events in history have been impossible to describe. But no one covered it like they did the Hindenburg. "Oh, the humanity!" The horror and the suffering and the incredible pain inflicted on ten thousand or more people on this night is virtually impossible to describe. Some people died quickly and didn't suffer very much. Others experienced all the pain and horror one can imagine, not only themselves but along with their families.

Meanwhile the ash was climbing high into the stratosphere. It was then blown by the upper air winds across much of the Northern Hemisphere, ultimately reflecting incoming solar radiation back into space, causing temperatures to plummet. In this case, the cooling ash particles overwhelmed the warming effect of the sulfur. Crop failure followed, not only due to the cold and frosty summer, but also the dimmed sunlight, which reduced photosynthesis.

The Yunnan province of southwest China was reduced to near starvation as one rice crop after another failed. As the famine dragged on for three years, the farmers tried to find a more reliable crop. It was the beginning of the opium trade. This in itself was a history changing event.

In India, a drought followed by unseasonable flooding altered the ecology of the Bay of Bengal. The bay had always harbored cholera, but the conditions caused the bacteria to mutate. The local population had no immunity to the new strain and it quickly spread along trade routes. By 1820, it had made its way back to Indonesia and then to China and Japan. British troops then picked it up and brought it all over the world from the Middle East to Russia and finally back home. The pandemic raged for six years until another severe winter in 1823 froze the water supply and the bacteria with it. All told, the pandemic killed at least one million people in India and perhaps as many as 8,750,000. The pandemic was spread by sea and land to other Asian countries, later arriving in Africa, Europe, and the Americas. with Java, Korea, and Vietnam each experiencing more than one hundred thousand deaths out of much smaller populations than exists today.

Throughout Europe there were record colds and increased rainfall.

The climate disruption even created a monster—Frankenstein's monster. During what the English called the "Year without a Summer," eighteen-year-old Mary Wollstonecraft, soon to be known by her married name, Mary Shelley, took a vacation to Geneva with her future husband Percy Shelley and her sister Claire Clairmont. There the sisters met Lord Byron and John Polidori. The literary band rented a villa together.

The weather was not convivial. Mary reported that "the thunder storms that visit us are grander and more terrific than I have ever seen before."[4] And in the introduction to her famous book, she called it "a wet, ungenial summer, and incessant rain often confined us for days to the house."[5] So the friends spent most of the time indoors, entertained one another with ghost stories, and did a lot of writing. This was well before the days of radio, television, movies, and of course the Internet.

Byron produced the grim *Darkness*, in which mankind dies as the sky is permanently darkened:

> All earth was but one thought—and that was death,
> Immediate and inglorious; and the pang
> Of famine fed upon all entrails—men
> Died, and their bones were tombless as their flesh;
> The meagre by the meagre were devoured[6]

John Polidori wrote *The Vampyre*, which later influenced Bram Stoker's *Dracula*. And Mary Shelley wrote *Frankenstein*.

The effects of the Tambora volcano also triggered a wave of German immigration to the United States. In Germany, temperatures were almost 9°F/5°C below historical averages during the summer of 1816, with heavy rainfall that caused landslides all over the Kingdom of Württemberg. Vineyards were wiped out and crops failed throughout the nation.

The German state, in an effort to reduce its spending, promoted emigration and paid for some of the hardest hit to leave the country. These immigrants founded many of the farming communities of the American Midwest. The early settlers set a pattern of migration for future waves of German immigrants as people back home read letters from their friends and family in America and decided to follow their path. They often migrated to the same town or city. Their influence was felt in the church denominations that predominated and the breweries the immigrants founded. At the beginning of the twentieth century, Germans were the predominant ethnic group in the United States, about eight million out of a total population of seventy-six million. Almost a century after the first wave of German immigration, the population of German-Americans was so dominant that its political clout delayed the United States' entry into World War I.

Getting back to 1816, North America was not spared the effects of Tambora's volcanic ash. It was not the coldest recorded winter in the northeastern United States, but the summer months of June, July and August set records for cold temperatures that have not been matched to this day. America then consisted of only eighteen states. Over one-third of the population resided in New York and New England, which was devastated by freezing temperatures, frosts, and even snow and ice storms in June and July in some regions. The late frost killed crops in several northeast states, and triggered a mass migration. Northern farmers settled in Ohio in great numbers, and some ventured even further west. Among the estimated fifteen thousand people who emigrated from Vermont alone was the family of eleven-year-old Joseph Smith, who went on to found the Church of Jesus Christ of Latter-day Saints (also known as the Mormon Church). According to the church, "even at this early age, Joseph had already seen plenty of life's suffering, including sickness, poverty, death, and the uncertainty of frontier farming life. He had no doubt heard the stories his parents had told of losing their farm, in part through the selfish actions of others. Traveling to New York gave Joseph new chances to witness and wonder at what people do when faced with others' vulnerability."[7] The difficult winter journey from Sharon, Vermont to Palmyra, New York shaped Smith into the type of young man who, in 1820, would go into the woods and pray. The visions he received in New York were the basis of the *Book of Mormon* and the foundation of a religion that now has seventeen million members.

The damage to crops in North America was severe, but not as severe as it had been in Europe. In the year before the Tambora explosion, 1815, English farmers had such a productive year that over supply led to a drop in the price of grain that had not been seen since 1804. Parliament responded by passing the so-called Corn Law forbidding the importation of foreign grain unless the price of a quarter of wheat reached eighty shillings. The unfavorable weather of 1816 led to a terrible harvest. As bread became scarce and food shortages led to violence, Parliament suspended the Corn Law, allowing the import of grain to resume. Because of this, in spite of their own shortages, American farmers found it more profitable to export their grain to England than to sell it at home. Scarcity and grim predictions for future harvests on both sides of the Atlantic drove export prices for wheat up. Many displaced New England farmers bought land on credit when the price of wheat suddenly rose.

It took a couple of years for Tambora's volcanic particles to work their way out of the atmosphere and settle back to the earth. More typical summer weather finally returned. Paradoxically, the return of normal temperatures and healthy crops led directly to the first sustained economic depression in the United States. When production in Europe returned to normal, England reversed its repeal of the Corn Law and stopped buying US wheat. Export prices for wheat, which had reached a high of $2.53 in 1816, plummeted. Prices fell to $1.72 at the end of 1818 and then to $0.99 by the end of 1819. As the price of wheat fell, the farmers who had moved west could not sell their produce at a high-enough price to service their debt. The result was the Panic of 1819, America's first Great Depression.

"There was no single cause of the collapse of America's post-war (War of 1812) economy," wrote Andrew Browning, author of *The Panic of 1819*, "but among the largest contributing factors was the desire to get in on the commodity export boom—and the inability to escape when that boom turned to bust."[8]

The economic fallout caused even more migration. Large numbers of Americans were encouraged by the Mexican government to settle in the Mexican state of Coahuila y Tejas. They established an American colony there led by Moses Austin. Over the next decade more than twelve thousand Americans had immigrated to the land they called Texas. The influx was so alarming to the Mexicans that they eventually passed laws prohibiting any immigration from the north. The Tejanos (Mexican Texans) and the US colonists fought for independence from Mexico in 1836. During the war, Mexican president Santa Anna was taken prisoner and in exchange for his freedom gave Texas its independence. The sometimes violent debate over whether Texas should be annexed by the United States continued until 1845 when it became a state.

Meanwhile, as banks began recalling loans, money became scarce, and anti-bank sentiment grew in the United States. The "King of the Wild Frontier" Davy Crockett, then a Tennessee politician, captured the mood of much of the nation when he dismissed "the whole banking system" as "a species of swindling on a large scale."[9] Several states tried to relieve the money shortage by taxing the federally owned Bank of the United States and using the funds to make loans to their citizens. In 1819, the Supreme Court heard the case of *McCulloch v. Maryland*. The court ruled that while the federal government had the power to tax state and private banks, the states could not tax the federal bank. Chief Justice John Marshall in his opinion wrote the now famous phrase "The power to tax is the power to destroy."[10]

The decision did nothing to stem the growing anger of debtors against financiers. Class divisions escalated, leading to the rise of Andrew Jackson, a populist who promised to defend the working-class against what he saw as the oppression of the wealthy elite. Jackson first ran for president in 1824. At the time, there were numerous political parties and four other strong contenders for the presidency. Jackson became the first presidential candidate to win the popular vote but to lose the election. Because he did not have more than 50 percent of the electoral college vote, the House of Representatives selected John Quincy Adams as the next president. In response, Jackson began actively campaigning for the next election, saying that the election had been stolen. Prior to the election of 1828, it was unusual for a candidate to go out and campaign, which was considered a bit vulgar. Instead they would persuade their followers to go out and make the case for them. By going directly to the people, Jackson positioned himself as a new kind of candidate, and ushered in an "Age of Jackson."

Jackson's tenure as president was controversial and spurred the creation of an opposition party, the Whigs.

By placing Jackson in power, the "Year without a Summer" also laid the foundation for the Trail of Tears. In 1830, Jackson signed the Indian Removal Act into law. It gave the United States the power to negotiate treaties to remove Native Americans to territory west of the Mississippi. On paper, the American government was not permitted to use force or coercion, but this was often ignored. In 1831, the Choctaw became the first nation expelled from the land they had lived on for generations. They were threatened with invasion. It was a forced march of expulsion overseen by the US military and ordered by Jackson. They marched west without any food or supplies. Thousands died on the march. A Choctaw leader gave the forced migrations their names when he told an Alabama journalist the march had been a "trail of tears and death."[11] Before the Indian Removal Act, nearly 125,000 Native Americans lived peacefully on millions of acres of land in eastern states on farms and in towns. More than forty-six thousand were forced to abandon their homes and move to a territory that eventually became the state of Oklahoma. More than four thousand died from exposure, disease, and starvation on the way.

Tambora is still an active volcano. It erupted again in 1880 and 1967, but never since—at least not yet—has a volcano erupted with such force or such consequence. Yet a major eruption of this scope undoubtedly will happen. Yellowstone (as noted in the chapter on dinosaurs) and Mt. Rainier in Washington State are just two "super volcanoes" with the potential to change the climate for years or decades, and possibly much longer, if they were to erupt, not to mention the great impact such an eruption would have on nations, civilization, and humanity itself.

Chapter

25

Rain and the Civil War

The mid-nineteenth century was a period of great technological advances. The US Civil War saw the first uses in combat of ironclad ships, the military telegraph, land mines, repeating rifles, and telescopic sights, but it did not produce a single weather forecast—something that could have been a greater advantage than all of the other inventions.

The study of climate and weather had been advancing since the turn of the century. In the lead-up to the war, strides were made in synoptic meteorology, which is the collection of information from various geographic sources. But accurate descriptions of what was happening in the atmosphere and sky were still a far cry from understanding what it meant in a larger sense. Remember that, in order to provide a weather forecast, you first need a current state of the conditions.

In the 1830s and '40s, prominent meteorologists were still arguing over what caused storms—was it electricity? Gravity? Something else? Meteorologists had not yet determined which correlations were significant and which were coincidences. Some of the most well-known figures in the field contradicted one another and espoused untested theories that proved to be as accurate as phrenology and mesmerism and which were seen in the same light. The controversial meteorologist James Pollard Espy's *The Philosophy of Storms* is a perfect example of the state of the art at the time. On one hand he correctly posited that the convective principle played a role in the creation of storms. On the other hand, he promoted a belief that smoke produced by the factories of Manchester, England generated rain clouds and therefore you could put an end to a drought by burning large areas of forest.

By 1850, largely due to military concerns, a network of weather reporting stations was developed in the United States. Given the general state of prediction, the data did little for the generals and soldiers of the Civil War. Yet culturally there was a great interest in the weather. During the war, the poet Walt Whitman filled his notes, essays, and letters with observations on what he called "the subtle world of air above and around us."[1] It was an era in which science held the promise that life could be more controllable and less arbitrary. The war challenged that faith.

The weather does not take sides, and it brought misery to soldiers from both armies. Throughout the course of the conflict, combatants had to contend with every condition imaginable. The biggest obstacle for the South was an unprecedented drought, while the North suffered its most disastrous defeat bogged down in heavy rains and mud.

Confederate forces began the August of 1862 with a number of important victories. They had captured Frankfort, the capital of Kentucky, and installed a confederate governor. Yet by October, these units were forced to retreat. The men were exhausted and starving.

A once-in-a-generation drought had depleted southern food production, while Midwestern wheat was spared. So while soldiers on both sides were affected by the heat, dust, and lack of water, the Confederacy found it impossible to replenish its supplies.

Ironically, months earlier soldiers had been up to their calves in Virginia mud. Flooding along the Mississippi and other rivers destroyed crops, and the dampness allowed a fungus called wheat rust to thrive in southern fields. The few crops that survived the flooding and disease were wiped out by the drought that followed.

Historian Kenneth Noe wrote: "The newborn Confederacy simply had been born at perhaps the worst possible moment in the 19th Century to launch an agricultural republic."[2]

On September 14, Brigadier General James Chalmers of Braxton Bragg's Confederate army and Colonel John Scott, commanding a cavalry detachment and acting without orders, attacked an entrenched federal garrison where they had heard there were large stores of wheat. The surprise attack was successful, but the bounty of rations did not materialize. The forces continued their delayed march, surviving on wormy flour. By mid-September, some troops were so hungry and frustrated that they walked home across the nearly dry Ohio River.

In October 1862, the Confederate soldiers reached what was to be their northernmost battle site in the Western Theater (as Gettysburg was to the Eastern Theater). The Confederates were greatly outnumbered, but outnumbered by another army of men who were also dehydrated and on the verge of collapse. Kentucky's largest battle was fought over water springs outside of Perrysville. More than 1,400 soldiers were killed in the battle and more than 5,500 were wounded. While Bragg's men won the day and held the springs, the general soon discovered that the supply house he had been counting on was empty. With nothing to feed the troops and no end of the drought in sight, he abandoned his Kentucky aspirations and retreated. The Western Kentucky drought raged on for another two years.

While the Western Theater was parched, the Eastern Theater was another matter entirely. Union morale was at a low point at the end of 1862. Richmond was under Confederate control, Thomas Jonathan "Stonewall" Jackson had defeated Union forces at the second battle of Bull Run, and the battle of Antietam had ended in a draw with huge losses on the Union side. President Lincoln, under great pressure from Congress, fired George B. McClellan and put Ambrose Burnside in charge.

Burnside planned to take Fredericksburg, VA, and to march from there to Richmond. His army of 120,000 troops arrived on the Northern side of the Rappahannock River the third week of November, but the pontoon train that was supposed to help him build a bridge to cross had not yet arrived. As the unit waited for the engineers, the entirely unsurprised Confederates, led by Robert E. Lee, patiently amassed a force to meet them.

When the Union soldiers finally did manage to get across, they found themselves in a muddy field ringed by Confederate soldiers hidden behind a stone wall. Wave upon wave of Burnside's men were easy, visible, slow-moving targets. Even so, Burnside kept ordering men onto the field. In the end, between eight thousand and twelve thousand Union soldiers were killed before Burnside retreated on December 14 to move his men downstream. The spot seemed ideal, as intelligence told the general that on January 20 the Confederates would be far from his position.

As the Union soldiers prepared to roll in so did a massive storm. The storm was a surprise, and the effects on the ground were more so. One of the solders, Colonel Régis de Trobriand, described it this way: "It appears as though the water, after passing through a first bed of clay, soaked into some kind of earth without any consistency. As soon as the hardened crust on the surface is softened, everything is buried in a sticky paste mixed with liquid mud, in which, with my own eyes, I have seen teams of mules buried."[3]

(The locals would not have made the same mistake. In Virginia, they had a name for pools of mud that formed from the red clay turning everything to muck. They called it a loblolly.)

The seventy-five thousand Union soldiers were so slow that it took them a full day to travel one and a half miles. As they continued their struggle with the soil, the Confederates didn't bother to attack. They stood out of rifle range taunting and laughing at their enemy as they tried to build dry roadways from logs. Burnside finally gave up and led the wet and demoralized team back to its original camp. The whole event was such a humiliation that Burnside was forced to resign.

Northern observers were outraged by the mud march and called on the government to do a better job of forecasting. The *Atlantic Monthly* ran an article that noted that weather and history have always been intertwined and the army should not have been taken by surprise:

> Americans have fretted a little because their 'Grand Army' could not advance through mud that came up to the horses' shoulders, and in which even the seven-league boots would have stuck, though they had been worn as deftly as Ariel could have worn them. They talked as if no such thing had ever before been known to stay the march of armies; whereas all military operations have, to a greater or a lesser extent, depended for their issue upon the softening or the hardening of the earth, or upon the clearing or the clouding of the sky.[4]

The following spring, a man named Francis L. Capen showed up at the White House and presented himself to Abraham Lincoln as "A Certified Practical Meteorolgist [*sic*] & Expert in Computing the Changes in the Weather."[5] He asked the president to recommend him for a job in the War Department and promised that the information he could provide would save the government thousands of lives and dollars. Lincoln was not impressed with Capen's abilities. "It seems to me that Mr. Capen knows nothing about the weather in advance," he wrote. "He told me three days ago that it would not rain again till the 30th of April or the 1st of May. It is raining now and has been for ten hours. I can not spare any more time to Mr. Capen."[6]

While it still outstripped their abilities, the need to develop a true system for predicting the weather had been powerfully demonstrated by the war.

Chapter

26

Drought Kindles the Great Chicago Fire, Then Rebirth

Sometimes history is altered by a tempest, and other times it is the lack of a tempest. If there had just been a bit more rain, the city of Chicago might have been spared its greatest trauma, the Great Fire of 1871. The fire killed an estimated three hundred people and left another 100,000 of Chicago's 298,977 residents homeless. (Some articles on the fire note the population of Chicago was 324,000, however, US Census figures from 1870 put the population at 298,977.) The fire destroyed 2,112 acres/8,546,961 sq m of the city, including the center of the business district.

In the summer and autumn of 1871, the entire Midwest was parched by a major drought. Rainfall in Chicago was 4 in/10 cm below normal that season. The city had recorded only 5 in/12.7 cm of rain, and, in the week leading up to the fire, it had not rained at all. It still ranks as the fifth driest July-October period Chicago has ever seen. On October 8, the humidity plunged to below 30 percent. A city comprised of wooden buildings and barns full of hay was ready to spread the blaze like so much kindling.

To make matters worse, the flames were fanned by a southwest wind of more than 20 mph/32 kph. As the hot air rose from the blaze, it came into contact with cooler air and began to swirl, creating what meteorologists call "convection whirls" and that the locals called "fire devils." Some reported seeing walls of flame as high as 100 ft/30.48 m. One witness called it a hurricane of fire "howling like myriads of evil spirits, [which] drove the flames before it with a force and fierceness which could never be described or imagined."[1]

Firefighters did all they could, but it was not until nature intervened with lighter winds and a light rain that the fire burned out on the morning of October 10.

To this day no one really knows what provided the spark that lit up the city. Some have speculated it might have been a meteor shower. A similar fire in Peshtigo, Wisconsin, blazed on the same date as the Chicago fire, both around the same time a large meteoroid was observed entering the Earth's atmosphere. On the same day, fires also flared in Holland and Manistee, Wisconsin, across Lake Michigan from Peshtigo, and in Port Huron, Michigan. Peoria and several other cities in the Midwest also reported major fires in the same period. All of these fires were hot and fast-moving, raging out of control within minutes due to abnormally dry weather that had occurred in the previous few months.

The Peshtigo fire, though little remembered today, was actually far more deadly than the Chicago fire. In Peshtigo, an estimated 1,200 people were killed, although the exact number will never be known as the town's records also went up in flames. The local newspaper managed to report on the blaze:

> The frenzy of despair seized on all hearts, strong men bowed like reeds before the fiery blast, women and children, like frightened spectres flitting through the awful gloom, were swept like Autumn leaves. Crowds rushed for the bridge, but the bridge, like all else, was receiving its baptism of fire. Hundreds crowded into the river, cattle plunged in with them, and being huddled together in the general confusion of the moment, many who had taken to the water to avoid the flames were drowned. A great many were on the blazing bridge when it fell. The debris from the burning town was hurled over and on the heads of those who were in the water, killing many and maiming others so that they gave up in despair and sank to a watery grave.[2]

Only one building was spared in the entire logging town. Many of the victims were so charred, similar to what was the case in the 2023 Hawaii fires, that they could not be recognized, and 350 were buried in a mass grave. In Chicago, the death toll was 250. But news of a fire in the larger city eclipsed that of the logging village.

The Chicago Fire spread so quickly that people could not be sure where it had begun. It was a reporter for the *Chicago Evening Journal* who first suggested it had started in a barn owned by a pair of Irish immigrants, Patrick and Catherine O'Leary. He had gotten the information by interviewing local children. In an era when the Irish were already targets of discrimination, the story gained traction. There were even whispers that the O'Leary's had started the fire on purpose. Mrs. O'Leary was one of the witnesses to testify in an inquiry on the cause of the fire held by the Board of Police and Fire Commissioners. The commission reached no conclusion as to what caused it, but most people, when they tried to remember the hearings, only remembered something about Mrs. O'Leary and a milk cow. There was a poetic quality to the idea that an entire city could be brought down by a cow kicking over a lantern that made the explanation spread like the fire itself. (With so many fires starting simultaneously, unless she was very speedy and well-traveled, Mrs. O'Leary's cow could not have been guilty. The meteor theory is much more plausible.)

Paradoxically, the fire, might have allowed the city to grow. Chicago historian Neal Samors posits that it was a post-fire building boom that created the modern city. In the twenty years following the fire, the population boomed from three hundred thousand to one million. Were it not for the fires, Samors wrote, "Chicago would probably have been a much smaller metropolis."[3] An important footnote is that balloon construction was used in Chicago; that is, the use of long timbers without floor breaks that allowed the fire to climb up building walls as if in a chimney. The long timbers only became available because of railroad transport from long distances. These timbers were not available before the Civil War. After these disastrous fires, balloon techniques were outlawed.

Chapter

27

Amazing "Drought Locusts" Bring Destruction and Change Attitudes

I n July 1874, the skies over Kansas became dark with what one observer described as "a moving gray-green screen between the sun and earth."[1] To some, the outline in the sky looked like smoke from a distant fire. To others it appeared to be an unseasonable snowstorm, but what was approaching was not precipitation. It was a massive swarm of locusts estimated to number 12.5 trillion.

As the insects descended upon them, the heavens roared with the ferocity of a thunderstorm or, as one witness described it, "a train of cars in the air."[2] There was horrible cracking and snapping, and everything was coated in a "seething, crawling mass"[3] several inches deep. When the swarm had passed, not an ear of corn was left in the field. It was the largest locust invasion in recorded history. As Jeffrey A. Lockwood, author of the book *Locust*, noted, "no people on earth, not even a pharaoh, had ever witnessed a swarm of such immensity."[4]

The plague of locusts, enabled by drought conditions in the Rocky Mountains, caused so much damage that western migration was stalled for a time, and the efforts at recovery set expectations for what the United States government's response should be in the face of natural disasters for years to come.

Most of the non-indigenous population of the plains states was made up of immigrants from Europe who had headed west to seek their fortunes after the passage of the Homestead Act in 1862. The act provided settlers 160 acres of public land. In exchange, they were required to complete five years of continuous residence before receiving ownership of the land. After six months of residency, however, homesteaders could buy the land from the government for $1.25 per acre. The Homestead Act was popular with Union veterans returning from the Civil War.

Settlers on the Great Plains had endured an unusually hard winter and dry summer caused by a severe El Niño event. (Please see sidebar at the end for a more in-depth description of El Niño/La Niña.) The climate was altered around the globe, causing mass famines in China and India and triggering epidemics. In 1873, Kansas had seen its driest year on record, but the rains were starting to return and the settlers were beginning to regain hope that their crops would be healthy. But the same dry conditions had stretched into the normal territory of the Rocky Mountain grasshopper. The drought had caused the grasshoppers to enter their "gregarious phase" and reproduce at great speed. The swarm then migrated south in search of food.

A Nebraska judge and amateur meteorologist, Albert Child, observed the swarm for ten days in June and telegraphed requesting reports from surrounding towns. He was shocked to find that the swarm seemed to cover an area of 110 mi/177 km by 1,800 mi/2,897 km, and as much as 0.5 mile/0.8 km in depth. Child noted that the wind was blowing at 10 mph/17 kph, but the locusts were outpacing it, traveling at 15 mph/24 kph. The swarm covered 198,000 sq mi/512,818 sq km.

The insect invasion laid waste to crops in Kansas, Nebraska, western Iowa, the Dakota Territory, Minnesota, Missouri, parts of Wyoming, Texas, and what is now Oklahoma. (Then it was called "Indian Territory.") As an 1880 US Entomological Commission report noted, the swarm devoured "a swath equal to the combined areas of Connecticut, Delaware, Maine, Maryland, Massachusetts, New Hampshire, New Jersey, New York, Pennsylvania, Rhode Island and Vermont."[5]

It was said that the swarm blocked out the sun in some places for as long as six hours. They blanketed everything. Fences and walls were covered a foot/.3 m deep. There were so many feasting on the leaves that their combined weight broke tree limbs. Entire corn crops were devoured. When all the leaves, grain, and vegetables were gone, the locusts started invading homes and barns gnawing on anything organic, from horse's harnesses to tool handles to clothing and blankets. One farmer quipped that the locusts "ate everything but the mortgage."[6]

It was the biggest natural disaster the country had experienced, causing an estimated $200 million in damage to farms, or about $200 billion in 2023 dollars.

Only one family in ten was left with enough supplies to make it through the winter, and many in western Kansas and Nebraska were forced to abandon their homestead claims and turn back east. Kansas was said to have lost as much as a quarter of its population, and migration to the plains practically stopped. Fortunately, the population decline was short lived. The swarm's long-term effect came from the debate that followed on the role of the federal government in providing disaster relief.

Early in the crisis, many newspapers in the east editorialized against the need for federal assistance, and they were joined by many voices from the affected region, as well. Local officials were afraid that negative publicity about the outbreak would make people shy about investing and settling in the area.

In east and west alike, editorials touted the values of hard work, resiliency, and self-sufficiency and argued that charity should come from local, rather than national, sources.

In the end, however, the crisis was too great for local organizations alone. As the federal government had assisted the victims of the Chicago fire three years before, journalists began to argue for equal treatment for the plains and urban disaster victims. The fact that many of the homesteaders were Union Civil War veterans who had clearly not lost their fortunes through laziness or a failure to plan brought many around to argue for assistance.

As a commentator wrote in the Worcester, Massachusetts *Daily Spy*: "While we would remember the charity which begins at home . . . we ought not to forget that the duty presses upon us with paramount claim of doing our utmost to relieve from the horrors of starvation a community made up largely of people . . . who are advancing the material prosperity of our country."

For several months, the homesteaders had to rely on a variety of local assistance programs, many of which were designed with strict requirements to weed out the undeserving. A homesteader had to prove he was entirely destitute with nothing left to sell before he could get any assistance. This left many homesteaders in a bind. If they took what resources they had left and moved out of the grasshopper area, they risked losing their claim and everything they had invested. Yet to get aid, a farmer would have to sell whatever resources he had left, creating a long-term problem for short-term gain.

One of the settlers who was forced into this catch-22 was Charles Ingalls, father of Laura Ingalls Wilder, author of *Little House on the Prairie*. In 1873, he sold the dwelling that Laura would one day memorialize as the *Little House in the Big Woods*. Pursuing the dream of a better life thanks to the Homestead Act, Charles moved the family from Wisconsin to Plum Creek, Minnesota and filed a claim on 172 acres/696,059 sq m. No sooner had he started to farm, however, than the locusts invaded. In the wake of this financial ruin, Charles was forced to sell the last of his horses so on November 30, 1875 he could give a sworn statement that he was "wholly without means."[7] Having thus divested himself of anything of value, he became eligible to receive two half-barrels of flour, worth five dollars and twenty-five cents. The children had something to eat as Charles Ingalls walked two hundred miles to find work on someone else's farm.

In the end, it became clear that the problem was too large for local governments and organizations to solve on their own. On January 25, 1875, Congress passed legislation directing the secretary of Agriculture to distribute $30,000 worth of seeds to areas that had been devastated by the locusts. The following month Congress approved an additional $150,000 to distribute surplus army blankets and clothing. Some state governments actually passed laws requiring men to work several days a season to help eradicate grasshoppers. The crisis had created a new-found acceptance of federal assistance, and from then on it has been assumed that in a disaster the federal government will step in.

As Lockwood noted:

> the locusts forced every level of government to come to terms with its obligations to the people in times of suffering and need. The conservatives, liberals, and libertarians had very different notions about the propriety of public assistance. These fundamental questions continue to lie at the center of our society in the twenty-first century: Should we value work and effort or wealth and success? Are poor people indolent beggars or unfortunate victims? And what are the ethical duties of society, community, and family during times of adversity? Perhaps the story of the Rocky Mountain locust holds more lessons for our modern culture than we might initially attribute to the tale of a lowly insect.[8]

The locusts continued to torment farmers, although in smaller numbers, until 1877. In April of that year, a snowstorm damaged many of the insects' eggs and the summers of swarms came to an end.

The insect that caused such devastation is now extinct, with the last reported sighting of a Rocky Mountain locust reported in 1902. Entomologists suggest that the changes brought by the settlers, including how they used the land and the new plants they brought with them, might have changed the locusts' habitat and led to the die-off.

ENSO (the El Niño Southern Oscillation)

Fishermen off the west coast of South America were the first to notice appearances of unusually warm water that occurred at year's end, giving it the name El Niño way back in the 1600s because of its tendency to occur around Christmas time. El Niño is Spanish for "the boy child" and is named after the baby Jesus.

(Continued on next page)

Today ENSO and its two components, El Niño and La Niña, are followed and well understood, and we even have the ability to predict them with a good degree of accuracy.

I first learned about ENSO from Dr. Hans Panofsky in a course I took at Penn State in the 1950s, when he told the class of an oscillation in the tropical ocean temperature that was detected because of variation in barometric pressure on a few islands with a long cycle averaging sixteen to twenty-four. I heard more about it from Jerome Namias, the first long-range forecaster for the National Weather Service, in the early 1960s when he spoke in our graduate seminar about the relationship between these long cycles of warming and cooling of the oceans, which at that time was mainly detectable through limited ship measurements of water temperature and the variations in barometric pressure in some tropical locations. In those days, we did not have satellite measurements of ocean temperatures, so measurements of variations in ocean temperatures across most of the oceans were very limited.

In recent decades we have recognized that ENSO is perhaps the most important of what are known as "teleconnections," patterns in the atmosphere that typically persist from weeks to years that influence the temperatures, precipitation, storm tracks, and jet stream over large areas.

Think of a teleconnection as being like construction on an urban highway—it may impact the traffic flow for months (much as a teleconnection impacts the flow of the atmosphere), controlling the traffic flow completely and causing it to back up for miles during rush hour (much as a teleconnection can lead to a series of major storms or bring a long period of very warm weather to a large area), while at night causing traffic to slow down only through the construction zone (much as a teleconnection may not control the weather continuously, with dry periods between the storms it brings).

It has been argued that in 2021 and 2022, La Niña caused the earth to be cooler than it would otherwise have been, but the warmer El Niño taking over is why more record high global temperatures have been occurring in 2023, and 2024 is likely to be the hottest year ever recorded averaged across the globe.

Chapter 28

Volcanic Sunsets Inspire *The Scream*

"**I** felt a great, infinite scream pass through nature."

Edvard Munch's *The Scream* is one of the best-known images in art. It has been called the Mona Lisa of modern art because it is so ubiquitous. Like the *Mona Lisa*, it is frequently parodied and it comes to mind whenever an illustration is needed for anxiety and dread. Originally part of a series of images exhibited as "The Frieze of Life" in 1893, it was not originally meant to represent individual angst. Munch's original title for it was *The Scream of Nature*.

The flash of inspiration came when Munch was out walking with two friends. "Suddenly the sky turned blood-red," he wrote. "I paused, deathly tired and leaned on a fence looking out across the flaming clouds over the blue-black fjord and towns. My friends walked on and there I stood, trembling with fear . . ."[1]

Like Mary Shelley's *Frankenstein*, *The Scream* was produced in a period of climate disruption caused by the eruption of a volcano in the Dutch East Indies. In this case it was Krakatoa, an island in the Sunda Strait between Sumatra and Java. In 1883 it was a spice trading hub, with everything an elegant world traveler could wish for.

It was a clear summer day in August 1883, and the circus was in town. When the ground started to rumble, people paid it little mind and stayed on the beach. It was not long, however, before it was clear that something was quite wrong. On Sunday, August 26, smoke began to spew from the mountain, and hot ashes began to fall. There were two small explosions and then a third—this one was deafening. Krakatoa's explosion was not as powerful as Tambora, but it was powerful enough.

The seismic activity set off a series of tsunamis, one of which carried a warship 2½ mi/4.02 km inland, where it perched on a hill for many years. Villages on the islands of Java and Sumatra were inundated, and thirty-seven thousand people were killed. As with Tambora, volcanic particles were pushed high into the atmosphere, and circled the globe thousands of times until they fell out, impacting global weather systems. In the year following the eruption, average global temperatures fell by as much as 2°F/1.2°C, meaning in some places, temperatures probably averaged ten degrees below historical averages. In other areas, it might have been even more extreme. Temperatures did not return to "normal" until 1888, five years later. During the intervening period, crops suffered from early frosts, from frosts late into the spring and early in the fall. The suspended dust particles not only reflected solar energy back into space, but also produced spectacular sunsets. Noctilucent clouds, also known as "night shining clouds," were first spotted by German meteorologists after the eruption. Scientists are divided on whether the cloud formations were caused by dust from Krakatoa seeding the mesosphere or whether the clouds existed before, but they were spotted because more people were observing the dramatic skies at that time.

And they were dramatic. Sunsets in Northern Europe and North America sometimes looked like fire dancing across the heavens. They glowed pink, purple, bronze, or blue with colorful rings around the sun. This is what Edvard Munch observed as he and his friends walked. There were four versions of *The Scream*. In 2012, one canvas sold at auction for a record $120 million.

Chapter

29

"Great White Hurricane" Creates the New York Subway System

When you think of New York City, your focus most likely turns upward to the towering skyscrapers. But the vertical city extends downward as well. The subterranean city includes thousands of miles of power, telephone, and water lines, a steam delivery system, and five hundred miles of subway tracks. On an average day, more than 4.3 million people travel beneath the urban concrete. But this was not always the case. The modern eastern cities with their vast hidden infrastructure owe their existence to a snowstorm that happened in 1888.

The first days of March 1888 had been unseasonably warm on the East Coast, and residents of cities like New York, Washington, DC, and Boston prepared for an early spring. On March 10, when early reports of a pending storm came in, the temperatures were hovering in the mid-fifties. Few people took the reports seriously. But a very cold Arctic air mass was moving southward and cold air, being more dense than warm air and already on the move, would quickly push the warm air out of the way, and created additional energy by undercutting the warm air.

The next day temperatures plunged. The rain became snow overnight. Initially the snow was light, and people headed out to work and school. But then the weather pattern changed dramatically. The movement of cold Canadian air feeding into a developing storm system in the Gulf Stream off the East Coast produced a massive surge of energy creating a bomb cyclone. It was called "the Blizzard of '88" or "the Great White Hurricane." It affected an unusually wide area, and, even by today's standards, it ranks as one of the worst blizzards in American history. Barometric pressure readings plummeted as the storm hooked north offshore, and wind gusts reached hurricane strength.

The storm stretched from Maryland all the way up to Maine and parts of Canada, but it was deadliest in New York City, which accounted for half of the four hundred fatalities directly attributable to the storm. Tragically, many were children trying to get home from school.

As many as fifteen thousand people found themselves stranded on the city's elevated trains. In some areas people with ladders took advantage of the situation by charging the stranded a fee to be helped down.

The most high profile victim of the storm was Senator Roscoe Conkling. He decided to brave the blizzard and walked three miles from his Wall Street law office to the New York Club. He did not make it to his destination. He got disoriented in the snow and collapsed. He was not rescued for two hours, and he suffered exposure. He seemed to recover initially, and recounted the experience to a friend in a letter:

> I had an ugly tramp in the dark—the lights out, from Wall Street up, over drifts so high that my head bumped against the signs, and dug-outs opposite the store doors suddenly letting a wayfarer down a foot or two over snarled telegraph wires and slippery places, with a blizzard in front not easy to stand against, and so cold as to close the eyes with ice, and drifts were not packed enough to bear up, in which one sank to the waist.[1]

After this his health took a turn for the worse, and he died of pneumonia on April 18 at the age of fifty-eight.

The snow continued to fall for another three days, paralyzing the Northeast. Saratoga Springs, New York had the highest reported snowfall with fifty-eight inches. In New York City, the big problem was the snowdrifts that piled up higher than three-story buildings. The tallest documented drift reached 52 ft/15.85 m or five to six stories high.

Telegraph lines, gas lines, and water mains, all located above ground, froze, fell, and were buried in snow where they could not be reached by repair crews. Brooklyn was entirely cut off from electricity and communication. Wall Street closed for three days. People were trapped indoors for days without adequate food or supplies, even though it was March, not midwinter. It took more than a week to clear the snow, and the elevated trains were stopped everywhere.

The event made it clear that above-ground infrastructure was vulnerable, and planning began to move everything underground. Boston and New York started planning underground train systems. Boston's opened first in 1901, followed shortly by New York's, which opened in 1904.

"GREAT WHITE HURRICANE" CREATES THE NEW YORK SUBWAY SYSTEM

The "Great White Hurricane" was not the only major blizzard to strike the United States in 1888. Tragically, New York had failed to heed the lessons of a storm that had hit the Midwest two months before.

January 12, 1888 began as a mild day in the Great Plains, with temperatures well above freezing. As children headed off to school in Minnesota and Nebraska with no hats or gloves, a massive cold air mass that had formed over Alberta was bringing its violent winds and extreme temperature drops across sparsely populated Montana and northern Colorado. The Army Signal Corps had been observing the phenomenon, but they chose not to issue a Cold Wave warning the previous night. As the storm raced across the states covering more than 780 miles/1,255 km in seventeen hours, Midwest settlers were entirely unaware of what was coming. Temperatures dropped to -40°F/-40°C in a matter of hours.

Iowa and Minnesota were both hit by the deadly storm, but the most damage was in Nebraska and the Dakota Territory in what is now South Dakota. An estimated 235–250 people were killed, although the precise number is hard to discern due to gaps in rural newspaper coverage, incomplete records, and the fact that many bodies were not found for weeks or even months. The actual number of fatalities was probably much higher. Tragically, the storm became known as the "Schoolchildren's Blizzard" because many of the victims were children trying to get home from school through snow drifts and deadly cold winds. "For a certain generation of upper Midwestern settler, the date January 12, 1888, rang with as much dark meaning as December 7, 1941, or September 11, 2001, would have today," wrote Minnesota journalist Alyssa Ford. "Everyone had a story of where they were that day."[2]

Until the twin disasters of 1888, weather forecasting had been the job of the military. (They called their forecasters "indications officers" in those days.) In the wake of these two devastating blizzards, it became clear that a better system of warning the civilian public of severe weather was required. Two years after the events, President Benjamin Harrison signed legislation that moved the meteorological service out of the War Department. The US Weather Bureau under the Department of Agriculture was created on October 1, 1890. In order to better coordinate with commercial aviation, it would be moved again in 1940 by President Franklin D. Roosevelt to the Department of Commerce.

Chapter

30

America's Worst Hurricane Boosts Houston

T he city of Houston, Texas, with 2.3 million residents, is the fourth most populous city in the United States behind New York, Los Angeles, and Chicago. It is third only to New York and Chicago in its concentration of Fortune 500 companies. Yet, this might have been the profile of another Texas city—Galveston—were it not for a hurricane more than a century ago. The Galveston hurricane was, and remains, the deadliest natural disaster in US history.

On the morning of September 8, 1900, Galveston was the fourth largest city in Texas, slightly behind San Antonio and Dallas. It had the biggest port in the state, it boasted the first telephones and electric lights, and it had the most millionaires. Then everything changed. The city was all but destroyed when a category four hurricane bore down upon it. Tragically, the natural disaster was compounded by a disaster of weather forecasting.

The US Weather Bureau, the predecessor of the National Weather Service, was then only a decade old. Its hurricane science was rudimentary. It relied on reports from ship captains in an era before most ships had wireless communication. In Cuba, where hurricanes are a fact of life, they had become good at tracking and even forecasting the storms. Cuba was reporting that the hurricane was heading to the Gulf of Mexico. The Weather Bureau, on the other hand, thought it would go across Florida and up to New England.

The bureau's director, Willis Moore, was so persuaded he was right and also so territorial, that he blocked the Cuban reports and ordered US forecasters not to issue any hurricane warnings that contradicted the official projections. Everything had to go through Washington, a slow process.

Two days before the storm hit, the Weather Bureau's chief observer in Galveston, Isaac Cline, could see firsthand that the national forecast was off and that the hurricane was headed his way. On September 7, he ordered hurricane warning flags to be flown. The next morning he hitched his horse to a cart and rode to the beach to warn the residents personally. He told everyone he saw to get to higher ground. Unfortunately, the highest ground in Galveston was only 8.7 ft/2.65 m above sea level.

When Cline told the former Chief Forecaster for the US Signal Office, Henry Harrison Chase Dunwoody, of his concerns, Dunwoody replied, "No sir. It cannot be; no cyclone ever can move from Florida to Galveston."[1] This hurricane is the basis of a book titled *A Weekend in September*, which chronicles how the arrogant US government forecasters ignored the warnings that the hurricane was heading toward Texas.

The hurricane (it had no name because, as noted earlier, they did not name hurricanes until 1953) brought winds of 135 mph/217 kph and a tidal surge of 15 ft/4.57 m. It destroyed more than 3,600 buildings. Between six and twelve thousand people were killed, among them Cline's wife.

With Galveston largely destroyed, Houston's growth accelerated. Its location, 50 mi/80.47 km farther from the Gulf of Mexico, made it safer, and with the invention of air conditioning (in 1902) its growth accelerated even more.

Damage from Hurricanes

In a recent book on the history of hurricanes, *Furious Sky* by Eric Dolin, the author estimates that, adjusted for inflation, the total damage from all the hurricanes in US history exceeds a trillion dollars.[2] I suspect this is an underestimate. Hurricanes have likely killed well more than a hundred thousand people in the United States. If they all happened in one year, I suspect the financial impact would be closer to $5 trillion, or 25 percent of the entire GDP of the country.

Chapter

31

A Gust of Wind Makes the Wright Brothers First in Flight

Who was Samuel P. Langley? He might have been remembered as the father of the airplane if not for an ill-timed burst of wind.

If anyone was going to invent an airplane, the government of the United States thought that it would be Langley. The secretary of the Smithsonian Institution, who had worked at the Harvard and Allegheny observatories and the US Naval Academy, he was considered the nation's foremost expert on the theory of heavier-than-air flight. The Board of Ordnance and Fortification of the War Department funded his experiments to the tune of $50,000 (about $2,000,000 in 2023 dollars. Of course, given the cost to do research today you would probably have to add another zero to that figure.)

Langley constructed a number of flying machines, some powered by steam and some by gasoline. He got his first unmanned flying machine off the ground in 1896. On its first test it flew 3,000 ft/914 m. He improved it later that year so it could go 4,200 ft/1,280 m. These successes allowed him to secure additional funding of $23,000 (about $10,000,000 today) from the Smithsonian Institution with which he believed he would be the first to fly a passenger.

In July 1903, Langley had worked out all of the glitches, and he brought his "aerodrome" to the shore of the Potomac River where it was to be catapulted off a barge and into aviation history. Unfortunately, the weather did not cooperate. Storms not only prevented the flight, but they also warped the plane's wings so badly that it took three months to fix them.

A GUST OF WIND MAKES THE WRIGHT BROTHERS FIRST IN FLIGHT

On December 8, Langley was ready to launch again. This time he was so sure he would be successful that he invited an audience of politicians, military members, and the press to watch the historic event.

On December 8, 1903, Langley once again attempted to become the first man to demonstrate a working heavier-than-air craft. The press, military observers, and members of Congress lined the shore to witness the historic event. Once again, the new invention was placed on a barge on the Potomac and faced into the wind. When the crewmen pulled the restraining pins away to ready the plane for its catapult launch, a heavy gust of wind moved the platform, the wings of the aerodrome collapsed, and the rest fell into the water. The scene was unintentionally comic, and the whole idea of the airplane started to seem ridiculous to many of the observers.

The Wright Brothers, meanwhile, planned a quiet test of their invention, the Flyer, in Kitty Hawk, North Carolina. Nine days after Langley's disaster, they invited a few people to watch their experiment.

On December 17, 1903, the brothers made four brief flights. The longest lasted twelve seconds and traveled 120 ft/37 m. It was the first successful flight of a human. Today the event is recognized as perhaps the most important milestone in aviation history. But this was not always the case.

Had Langley not encountered the fateful gust of wind, it is possible that the United States would have been recognized as first in flight much sooner than it was.

There were no reporters on the scene when the Wright Brothers made their now-famous flight. The Wright Brothers had contacted someone in the Weather Bureau to select a location to do their first test flight and to find out where the best prevailing wind conditions would be and were told to go to the Outer Banks of North Carolina. That was a good forecast (although technically, this was not a weather forecast, but a decision based on climatological statistics). The next day a small article in the *Virginian-Pilot*, pieced together from the statements of witnesses, announced what the Wright Brothers had achieved. The notice did not gain widespread attention. In fact, according to Larry Tise, a historian and author of *Conquering the Sky: The Secret Flights of the Wright Brothers at Kitty Hawk*, the public was mostly unaware of the feat for another five years. The Wright Brothers intentionally worked "privately and secretly," because as their patent No. 821,393 for a "flying machine" was pending, the Wrights were afraid "other people would immediately replicate what they were doing."[1] They were so secretive that they refused to demonstrate their aircraft's unique features to prospective buyers. The US War Department, having already sunk $50,000 into Langley's failed aerodrome, was not willing to take the Wright Brothers' claims on faith.

In the meantime, a Brazilian named Alberto Santos-Dumont made his own powered flights before cheering crowds in Paris in 1906 and 1907. In Brazil, he is still widely credited with being the inventor of the airplane. The opening ceremonies at the 2016 Olympics in Brazil contained a tribute to their own aviation pioneer.

Even when the Wright Brothers saw the fanfare surrounding Dumont, they refused to take part in the aviation competitions that made other pilots and inventors famous. Over the next year the French designers Charles and Gabriel Voisin and Louis Blériot dominated the field of aviation development, and, in January 1908, another Frenchman, Henri Farman, won the Deutsch-Archdeacon Grand Prix for flying a circle over a Parisian field.

It was only then that the Wright Brothers realized they would have to let the world know about their work or they would be left behind. The now-famous photo taken after the Wright Brothers' 1903 flight was not made public until 1908. That year the Wright Brothers did a demonstration of their invention in Paris and became instant celebrities. It was clear that the Americans had a much more developed machine. Dumont's flight was powered, Tise said, "but how controlled it was is another question."[2] Dumont got off the ground, flew in a straight line, and "didn't crash." But the Wright Brothers were able to fly in a circle and land in the same spot from which they had taken off.

By now, however, they had new domestic competition from a fellow bicycle builder turned aviator, Glenn H. Curtiss. The Wrights were able to defend their patent on every occasion, but it was a Pyrrhic victory. The years of legal wrangling took their attention away from their true talent, designing airplanes. Some historians argue that the conflict had larger ramifications.

According to the *Wall Street Journal*, the bitter patent battle slowed US aircraft design and production as a whole. By the time the Wrights' patent was upheld in 1914, the United States lagged behind other nations in aircraft design. That August, Germany had 180 fighter planes, France had 136, England forty-eight, and the United States less than a dozen. In 1917, the American military flew into battle almost entirely in European designed and built planes.

Ultimately, the US government put an end to the aviation patent wars in 1917 by buying up aviation patents so they could be used by American builders without paying a royalty, thus speeding up development.

Not all experts believe the Wright-Curtiss patent battle was to blame for America's lag in airplane production. In the Wright Brothers' day, the United States was not yet the major power it would become after WWII. Given its status on the world stage, it is perhaps not surprising that it would rank fourteenth in government aviation funding.

In the end, the former patent rivals merged. Today Curtiss-Wright Corporation, with headquarters in North Carolina, has eight thousand employees and revenues of $2.5 billion. And the number of daily flights in the world each day in 2019 reached 38.9 million, serving around four billion passengers, before declining during the COVID-19 pandemic.

Chapter

32

Invisible Iceberg—A Mirage Sinks the *Titanic*

It was called the "Ship of Dreams." At the time of its maiden voyage on April 15, 1912, it was not only the largest passenger ship, but it was also the largest man-made moving object on Earth. The story of its collision with an iceberg and the plight of its passengers is one of the most familiar stories in history. More than five hundred books have been written on the subject and more than a dozen films, including James Cameron's Oscar-winning 1997 blockbuster, have been made. The name *Titanic* is said to be the third most widely recognized word in the world, after "God" and "Coca-Cola."[1]

The sinking of the *Titanic* captures our imagination as the end of a romantic era, as a metaphor for technological hubris, and as a great human drama. Stephen D. Cox, author of a book on the *Titanic*, explained the enduring fascination with the tragedy. "The *Titanic* sank in two hours and 40 minutes," he wrote, "the length of a classic play. Its cast of characters included people of every rank and station and personality. The cast was large enough to represent the human race, yet small enough to form a self-contained society, in which individuals could see what other individuals were doing, and think carefully about their own responses. The *Titanic* had what every great drama needs: a relentless focus on the supreme choices of individual lives."[2]

The stage for this grand drama was set years before the ill-fated ship was ever launched with a series of warm years in the Arctic that increased the rate of melting of glaciers in Greenland. North Atlantic icebergs travel from the western coast of Greenland. Every year chunks of ice cleave from the glaciers and are transported by the West Greenland Current. Most of the ice travels north, but some is diverted into the Labrador Current along the Canadian coast into a part of the Atlantic known as "iceberg alley."

In an average year, few make it all the way down to a latitude of 48°N, which takes them into the important shipping corridors. But in a warm period, more cracks appear in the ice and the meltwater at the base of glaciers acts as a lubricant, allowing the ice to slip into the sea more quickly. This means more icebergs form and move. The more icebergs there are, the more likely it is that a few will float into the most important shipping lanes. While normally only a few hundred icebergs migrate south of 48°N, in 1912 more than 1,038 did, four hundred of them in April 1912. As the *Titanic* embarked from Southampton on April 10, 1912 with New York City as its planned destination, an iceberg was making its way to latitude 41°N, the same latitude as New York City.

On board the ship was a cross-section of British and American society. A Minnesota salesman named Alexander Holverson wrote a letter to his mother describing an encounter with the man who was then the wealthiest in the world. "John Jacob Astor is on this ship," he wrote. "He looks like any other human being even though he has millions of money. They sit out on deck with the rest of us." He noted that the *Titanic* was "giant in size and fitted up like a palatial hotel." "If all goes well," he wrote, "we will arrive in New York Wednesday A.M."[3]

All did not go well. Iceberg and ship were on a collision course.

The *Titanic* had received warnings and was aware that there was ice in the area, but the crew did not know the exact locations of the icebergs. A ship, the *Californian*, had spotted the large iceberg and saw a ship approaching it. Radios were not standard in those days, but the *Californian* and the *Titanic* both had them, and yet the *Californian* did not try to radio the *Titanic*. Why?

Icebergs were not the only natural hazard that night. A century after the *Titanic* foundered, historian Tim Maltin traveled the world to analyze witness accounts, weather reports, and more than seventy-five ship's logs from April 1912. The logs recorded strange reflections and mirages.

Maltin believes the *Titanic* was the victim of what he calls "a killing zone of nature due to atmospheric conditions. A mirage, high pressure and darkness just came together."[4]

On April 14, as the *Titanic* sailed from Gulf Stream waters into the Labrador Current, it encountered a cold front. The 60°F/15°C temperature began to drop. By noon it was 50°F/10°C and falling. By 7:30 p.m. it had dropped to 39°F/3.9°C. The northwestern winds reached 25 mph/40 kph. Later that evening, temperatures were below freezing.

Even with that cold air temperature, the ice-filled waters were colder than the air above, creating a phenomenon known as thermal inversion. It refracted light in a strange way, creating a false horizon that made objects seem smaller and closer than they actually were. Most importantly, you could not see objects until they got closer. The area between the false and true horizons appears as haze.

The optical illusion led the *Californian* to misjudge the size of the *Titanic*. They knew only one other ship had such modern technology on board, and because they thought the ship they were seeing was too small to be the *Titanic*, they tried to signal it with Morse lamps. Tragically, the abnormally stratified air prevented the *Titanic* from seeing the signal. The captain of the *Californian* later said he could not understand why the other ship "did not take the slightest notice" of it.[5] Icebergs consist almost entirely of fresh water since they originate from snow falling over land. Anyone who has put ice into a glass of water or soda realizes that the ice cubes float and the bulk of the ice is below the water line. Less than 10 percent of the ice is above the water line, which means that about twelve times as much ice is below the ocean and invisible, than is above the water level. This is another reason why icebergs are so dangerous to ships.

The *Titanic* continued to race toward the deadly iceberg obscured by the haze of the thermal inversion. To make matters worse, it was a clear, moonless night with calm seas. This robbed the lookouts of their main clues as to the position of icebergs—waves driven by the wind breaking around their bases. The lookouts spotted the berg and sounded the alarm only one mile from the hazard. It was too late for a ship the size of the *Titanic* to change course.

"For years *Titanic's* lookouts were not believed when they said the iceberg came out of a haze on that clear night," Maltin said, "but now we know they were telling the truth."[6]

At 11:40 p.m., *Titanic* and iceberg met. The *Titanic* sideswiped the iceberg and tore a gash in its side. Six of the ship's watertight compartments started to fill. The ship could have survived had only four compartments been breached; the *Titanic* would have stayed afloat.

It was some time before the passengers became aware of how serious their plight was. When the crew started to lower the lifeboats, some passengers decided not to get in them because the ship seemed more stable. They found it hard to believe the ship could sink. Passengers did not want to shiver for potentially hours in the lifeboats, not realizing that if they did not get in the boats they would be doomed. They believed the situation would be sorted out and they would be brought back on board. Some of the lifeboats were launched half empty.

Contrary to popular belief (a myth perpetuated by the film *Titanic*), the company that operated the *Titanic*, the White Star Line, had not reduced the number of lifeboats on board to save deck space or money. In fact, the ship was carrying more than the law required. The problem was that nineteenth-century regulations based the number of lifeboats required on the gross tonnage of the ship rather than the number of passengers on board. With a gross tonnage of 46,000 tons, the *Titanic* was required to have enough boats for 1,060 people. It was actually stocked with enough to carry

1,178 people, but this was still far fewer than the 2,208 people on board, including 908 crew members.

As the ship started to sink, the crew tried to signal the *Californian* with their Morse lamps. The temperature inversion again disrupted the signals. Although some on the *Californian* spotted the *Titanic's* distress flare, which was launched six hundred feet into the air, it appeared so low that they did not know what it was.

At 2:20 a.m. on April 15, 1912, the *Titanic* was on its way to the bottom of the ocean. Those on the *Californian* believed the small vessel had sailed away.

By the time the *Titanic* went down, the air temperature had dropped to 29°F. Although many of the passengers survived the sinking of the ship, most of those who ended up in the ocean suffered hypothermia and died from exposure. In all, more than 1,500 perished that night.

Among them were a number of people who were prominent enough that their passing could have altered the course of history. Along with millionaires like John Jacob Astor and Benjamin Guggenheim, there were political luminaries like Major Archibald Butt, who had served as an aide to President William Howard Taft and President Theodore Roosevelt. And of course, we don't know what all the other people who were lost could have contributed to society. For the moment, however, we will highlight a man who is less well-known today, the pioneering journalist W. T. Stead.

Stead was one of the first, if not the first, investigative journalist, and his sensational reports had the power to shape public policy. In 1885, his four-part series on London's underworld of underage prostitution called "The Maiden Tribute of Babylon" shocked the public and led to the Criminal Law Amendment, which raised the age of consent in England from thirteen to sixteen, cracked down on prostitution, and created the crime of "gross indecency," outlawing consensual same-sex activity. This, a decade later, led to the arrest and early death of the playwright and famous wit Oscar Wilde.

Had Stead lived to see World War I, one can only imagine what social ills he might have taken on with his pen, and how it might have changed the world.

Following the sinking of the *Titanic*, a number of new maritime safety measures were enacted. The Radio Act of 1912 required ships to maintain radio communications with other ships and with stations along the coast. It regulated the use of certain bandwidths for shipping. The International Convention for the Safety of Life at Sea Treaty passed in 1914 and required every vessel to include enough lifeboat space for every person on board. The treaty also created an International Ice Patrol, which continues to warn ships of iceberg danger to this day.

This job is more important than ever as the number of icebergs in the North Atlantic is expected to increase thanks to climate change, which is melting Greenland's glaciers.

This continues to have economic repercussions as ships are forced to slow down or take detours of hundreds of miles. The North Atlantic corridor is still one of the most important shipping lanes in the world. Another interesting sidebar to the *Titanic* story: Had the *Titanic* encountered the iceberg an hour earlier in the cruise, the air temperature would have been significantly warmer and the water temperature would have been about 50 degrees. People could have survived in 50-degree water perhaps long enough for help to arrive. Furthermore, passengers might have been more willing to get into the lifeboats if the temperature was much more moderate. The air temperature dropped from 50°F to 29°F in a little over an hour's sail. The *Titanic* collided with the iceberg in the very cold Labrador current.

Why Hollywood Is in Hollywood

Believe it or not, the first dramatic film about the sinking of the *Titanic* was released in 1912, just a month after the disaster. It starred Dorothy Gibson, a well-known actress, who was a *Titanic* survivor. Gibson was already under contract to the American branch of the French film company Éclair, and they sensed opportunity in their star's survival. They had her write and star in *Saved from the Titanic*. Like most silent films of the era, it was short with a running time of just ten minutes. It was filmed in what was then the film capital of the world: Fort Lee, New Jersey.

In those exciting early days of cinema, the biggest stars could be found in Fort Lee. Were you lucky enough to live there in the first decade of the twentieth century, you might run into Rudolph Valentino, Roscoe "Fatty" Arbuckle, Will Rogers, Lillian Gish, Mary Pickford, or Lionel Barrymore on the city's streets.

The world's first movie camera, called the kinetoscope, was invented in 1893 by Thomas Edison and his assistant William Dickson on the grounds of his laboratory in West Orange, New Jersey. After taking out a string of patents related to his invention, Edison created the Edison Trust and took control of the fledgling industry. Neighboring Fort Lee seemed to be the perfect place to make movies. It had a diverse landscape, with waterfalls, farms, and forests that could double for many different parts of the world, and it was just a short ferry ride for Broadway stars. MGM, Universal, and 20th Century Fox all got their starts in Fort Lee. By 1918, there were eleven major studios in operation.

That was the peak of the New Jersey film industry. The death knell came from the bitterly cold winter of 1918–1919 and the Spanish Flu epidemic at the same time. These events triggered a mass exodus to Southern California where land was cheap and the sun shone year round. By the early 1920s, nearly all film production had moved west. More about these events in the following chapter.

Chapter

33

Climate Catalyzes the 1918 Flu Pandemic

I t was an invisible killer, a strain of the flu that swept the world reaching even isolated islands and the Arctic Circle. According to the Centers for Disease Control and Prevention, "Although there is not universal consensus regarding where the virus originated, it spread worldwide during 1918–1919. In the United States, it was first identified in military personnel in spring 1918."[1] An estimated five hundred million people worldwide, or one-third of the world's population, became infected with this virus. The number of deaths was estimated to be between fifty million and one hundred million people. Some historians believe that figure is on the low side and many millions more may have succumbed to the virus.

The pandemic came to be known as the Spanish flu, not because it originated in Spain, but because it was one of the few European countries that had remained neutral during World War I. The combatants had put in place strict media censorship, which suppressed information about the flu because such information was considered bad for morale. Unconstrained Spanish journalists sounded the alarm by first reporting on the health crisis in May 1918. Spanish King Alfonso XIII was inflicted with the illness shortly thereafter. The Spanish, however, did not call it the Spanish flu. They blamed it on their neighbors and called it "the French Flu." Actually, it might have originated in crowded Army camps in Kansas.

One reason the flu was so deadly and spread so quickly was the climate. In 1918, the waters of the tropical Pacific were cooled by a La Niña. The cooling caused a change in the migrations of wild birds, which brought them into contact with different animals and people. This aided the genetic mixing of various strains of the flu virus, creating a new strain for which humans had not yet developed immunity. The strain was especially insidious thanks to a group of genes that allowed it to weaken a victim's lungs and bronchial tubes, leaving them susceptible to bacterial pneumonia.

The La Niña was followed later that year by a powerful El Niño system in the Pacific. According to a new National Oceanic and Atmospheric Administration (NOAA) study, it was one of the strongest El Niños of the twentieth century. This caused the unusually cool temperatures over the Pacific to heat quickly, which in turn played havoc with weather patterns around the world. The extreme weather affected health, leaving many people more vulnerable to the virus.

In India, for example, as a result of the El Niño, regular monsoon rains failed to develop, causing a severe drought. The drought happened at the worst possible time as the new strain of flu was making its way around the globe. With the combined punch of the drought, famine, and disease, India was especially hard hit and lost an estimated seventeen to eighteen million people to the pandemic.

Influenza viruses tend to spread in waves. They thrive in cold, dry environments. That means the risk of catching the flu is greatest in the two- to three-month period between November and March in the Northern Hemisphere and between May and September in the Southern Hemisphere. Epidemiologists have suggested a number of reasons for this. First, influenza viruses are more stable in the cold. They "like" a temperature around 41°F/5°C but are blocked or inefficient at 86°F/30°C.

Dry indoor spaces that people inhabit in winter also play a role. Scientists also know that influenza is stable at low relative humidity, but unstable at higher humidities. This means that the virus spreads more easily in dry environments and less easily in more humid environments.

Temperature and humidity affect how the body reacts to a viral threat. Researchers have found that low humidity hinders the immune response by preventing cilia, the hair-like structures in the cells of the airway, from removing viral particles and mucus. It also reduces the ability of the cells in the airway to repair damage caused by the virus and the ability of infected cells to alert neighboring cells to a threat. The 1918–1919 winter was particularly cold and the colder it is outside, usually the drier it is inside. As air from the outside comes into a building and is heated, the temperature goes up, but the relative humidity goes down. Both cold and dryness caused the virus to spread more rapidly.

After communities recovered from the first wave of the flu in the spring, a second, more contagious wave appeared in the fall. What made the Spanish flu so frightening was that it cut down previously healthy people in their prime. More US soldiers died from the 1918 flu than were killed in battle during all of World War I.

An unintended consequence of the outbreak was that it helped make smoking more popular after cigarettes were promoted to soldiers as a prophylactic. The flu also made aspirin use more widespread. Bayer had developed aspirin in 1899, and its patent expired just ahead of the outbreak in 1917. This meant that more companies were able to produce the drug. Doctors started to recommend it to patients to help with flu symptoms. It helped reduce the pain and discomfort from the symptoms, but was highly unlikely to actually combat the flu.

Scientists never did develop a cure. The pandemic had run its course by the summer of 1919, as those who were infected by the flu had either died or developed immunity.

Prior to the pandemic, most doctors worked independently. Some were funded by charities or religious institutions, but there were no centralized systems to make sure citizens had warnings about developing pandemics or access to health care. This all changed after the outbreak. The science of epidemiology became a serious discipline. By 1925, the United States had organized a national disease reporting system.

The first international organization for fighting epidemics was formed in 1919. It was the forerunner of today's World Health Organization. Meanwhile countries around the world also developed systems to improve the availability of health care. Throughout the 1920s many governments adopted centralized public health care systems. Russia was the first, followed by Germany, France, and eventually the United Kingdom. The United States focused on employer-based insurance systems, which started to take off in the 1930s.

Chapter
34

Drought Triggers the Dustbowl Migrations

They were called "human tumbleweeds." In the late 1930s, California was inundated with domestic migrants who were trekking west from Oklahoma, Kansas, Arkansas, Missouri, and Texas. The migrants were not all poor, but many were, and what they all had in common was that their old way of life had been imperiled by one of the hottest and driest periods in American history.

The all-time highest recorded temperatures in twenty-three states (twenty-four counting the District of Columbia) happened in the 1930s. The year 1936 saw the Dust Bowl subsiding but July of that year was extremely hot, with ten states reporting their all-time high temperatures, records to this day. The result was a severe drought across the Midwest and Southern Great Plains, which dried up the top soil. Winds from the Rockies picked it up and created massive dust storms sometimes called "black blizzards."

In mid-latitudes, the upper air winds almost always blow west to east. While less prevalent at the surface where people live, the west wind is predominant, although at any given time winds can blow from any direction.

Some of these billowing dust clouds were blown as far as New York City and Washington, DC. On May 12 1934, the *New York Times* reported that there was so much dust in the city atmosphere that it seemed like night at lunch time. People who lived in the thick of it found their homes coated with grit and some people developed an illness called "dust pneumonia." We didn't measure this in those days, but undoubtedly lung disease caused by inhaling particulates during the Dust Bowl killed tens of thousands of people, perhaps even one hundred thousand people.

The particles in the air only exacerbated the drought. As with some of the volcanoes we have read about, they reflected sunlight back into space. As the surface temperature cooled in the darkness, there was less evaporation. Less evaporation means fewer clouds. Fewer clouds mean less rain. And so, once a usual drought began, the combination of farming practices and physics caused it to worsen until it reached historical proportions. Arriving at the height of the Great Depression, the drought was a crippling blow to already cash-strapped farmers.

And, as we saw with the plagues of Egypt, the disruptions in the climate led to a change in the ecosystem. One result was a major infestation of grasshoppers with clouds of as many as twenty-three thousand insects per acre. Whatever crops had survived the drying were eaten by the bugs.

An AP reporter named Robert Geiger first coined the term "Dust Bowl" in 1935 to describe the hardships, and the term came to symbolize the struggles of an entire nation as the crop failures exacerbated the Great Depression. More than 3.5 million people were displaced, and unscathed California, where the agriculture industry was booming, was the main destination. Populations in several Plains states dropped and for some places it took forty years to recover to pre-Dust Bowl population levels.

The Providence Journal described the migrants in dramatic terms, "An army is marching into California—an army made up of penniless unemployed, desperately seeking Utopia. 'Here we are,' say the invaders, 'what're you going to do about us?' And nobody knows the answer."[1]

The term "Okie," which had previously been a neutral way of describing someone from Oklahoma, as one might call someone from Texas "Tex," took on negative connotations. The movement of Dust Bowl refugees came to be known as the Okie Migration, even though the displaced were from a number of plains states including Missouri, Arkansas, and Texas.

President Franklin Delano Roosevelt enacted the first of several mortgage and farming relief acts under the New Deal in 1933 to help keep farmers afloat. He also formed several agencies focused on land management and conservation.

The work of such artists as John Steinbeck, Dorothea Lange, and Woody Guthrie popularized the image of the Dust Bowl migrant as a farm worker, but in fact, at least half were working in other blue-collar professions.

The worst of the drought and dust storms were waning when John Steinbeck's *Grapes of Wrath* was released, becoming an instant classic. But the sympathetic portrait Steinbeck and his fellow artists painted of the poor had profound and long-lasting effects on public policy. America's welfare and financial programs such as social security and the US Securities and Exchange Commission (SEC) and Federal Deposit Insurance Corporation (FDIC) were created in response to the Great Depression and the simultaneous heat wave and drought.

How Drought Begets More Drought

Once a drought or heat wave begins, in some circumstances it can create the very conditions that perpetuate it and even make it stronger. During the Dust Bowl, a prolonged hot period dried out the soil and, with low soil moisture, this reduced evaporation and the potential for rain. The farming practice at the time was to clear the vegetative cover and till the land between crops, increasingly using machinery rather than animals. This left the dry soil very loose and easily eroded and picked up and carried by the wind. Many soil scientists, agricultural researchers, and historians have blamed the Dust Bowl catastrophe on inappropriate cropping practices, especially clearing trees and other vegetative cover from the land surface, as well as the advent of mechanized agriculture, which accelerated over-cultivation.

With hot temperatures, evaporation of moisture from the soil and plants increased, which dried the soil further and made it even more susceptible to being picked up by wind. This exacerbated and accelerated the drought process for several reasons:

First, the drier soil had little additional moisture to evaporate, limiting the amount of water vapor in the atmosphere that was available to produce rainfall. Second, the proliferation of a great quantity of dust particles in the air were carried upward, where they competed with each other and any ice particles in the cloud for available moisture. The result was clouds with tiny water droplets. In a vacuum, all particles accelerate to the ground under the force of gravity at the same rate. However, because of air resistance, small water droplets in clouds hardly fall at all, and the only way you can get rain is by producing droplets large enough to fall fast enough to reach the ground before they evaporate. When there is a high concentration of small droplets, they remain suspended in the air, and drought results.

Water also has a high specific heat so it takes more than ten times as much energy to raise the temperature of a cubic inch of water as a similar amount of soil. So when there is less moisture in the soil, the heat from the sun will be more effective in raising the temperature of the earth.

Drought begets more drought. A lack of rainfall and clouds allows temperatures to get even higher. The higher the temperature, the more rapid the rate of evaporation from the soil and the plants. If the soil is dry, there is a lack of moisture to conduct the heat into the ground, so the top soil becomes hotter and makes the air hotter still. This in turn reduces the humidity further and causes even more rapid evaporation.

Water has many properties that keep the temperature from rising. Not only does it conduct heat into the ground, but when it evaporates, it has a cooling effect, just like how you feel when you step out of the shower into a drafty hallway. That evaporation is a very powerful cooling effect, but if there is less moisture to evaporate, the ground gets even hotter.

When settlers first arrived in the Plains in the 1870s–1900s, it was known as the Great American Desert. This area was very dry for at least the last few thousand years. At some point, the Great Plains might have been a great lake that resulted from the melting glaciers to the north, and that lake and the sediments at the bottom of that lake may have been the reason for the fertile fields of the American Midwest. As we know, climates go through cycles and after a long period of dry weather, the Plains became relatively wet, starting after 1910 and lasting into the late 1920s. Then the climate turned dry again. The long-rooted Plains grasses that held the soil in place were plowed under during the wetter years in order to plant agricultural products with much shorter roots. When the rains failed again, the soil blew away, because it was no longer held by natural grasses. Plowing techniques were poor. The farmers learned new ways to plow to hold soil in place, and today the crops that are grown in this region are more suitable and tailored for each particular locale.

Chapter

35

An Electric Charge Ends the Airship Era

When a dramatic event occurs, it is natural to look for a dramatic cause. When the *Hindenburg* burst into flames in front of newsreel cameras in 1937, people speculated that it must have been a lightning strike or sabotage. In fact, it was something much more mundane. The *Hindenburg* was destroyed by ordinary rain clouds.

For a brief, shining moment in the early 1930s, luxury travel was defined by the airship. Dirigibles had lower fuel costs, were quiet, and their interiors were roomy. The Zeppelin Company's *Hindenburg*, which launched in 1930, was one of the finest examples. At that time it was the largest man-made object ever to fly. Its interior was decorated in a modern Bauhaus style and featured private passenger cabins, a restaurant, cocktail lounge, airy promenades, and a smoking room. It even had a specially designed lightweight piano on board. Airships were admired—and feared.

In the interwar years, the United States, which was the only large-scale producer of helium, worried about the use of the craft in a future war and adopted the Helium Control Act. This kept US helium out of German airships so the *Hindenburg* was filled with more combustible hydrogen gas. But what sealed its fate was what was on the outside, not the inside. In order to protect it from moisture, the blimp's skin was coated with iron oxide covered with cellulose acetate. This flammable mix—nearly identical to rocket fuel—was stiffened with another flammable material, powdered aluminum.

The *Hindenburg*'s arrival in Lakehurst, New Jersey, on May 6, 1937 was not its maiden voyage. It had landed there nearly a dozen times, but such was the glamour of the *Hindenburg* that there was a large audience, including journalists, there to see it come in.

AN ELECTRIC CHARGE ENDS THE AIRSHIP ERA

It was arriving late. Headwinds over Newfoundland had delayed it, and stormy weather in New Jersey kept it circling the airport, unable to dock. It continued to circle for more than an hour. As it did so, it passed through rain clouds and became negatively charged. When the crew dropped its lines to dock, they acted as a ground. The flammable skin became heated and ignited. It took just thirty-four seconds for the pride of German engineering to be engulfed in flames.

This is one of the worst catastrophes in the world, radio reporter Herb Morrison famously observed. "Oh, the humanity, and all the passengers screaming around here!!"

The *Hindenburg* disaster was not the deadliest airship accident. That distinction belongs to the US Navy's USS Akron, a helium-filled craft, which killed seventy-three of the seventy-six on board in April 1933. Thirty-six lives were lost in the *Hindenburg* accident, including thirty-five people on the ship and one member of the ground crew. Amazingly, sixty-two of the ninety-seven people on board the ship survived.

The much more deadly wreck of the *Akron*, however, did not have the same impact for a number of reasons. The *Akron* was called "the giant of the skies" when it was launched in 1931. The victims were members of the military, not civilians. The USS *Akron* left the Naval Air Engineering Station at Lakehurst, approximately 25 mi/40 km east-southeast of Trenton, New Jersey, on the evening of April 3, 1933 on a mission to calibrate radio equipment along the northeastern coast of the United States.

Shortly after midnight on April 4, the ship encountered a series of strong updrafts and downdrafts. The *Akron* dropped in altitude and the ship's altimeter was giving inaccurate readings due to the low pressure of the storm. In those days, they often did not correct the altimeter, which is simply a barometer converted to measure the height of a plane or dirigible in the atmosphere, because normally atmospheric pressure decreases with height. The average pressure corrected to sea level is 29.92 in/76 cm of mercury. The record lowest surface pressure ever during the most intense hurricane has been under 26 in/66 cm, and the strongest high pressure area had a barometer reading of close to 32 in/81.28 cm. Near sea level, the pressure drops about 1 in/2.54 cm of mercury for every 1,000ft/304.8 m rise in the atmosphere. If a pilot does not correct the altimeter for the actual surface barometer pressure and uses the standard (average) pressure, it can lead to a deadly result. If the normal pressure is 29.92 in/76 cm, and the pilot is reading the equivalent of 28.92 in/73.41 cm, he might think he is 1,000 ft/304.8 m above the surface. Usually, he would be. Yet, in a low pressure area, with a sea level reading of 28.92 in/73.46 cm, his actual height would be at sea level. If the ground level is above sea level, he will crash into the ground.

Thus the captain believed the ship was higher than it was as he attempted to climb out of a downdraft. As the nose rose the tail fell into the ocean. The lower fin was torn off, and the ship disintegrated. Instead of a dramatic fireball captured on newsreels for the world to see, the victims of the Akron suffered death by hypothermia in the frigid waters of the stormy Atlantic.

The deadlier helium-airship accident was not enough to put an end to the industry. Over the years, there have also been many airplane crashes, yet none of them halted the production of airplanes. Why did the *Hindenburg* accident bring the age of the airship to an end?

The answer is probably found in the power of visuals. In the days before universal surveillance cameras and smart phones, it was unusual to capture an accident on film for the simple reason that usually someone would have to know it was going to happen and have cameras ready. Because the arrival of the glamorous *Hindenburg* was a society event, a number of journalists happened to be on hand.

Sam Shere, a photojournalist with the International News Photo Service, captured one of the most famous images in history. "I had two shots in my [camera]," he said, "but I didn't even have time to get it up to my eye. I literally 'shot' from the hip—it was over so fast there was nothing else to do."[1] Shere's photograph of the explosion of the *Hindenburg* went out over the wires and was printed in newspapers across the country, including on the front page of the *Washington Post*. Millions of people saw it, and the frightening image became indelibly associated with airships. Newsreel footage, which played in movie theatres across the country, allowed audiences to witness the majestic craft disintegrate into wire frame and flame.

If the *Hindenburg*'s final journey had been less documented, a single accident might not have been enough to cause airships to fall out of favor. The German and Allied forces would likely have made use of them in WWII for reconnaissance and bombing raids. Modern travelers might still have the option of crossing the ocean in a luxurious airship. Airplanes became more powerful and faster over time, and would no doubt have eclipsed airships for everyday international travel, but one can imagine a world in which a ship like the *Hindenburg* was a popular mode of slow-speed vacation travel, like a cruise ship.

On the other hand, because of their relative inability to navigate around severe storms and since weather observations over the oceans were not nearly as precise and complete in the late 1930s, if it had not been the Hindenburg, it is likely that some other airships would have met a spectacularly bad end and halted the era of the airship.

To this day aviators and engineers continue to imagine a place for dirigibles hauling cargo to remote areas. Traditional air travel requires substantial airport infrastructure. Airships could reach remote villages and natural resources that are not accessible by road all or part of the year.

In the 1980s, blimps—nonrigid airships—appeared in the air with advertising logos, with Goodyear being the most famous. Unlike the *Hindenburg* and airships of its era, the

Goodyear blimp, with no rigid structure inside, could carry a maximum of fourteen passengers and very little cargo.

The 1977 World Book Encyclopedia *Science Year Annual* announced "Airships Make a Comeback." Similar articles emerge every few years documenting the efforts of an enterprise here or there. Most recently the *Financial Times*, in February 2020, reported on a firm called OceanSky that announced plans to send a passenger airship to the arctic.

The main problem with bringing back the airships on any grand scale is the fuel. Helium, which is used in MRI scanners and rocket engines, is being depleted. In recent years, prices have skyrocketed as stores of the non-renewable resource become scarce, and since the *Hindenburg* disaster, hydrogen has been viewed as far too dangerous.

Claire Benson, a research fellow of the Explosions and Fire Research Group at London South Bank University, suggests in *Chemistry World* that our view of hydrogen may have been skewed by the *Hindenburg* accident:

> Hydrogen has many advantages as a fuel. It is 'cleaner' than hydrocarbon fuels, burns easily, and is safely managed in difficult environments. However, today it is almost impossible to discuss hydrogen use in any context, let alone aeronautics, without the '*Hindenburg* effect' surfacing: people remember the speed and size of the fire and decide to avoid the use of hydrogen altogether. The visibility of the *Hindenburg* disaster dramatically changed people's perceptions, much like other catastrophic disasters are so often the catalyst for change.[2]

With hydrogen now being used in applications ranging from research to power to public transportation, could the world be ready for a new generation of hydrogen dirigibles? If not, there is one theoretical option. An airship could be lifted by a vacuum. Such a ship would be constructed of a material that would be empty but which could withstand the atmospheric pressure from the outside. It would then rise because it would be lighter than the air it displaced. Nothing like this has yet been created, but NASA scientists have considered such an idea for exploring the surface of Mars.

A new day may yet dawn for dirigibles at the hands of human ingenuity. For now, the glamorous promise of spacious airships has been sidelined for almost a century due to the infamous *Hindenburg* tragedy and challenges of our atmosphere. The *Hindenburg* even left its mark on the stock market. There is a signal that is used by technical traders of stocks called the *Hindenburg* Omen. It occurs when both the number of new highs for the year and the number of new lows for the year exceed a certain number on the same day. It has proved itself a good predictor of significant stock market drops.

Chapter

36

Calm Seas and Cloudy Skies Aid the Dunkirk Evacuation

Victory in a battle gets all the glory, but as we have seen with George Washington in the American Revolution, a successful retreat after a failure can be equally vital over the long term to ensure victory in the war.

After the German conquest of Poland in September 1939, the European powers entered a period of stalemate in which France and Britain assembled defensive troops but did not engage. Journalists dubbed the period of inactivity the "Phoney War." (In French *Drole de Guerre* and in German the *sitzkrieg* in contrast to the *blitzkrieg*.)

Then on May 10, 1940, the day Winston Churchill became British prime minister, the Germans sprang into action by launching a *blitzkrieg* attack on the Netherlands and Belgium. By May 15, they'd broken through French defenses and turned toward the English Channel. The British and French had been taken by surprise by German forces who took a route through hilly, forested terrain that was previously believed to be too difficult for tanks. The Germans, however, had constructed narrow paved roads that allowed them to quickly cross into northern France. The German army divided the French and British allies, and left four hundred thousand Allied soldiers all but surrounded near the coastal city of Dunkirk.

But rather than strike while the troops were stuck on the beaches, Hitler gave his Panzer troops a halt order. Some people were perplexed as to why he paused, but the tank corps had been moving non-stop for days and the troops were exhausted. They had outrun their supply lines and the Germans did not believe the British had a sufficient number of boats to evacuate all of the stranded troops. Whatever the reason, it gave the British just enough time to plan their retreat.

CALM SEAS AND CLOUDY SKIES AID THE DUNKIRK EVACUATION

By May 19, it was clear to the British commanders that they would have to withdraw the entire British Expeditionary Force to avoid catastrophic losses. The sea provided the only escape route. The evacuation plan, dubbed Operation Dynamo, was ordered by Winston Churchill on May 24.

Dunkirk is forty miles by sea from the English port of Dover. It lies at about fifty degrees north of the equator. The most favorable seagoing weather generally occurs in April. As the season progresses, mid-latitude cyclones become more frequent as the weather gets more stormy. In a typical year, the seas in May would be choppy and stormy. Instead Allies were fortunate to have a week with overcast skies but no storms. Military geographer Harold A. Winters noted, "Without favorable weather the evacuation in 1940 would have been much less successful and the Normandy landings in 1944 surely delayed."[1]

Dunkirk's inner harbor had been rendered useless by German bombing. Still unscathed, however, were two long barriers called moles that had been constructed to protect the harbor from storm waves and to aid in navigation. Each of the moles was made of stone or concrete with a wooden walkway. The east mole became the most important evacuation route allowing soldiers to access the beach and wait for ships.

With the harbor bombed out of commission, large ships could not dock, and small boats would be needed to transport the troops in small numbers to ships anchored off the coast. The admiralty called on the British public to take to the seas in anything that could float. Hundreds of fishing boats, yachts, ferries, and paddle-wheeled pleasure boats answered the call and, sailed by average citizens, set sail for Dunkirk, risking mines, torpedoes, and air raids along the way.

As the British planned the extraction of its soldiers on May 26, an intense storm was heading from the mid-Atlantic to the English channel. If it had remained on this course, it would have made evacuation much more difficult than it already was.

Fortunately for the Allies, by May 28, the upper air wind flow pattern developed a blocking high pressure system over western Europe, which caused the storm to turn northward and avoid Britain. The skies were overcast with a ceiling of only 300 ft/100 m. This kept the German aircraft from engaging the evacuating soldiers on the ground. The temperature was mild and the seas were rough but not so rough as to prevent boarding the troops onto ships via the east mole. Above the clouds, the Royal Air Force and the Luftwaffe battled in the skies, while on the ground 17,804 soldiers boarded boats for home.

Winters noted that the weather patterns that aided the British were not the most statistically probable for the Dunkirk coast in late May.[2] More likely is a progression of wave cyclones (well-developed low pressure areas), which usher in stormy weather and rough seas. Another possibility is that dominant air masses from the Azores High would have kept skies clear and allowed for constant aerial attacks by the Luftwaffe.

"By a twist of fate, or better yet a meander of the jet stream, neither of these two most-likely weather patterns dominated Flanders in late May 1940," Winters wrote. "Instead the one set of conditions that most favored the Allied evacuation persisted for days."[3]

As the evacuation was taking place, two corps of the French First Army led by General Jean-Baptiste Molinié were valiantly holding back seven German divisions forty miles to the southeast. They were badly outnumbered with just forty thousand French standing against 110,000 Germans, but from May 28–31 they held their ground and kept the tank divisions from entering Dunkirk. Their efforts probably saved one hundred thousand Allied lives.

On May 29, the Germans remained largely grounded because of scattered rain and low visibility due to a mix of clouds and smoke from a burning port. These conditions remained until early afternoon when the skies cleared enough to allow German reconnaissance pilots to get a good view of where the evacuation was taking place. Dive-bombers were dispatched to attack the breakwaters.

The German Junkers Ju 87 dive bombers were equipped with a siren known as the "Jericho Trumpet," which was designed to spread terror with its wail as the planes attacked. A British gunner on the beach that day remembered the "diving, zooming, screeching, and wheeling over our heads like a flock of huge infernal seagulls."[4]

A number of ships were destroyed or damaged, including the destroyer *HMS Grenade*, which sank after being hit by three bombs, the minesweeper *HMS Waverly*, sunk with six hundred troops onboard, killing 350, and the destroyer *HMS Jaguar*, which was badly damaged. After that small window, however, the clouds returned and the Germans were grounded again by the next morning.

The British evacuation resumed throughout the day, both from the mole and from the beaches in small boats. There were occasional breaks in the cloud cover that allowed for intermittent air raids but even so, more than twenty-nine thousand more soldiers left Dunkirk via the beach and another twenty-four thousand via the moles.

On May 31, a southwest breeze blew over the channel causing choppy surf that slowed the evacuation from the beaches. The skies cleared, but in spite of three rounds of German bombing, the English sent the largest number of troops home yet, 68,014.

By June 1, most of the British soldiers had been evacuated. At this point the weather started to benefit the Germans. A large anticyclone (high pressure area) had drifted toward England leaving the beach at Dunkirk clear and sunny. With evacuation too risky during daylight, the British were forced to shift to nighttime evacuation. The last boat left on the evening of June 4. In all, 338,000 British soldiers had been sent home. And forty thousand French troops remained.

The Dunkirk evacuation inspired one of Winston Churchill's most famous speeches on June 4, when he summed up what had come to be known as the "Miracle of Dunkirk" in a speech before the House of Commons: "We shall go on to the end . . . we shall fight on the seas and oceans, we shall fight with growing confidence and growing strength in the air, we shall defend our Island, whatever the cost may be, we shall fight on the beaches . . . we shall fight in the hills; we shall never surrender."

The way that everyday citizens had come together to rescue the troops became a source of motivation and morale for the nation as it entered a full-blown war with Germany. As a witness to the events at Dunkirk said, "Unless the men of the B.E.F. are exterminated and the men who brought them off the piers and beaches are exterminated and all memory of them is blotted out, we cannot lose the war."[5]

Yet, what if the seas that week had been too rough for small boats to sail? What if the skies had been clear and the Germans had bombed the Allies out of existence? Ian Kershaw, professor of Modern History at the University of Sheffield, calls this "a nightmare fantasy."[6] In an article for *Lapham's Quarterly*, he imagines a world in which the Belgian and French allies fell to Hitler and all of the Allied troops not killed or wounded at Dunkirk were taken prisoner in "a defeat unparalleled in British history."

From there he imagined Hitler and Mussolini dividing up areas of influence in Europe:

Although Hitler permitted the British Empire to survive, he reduced it to a mere semblance of what it had once been. British rights in the oil fields of the Middle East were to be ceded to Germany, along with the mandated territories in the region and control over the Suez Canal. Backed by his bellicose foreign minister, Ribbentrop, Hitler insisted on acquiring a swathe of British, French, and Belgian colonies in Africa, establishing German rule over much of the African continent. With Malta, Gibraltar, Algeria, and Tunisia in Mussolini's hands—his part of the spoils from the Brussels Conference—the Axis powers now dominated the entire Mediterranean.[7]

Fortunately for the world, the winds were blowing in the right direction in May 1940 to prevent any of that from happening.

Chapter

37

Russian Winter Thwarts Hitler

Adolph Hitler had the benefit of history when he set his sights on the USSR. He knew of Napoleon's ill-fated invasion and he had no intention of repeating it, so he consulted a meteorologist, one of the first to experiment with long-range forecasts. After consulting 150 years of Russian weather records, Franz Bauer observed that there had never been four cold winters in a row and because the previous three winters had been especially cold, it was statistically impossible that Russia would experience another cold winter; ergo the winter of 1941 would have to be mild.

Reassured by this, Hitler planned a short, dramatic campaign intended to topple Stalin in a matter of weeks. So as not to repeat the errors of Napoleon, Hitler issued a directive on December 18, 1940 that his forces should attack with great force in the spring and avoid following Russian troops as they withdrew into the vast interior of the largest nation in the world. Modern Russia is large, but the Soviet Union was huge, occupying nearly one sixth of the earth's surface. To capture it, and all of its resources, would require a theater of war several times larger than all of the territory Hitler had annexed in Western Europe.

Hitler's Operation Barbarossa was to be a three-pronged attack. While one division was striking Moscow, another would seize Leningrad (now St. Petersburg), and the third would capture Kiev. Hitler believed it would all be over, and Russia would be defeated by fall. The German army was so confident with this timeline that several units brought dress uniforms for a victory march in Red Square, but did not bring any winter clothes.

The plan was launched on June 22, 1941. The June launch avoided the Soviet snow and ice, but it came with its own challenges. The summer was exceptionally hot and dry with temperatures climbing as high as 104°F/40°C. The Germans were surprised at the backwards conditions of the roads in Russia. The parched earth made for dusty unpaved roads, which damaged German tanks as their radiators and filters became clogged. To avoid heatstroke, many of the soldiers left their winter gear behind. They did not expect to need it, as they believed the forecasts that they would be victorious and home before winter.

None of this impeded the German progress much. The Red Army had been taken by surprise because Stalin had entered a non-aggression pact with Hitler not long before the invasion. By July they had already made it most of the way to Moscow. The Germans were aided, incidentally, by the many British vehicles that had been abandoned at Dunkirk. Although the soldiers had all been successfully extracted, they had been forced to leave most of their gear behind, including seventy-six thousand tons of ammunition, four hundred thousand tons of supplies, 2,500 weapons, and sixty-four thousand vehicles. Although the retreating British had poured sand into the radiators and fuel tanks of the vehicles, a large number could be salvaged and many were used against the Soviets in Operation Barbarossa.

The German advance was disastrous for the Soviets. In the first month, 747,850 soldiers had been killed and another three hundred thousand were taken prisoner.

As it had so many times before, the threat from outside drew the Soviet people together, and though they were badly outgunned, they were fighting for their very existence. Soldiers and citizens alike battled back, and when they were forced to retreat, they destroyed all provisions, burned houses, and poisoned wells, leaving their invaders to try to survive in the elements.

On July 28, the Soviet Supreme Command issued the order "Not a single step back!" Russian soldiers would defend the capital or die trying. By the end of August, Hitler decided to pause the advance on Moscow and to have his forces first go through Ukraine where the farms would allow them to stock up on provisions. The delay meant that they would make the final push to Moscow in autumn.

Hitler was not able to deploy as many reinforcements in early fall as he had wanted. The troops of his ally, the Italian dictator Mussolini, were bogged down in Africa, so Hitler dispatched German General Erwin Rommel's troops to Africa to prevent an axis defeat.

Hitler had been warned that the spring melt in these northern climes caused the soil to turn into a messy quagmire. He did not listen to those who advised him that there was often another muddy period in the fall. So the Germans were delayed again.

As the Germans began their march to Moscow on October 2, 1941, the residents of Moscow started evacuating their cultural treasures, digging an anti-tank trench, and launching anti-aircraft balloons. As civilians moved out, battalions from Siberia moved in. As the German tanks became stuck in the mud, Soviet tanks, which had wider tracks and higher ground clearance, continued to operate. This state of affairs continued until the frost came in November.

With solid ground beneath them, the 6th German Panzer Division made a steady advance. They got within 15 mi/24 km of the Kremlin. And some German troops saw the spires of Central Moscow churches in the distance. But on December 1 they had their first experience of the full force of the Russian winter. Temperatures plummeted to -40°F/-40°C. When the generals on the front lines asked the Third Reich's meteorologist if he still believed the winter would be mild, he said that it would be, and that the observations in the field must be wrong.

If they were mistaken about the weather conditions, their weapons didn't know it. The frigid temperatures caused their machine guns to freeze and firing pins to shatter. The shells that they fired thudded into deep packs of snow. The troops who had discarded their coats months before were now suffering from frost bite. Their boots, made with conductive iron nails, actually made their feet colder. This battered force was about to go up against reserves from Siberia who had lifelong experience with such cold. Their uniforms included padded jackets, felt boots, fur caps, and white camouflage gear.

With his men succumbing to the weather, Hitler was forced to have them retreat from Moscow. If they were going to make another attempt on the capital in spring, they would have to take the oil fields of Baku. The route took them through a city which was then named for the Soviet leader—Stalingrad. (It is now, as it was before Stalin, called Volgograd for its position on the Volga River.) If he could not take Moscow, at least Hitler could claim the prize of Stalin's namesake city.

The following summer, June 1942, the Germans stormed Stalingrad, burning it to the ground with air raids in preparation for an invasion by a force of a hundred thousand men. Over the next months, Russian General Georgy Zhukov continued to defend the city with a small force while secretly amassing a large force east of the city. Meanwhile, civilians and soldiers fought in the rubble of their buildings. With a small number of snipers they were able to hold off the Germans until September. The Germans had reached the city center with 330,000 soldiers, but they had expended almost all of their energy to get there.

Zhukov kept his second wave hidden, waiting for the first snowstorm, which finally came on November 19. Once the Germans were socked in with snow, the Soviet troops surrounded the city. They managed to take a hundred thousand Germans prisoner. Those they did not capture were trapped to fight for survival in the rubble of the buildings they had destroyed.

The Luftwaffe tried to airdrop supplies, but they were only able to drop a third of what the men needed—when their planes were not shot down by the Soviets. Between the Soviet attacks and the increasingly difficult weather, the Germans lost 490 planes and their crews. The soldiers were left to fight over meager provisions as they died of cold and starvation.

The Russians, meanwhile, were making good use of the cold. In mid-December, when the Volga froze, it became an ice bridge allowing the Russians to bring in thousands of trucks full of food, weapons, and warm clothing. They had everything they needed to maintain their blockade.

By January, the badly depleted force of starving, sick men sent a request to Berlin that they be allowed to surrender. They were told to hold their position, and that they would be hailed as heroes and patriots. They did not have to endure much longer. On February 2, 1943, the Germans were finally forced to surrender and the bloodiest battle in history came to an end. When the two hundred–day battle was finished, more than a million people had been killed. The Soviet Union had lost more people in the battle for Stalingrad alone than the British and Americans combined lost in the entire war. Yet suffering so much at the hands of the Germans only strengthened the Russian resolve. The Russians did not stop fighting until they had taken Berlin. The battle of Stalingrad is seen by many historians as the beginning of the end of the Third Reich.

Between the German invasion and Stalin's scorched earth tactics, the war left the Soviet Union, especially the western regions, in a state of absolute ruin. More than 1,700 towns and seventy thousand villages had been completely destroyed. Factories and infrastructure had crumbled. World War II, as a whole, was the bloodiest war in history, killing an estimated sixty million people or about 3 percent of the world's population. No nation lost as many souls as the Soviet Union. The estimates vary, but somewhere between twenty million and twenty-seven million Soviets died out of a pre-war population of about 170 million. That means between 12–16 percent of the Soviet population was lost. Of these, two thirds were civilians. No family was left untouched, and the sense of shared endurance and pride is central to the sense of Russian identity.

In the wake of such devastation, the Soviets resolved to build a defense system so powerful that no nation would ever dare invade them again. This was one of the major Russian motivations behind its domination of Poland as well as what was behind the nuclear arms race with the United States and Western Europe. As both sides amassed weapons to achieve balance and the deterrence of "mutually assured destruction," an entire generation on both sides grew up in the shadow of the bomb. In the United States, children had air raid drills and practiced "duck and cover." There was a widespread fear that a leader would make a mistake and launch an attack that would end in the extinction of the human race.

Because the weapons were too deadly to use, the United States and the Soviet Union engaged in a political and propaganda war that author George Orwell was the first to dub the Cold War. Rivalry between the two super powers dominated international affairs from the end of the war until the collapse of the Soviet Union in 1991.

As the United States had a stronger economy, built on capitalism, the Soviet Union, with central planning and inefficiencies had to devote more and more of its resources to maintaining its arsenal. In the mid-1980s, about 70 percent of the Soviet's industrial output went to the military. This was one of the leading causes of the collapse of the Soviet system.

Russians call World War II the Great Patriotic War. To this day, it is evoked to instill a sense of patriotism and national pride. Vladimir Putin regularly invokes it to stir a sense of national purpose in support of his foreign policy goals. In 2014, Putin signed a law criminalizing criticism of the Soviet war effort. Thus the frigid winter in Stalingrad is still felt in our politics today.

Chapter

38

Forecasting
D-Day

I n spite of Hitler's disaster in Stalingrad and his failed attempt to take Moscow, the war continued to rage on. If the Allies were to turn the tides of the war, they would need a massive operation to establish a beachhead in France.

The mission, Operation Overlord, was nearly two years in the planning. It encompassed nearly three million Allied troops—British, American, Canadian, Polish, French, and Czech—in four thousand ships and eleven thousand planes. It would need to take place in early summer to coincide with a planned Eastern offensive by the Soviets, which would strain German resources.

The planners needed a set of specific conditions to make the mission a success. It would need to happen at low tide with calm seas and 3 mi/5 km visibility. It would have to remain that way for at least thirty-six hours to give many of the forces time to land. The convoys would cross the channel at night to make it difficult for the enemy to gauge their strength and direction. They needed enough moonlight for airborne assaults, and forty minutes of daylight before the ground assault. Timing was critical. The decision on the exact time to launch would be guided by meteorologists in what has been called "the most important weather forecast in history."

Military planners on all sides understood the vital importance of weather forecasting. In the lead-up to the war, the British Met Office grew from seven hundred to six thousand employees. In the United States, the Air Force Weather Service employed nineteen thousand officers and other personnel in nine hundred weather stations around the world.

From this group, a team of six meteorologists—two each from the Met Office, the Royal Navy, and United States Air Force—made their own calculations and submitted their recommendations to the chief meteorological adviser, J. M. Stagg, who had to reconcile the sometimes contradictory advice. The forecasters from the different divisions had different approaches. The Americans mostly relied on past records in order to identify patterns. The British preferred mathematical models, but in an era before computers, complex calculations were laborious. Predicting conditions more than a day or two in advance was all but impossible.

The team had two great advantages over the Germans. First, because weather generally travels from west to east and the Allies had much more control over the Atlantic Ocean, they were able to make more observations of the patterns of high and low pressure and weather moving in from the Atlantic. Perhaps even more significant was that they had cracked the German Enigma code used to encrypt communications. This meant they were able to use not only their own observations but those of the Germans as well. While the Germans had almost no observations from the United Kingdom and the waters around it, the Allies had access to weather observations throughout the region. This gave them insight into a time window in which conditions were likely to be most favorable. The invasion would take place sometime between June 4 and 6, 1944.

On June 4, conditions were stormy. The two US meteorologists, Irving Crick and Ben Holtzman, believed the situation would change by morning and the mission should go forward on June 5. The Royal Navy team of Lawrence Hogben and Geoffrey Wolfe of the Royal Navy and the UK Met Office team of C. K. M. Douglas and Sverre Pettersen disagreed with their assessment. The Americans were so certain their forecast was right that they called the Met Office team to try to persuade them to change their own forecast to match it. The Met team refused, and without the full agreement of the forecasters Eisenhower decided to postpone the landings by one day.

The British team had been right to stand by their forecast. On the morning of June 5, 25–30 mph winds created rough seas in the English Channel. Would the weather be favorable for the mission the next day? It was not an easy call, and the stakes were incredibly high. If the weather was not favorable, the next window of opportunity for the attack would not be until June 19, two weeks later.

A Royal Navy ship off the coast of Iceland reported sustained rising barometric pressure, suggesting a fair weather high pressure area was developing behind the cold front that was over the channel. This could make the conditions on the morning of June 6 barely within acceptable parameters. The teams could still not reach a consensus. But two of the three teams now felt that the conditions would be favorable, so Eisenhower decided not to wait for full agreement and to go with the analysis of the majority.

It was a fateful decision. The storms on June 4 and 5 had kept German reconnaissance planes on the ground and persuaded them that the Allies would not invade at that time. In fact, the commander of Germany's troops in north-west France felt comfortable enough to take a trip home to Germany for his wife's birthday.

At 6:30 a.m. on June 6, five thousand vessels started their journey across the English Channel. The five divisions would land along a 50-mi/80-km front with the British and Canadians landing to the east and the Americans to the west.

Although the worst of the storms had subsided, the conditions were still far from ideal. High winds caused large waves, which rocked the ships, leaving the soldiers seasick and wet. In fact, most invading soldiers had been sitting on their invasion ships for more than twenty-four hours, rocking in heavy seas. When the Americans arrived at Omaha Beach, they found the Germans had blocked their way with barbed wire. To get to the shore, they had to jump into water up to their necks as the Germans fired down from high ground. Many of their armored units foundered in the waves. Of the first thirty-two ships launched, twenty-seven sank. In spite of these setbacks, the Americans were able to advance to the cliffs and move inland.

The 3rd Canadian Division, slated to land at Juno Beach, was delayed by an hour and a half. By the time they arrived, the Germans were prepared for them. The cost of securing their three beaches was high. An estimated three thousand British and 946 Canadians lost their lives. Among the Americans, 1,465 were killed. The Germans lost an estimated four to nine thousand men. But the Allies had secured the beaches, which gave them a doorway to bring food, ammunition, supplies, and soldiers to the continent. Germany was now forced to fight on three fronts: the Soviet Union from the east, Italy from the south, and France coming from the west.

Had Stagg not recommended the operation go forward on June 6, it would have been delayed so long that the Germans would have learned of the plan. As it turned out, on the backup dates of June 18 and 19, a storm pummeled the coast of Normandy, which would have caused another postponement. It was the advice of meteorologists, correctly forecasting a change to favorable weather, that gave the Western Allies their most significant victory of World War II.

Consensus Forecasting

Consensus forecasting has been an important concept in the success of AccuWeather's development of superior accuracy and greater precision of weather forecasts. For twenty-one years, I taught the upper-level forecasting classes at Penn

(Continued on next page)

State. When I retired from teaching, I had taught 17 percent of all the practicing meteorologists in the United States their basic skills in weather forecasting. As part of the class activities, I had each student make a forecast for various time periods and various locations for each day. These forecasts included high and low temperature, amounts of precipitation, and a dozen or more other parameters. These forecasts were then scored according to a known scale. The greater the inaccuracy of the forecast, the more points were accumulated. A perfect forecast would give a forecaster zero points. We computed and scored all the forecasts each day, and ranked the forecasters by the number of "error-points" they accumulated. As an example, at the end of the semester, the best student might have had three hundred errors and the worst might have had 1,400 errors. I found that if you took an average of any of the weather parameters predicted by the ninth and tenth forecaster out of a class of forty, the overall forecast would, on average, be even better than that of the top forecaster in the class.

When I founded AccuWeather and started providing weather forecasts initially to businesses, industries, schools, and county snow clearance operations, I incorporated this consensus approach into our commercial forecasting operation. What I found was that we could make our forecasts even more accurate if, rather than simply taking the average of the forecasters' opinions, the meteorologists discussed the forecasts and their reasoning until an agreement was reached. This approach worked best because the final forecast that resulted was shaped by consideration of how strongly each meteorologist felt and also weighted by how successful they had been in their previous forecasts (in other words, how much skill they had).

This approach formed a foundation for the AccuWeather Philosophy, which utilized a scientific approach toward maximizing the accuracy and value of the forecasts we provided. Of course, forecast accuracy is very important—the more accurate the forecast, the more valuable it can be. But value also includes concepts such as timeliness, format, understandability, consistency, and language—which all determine how effectively forecasts that have greater accuracy will be utilized to produce the best decisions.

This basic concept of consensus has been refined and expanded in ever-increasing ways over the decades to further improve the accuracy and superiority of AccuWeather forecasts.

For example, there are now numerous computer-generated forecast models, each one with its own strengths, weaknesses, and biases. By utilizing a weighting of these models as the basis for AccuWeather forecasts rather than simply choosing one, we made our forecasts more accurate than any of the individual models and more accurate than those available from any other source.

This approach has also proven useful as the computer-generated forecast models grew from single forecasts to ensemble forecasts. The way this approach works is that if the initial conditions in the model are varied slightly, sometimes it will make no difference in the forecast but sometimes the forecast weather will be much different. Today, most models are run as ensembles, where the model is run many times to generate forecasts, each based upon slightly different initial conditions, and the variation in the resulting forecasts gives an idea of the level of certainty of the forecast, as well as the range of possibilities.

In addition, we have developed microscale models based upon statistical and other analyses to better take into account the small-scale differences in weather caused by land-use, buildings, hills and valleys, rivers and streams, and other variations. These have been incorporated into our consensus melding of computerized forecast models to ensure that AccuWeather forecasts provide Superior Accuracy™.

We have refined this concept in several new ways by picking the best components of each forecast model and ensemble forecast models to develop a consensus of the models—taking the best pieces of each model, weighting them appropriately, and using the best combination, ultimately based on AI and segmented by location, time period, and parameters such as temperature, humidity, cloud cover, region, how far ahead, etc. This was very, very important in the advancement of weather forecasting, bringing sustained and increasing accuracy, credibility, and usefulness to AccuWeather's weather forecasts.

Chapter

39

Cloud Cover Spares a Japanese City

U sually people consider it a good thing when the sky is clear and sunny. This was not at all the case for those in Hiroshima, Japan on August 6, 1945. Hiroshima, an industrial city with a population of about 350,000 on the southwestern coast of the Japanese island of Honshu, had so far been spared the worst in Japan's war with the Allies. When other cities were firebombed, tributaries of the Ota River kept the flames from spreading there.

At 7:09 that morning, the air-raid sirens sounded, but there was no attack. A single foreign plane traveled across their airspace and disappeared. After forty minutes the residents of the city went back to their normal activities, not realizing that a lack of cloud cover had condemned them. The single aircraft had been a weather plane, the *Straight Flush*, commanded by Claude Eatherly. Eatherly had radioed back the fateful message, "Cloud cover less than three-tenths. Advice: bomb primary."

Hiroshima had not been the first choice of a target for the first nuclear bomb ever used in war. That distinction belongs to Japan's ancient capital Kyoto. The object in using the deadly weapon was to display such overwhelming force that the Japanese would have no choice but to promptly surrender, preventing the loss of countless American lives, which surely would have occurred if the war dragged on for months and years. The director of the Manhattan Project, General Leslie R. Groves, thought that the loss of Kyoto would shock the enemy into submission as no other target could. But Henry Stimson, the secretary of war, was not willing to vaporize centuries of cultural and religious artifacts in Kyoto. Believing the weapon would be shocking enough on its own, he overruled Grove.

Stimson received the go-ahead from President Harry Truman to use the atomic bomb on July 30. The mission could not proceed immediately because an approaching typhoon made it too dangerous to fly from August 1 until August 5. Again the weather played a role.

During the pause, the list of possible targets was finalized. Hiroshima had become the primary target. Not only was it an industrial center, but it also was surrounded by mountains that would increase the effect of the bomb by focusing its blast. There were, however, three backup targets: Kokura, Nigata, and Nagasaki. If it had been cloudy over Hiroshima, the site with the least cloud cover would become the new primary.

On August 5, the first nuclear bomb to be used in war was loaded into Air Force Colonel Paul W. Tibbets B-29 bomber, which he had named *Enola Gay* in honor of his mother. The *Enola Gay's* navigator, Theodore "Dutch" Van Kirk, laid in a course for Hiroshima.

At 8:15 a.m., the bomb, nicknamed "Little Boy," was released. "Little Boy" was a nuclear-fission bomb containing about 140 lbs/64 kg of highly enriched uranium. The bomb itself weighed about 9,700 lbs./4,400 kg. The blast destroyed 90 percent of Hiroshima and killed between seventy thousand and one hundred thousand people instantly. Another 140,000 died during the ensuing days, months, and years as a result of radiation sickness.

The United States expected that the display of power would cause Japan's Emperor Hirohito to surrender immediately. He did not. One explanation is that the destruction in Hirosima had been so complete that it took time for reports of the devastation to reach him. He would have had more time to assess the situation and avoid another attack were it not for bad weather. The United States had already planned a second bombing raid for August 11 in the event Japan did not surrender. Meteorological reports suggested that the weather would not be ideal at that time and so the operation was moved earlier.

The second atomic bomb was destined for Kokura (present-day Kitakyushu). With a population of 178,000 it was about half the size of Hiroshima, but it housed Nippon Steel's main works, as well as a major weapons arsenal. The United States was also aware that the munitions factory in Kokura was secretly producing chemical weapons.

On August 8, the second nuclear bomb, known as "Fat Man," was being placed into the bay of pilot Charles W. Sweeny's B-29, *Bock's Car*. "Fat Man" was a larger bomb than "Little Boy," with a plutonium core. It was about 10,300 lbs./4,670 kg and had a payload roughly the equivalent of twenty-one kilotons of TNT. The *Enola Gay* took off again. This time it was acting as a weather plane. The pilot radioed back that the conditions over Kokura were good.

At 3:47 a.m., pilot Charles W. Sweeny took off, flying into dark and stormy skies. By the time he arrived at his target, conditions had changed. The weaponeer's flight log records that the target was "obscured by heavy ground haze and smoke." There are a number of theories as to why Kokura was overcast when the *Enola Gay* had reported clear skies. One is that the smoke from the firebombing of a nearby city had rolled in. Another possibility is that technicians at the electrical power station in Kokura had intentionally released steam when the *Enola Gay* was spotted. Perhaps the weather conditions simply changed. In any case, Sweeny could not see the target. After circling three times, he gave up and turned toward a secondary target, one that had been added to the target list only the day before: Nagasaki, home to Mitsubishi Steel and Arms Works. Mitsubishi had begun as a small ship building enterprise but quickly expanded. By the 1930s, it dominated the production of cement, flour, and paper. It was one of Japan's top companies in warehousing, coal mining, heavy electrical equipment, aircraft, and munitions. By 1945, Mitsubishi alone accounted for 90 percent of Nagasaki's industry.

The skies over Nagasaki were cloudy that day, but not cloudy enough to save it. At 10:58 a.m., with fuel reserves critically low, the clouds broke and the target became visible. Or did it? Some historians are skeptical, noting that the bomb went off three quarters of a mile off target, an error rate consistent with radar, rather than visual bombing.

Although "Fat Man" had been a more powerful bomb than "Little Boy," the death toll in Nagasaki was less than that of Hiroshima, due in part to the bomb landing off target and in part to geography. Nagasaki was a river valley surrounded by alternating hills, which absorbed the blast, but did not focus it. In all, seventy thousand people were killed in the bombing.

Had the bomb fallen on Kokura, the explosion would have been much more devastating. As Masao Araki, who wrote a book on Kokura, noted: like Hiroshima, Kokura is built on a flat plain. He believes that because of this many more people would have been exposed to heat and radiation. The devastation would have been compounded by the explosion of the city's arsenals. In addition, as many as 1,300 workers would have been trapped in a coal mine.[1]

The Japanese Supreme War Direction Council did not surrender upon learning of the Nagasaki bombing on August 9. Instead the council declared martial law and vowed to keep fighting to the end. That night, Emperor Hirohito called the council to a meeting. Discussions continued until 2:00 a.m., at which point the emperor declared that Japan could not keep fighting the war and would accept the Allies' terms of surrender. On August 10, the Japanese Foreign Ministry sent its response to the Allies, offering to accept the terms of the Potsdam Declaration as long as the agreement did not "comprise any demand which prejudices the prerogatives of His Majesty as a Sovereign Ruler."

The United States, however, was adamant that "the authority of the Emperor and the Japanese Government to rule the state shall be subject to the Supreme Commander of the Allied powers who will take such steps as he deems proper to effectuate the surrender terms."

Newspapers in the United States were already celebrating the news that Japan had offered to surrender. The Japanese public, however, was unaware of the fact. Japanese newspapers on August 11 quoted a general addressing the army, "The only thing for us to do is fight doggedly to the end . . . though it may mean chewing grass, eating dirt, and sleeping in the field."[2]

On August 14, US bombers dropped leaflets over Tokyo that contained the messages between the Japanese officials and the Allies. Afraid that the messages would fall into the hands of the military and enrage the troops, the emperor had no choice but to officially surrender. Emperor Hirohito formally announced Japan's surrender on August 15, and it was formally signed on September 2, 1945.

The rebuilding of Hiroshima and Nagasaki began immediately. If the United States had bombed its primary target, it might have taken longer to recover. But thanks to the "Mitsubishi wealth," the United Press reported in 1955, "Today, 10 years later, there is no wreckage. Mitsubishi rebuilt its shipyard and Nagasaki vessels are sailing on every sea. New factories are making induction and direct current motors, turbo-generators, hoisting machines, winches, forged products, steel plate, high-grade steels and a popular tourist item turquoise shell wear."[3] On the day the bomb was dropped, Nagasaki had a population of 263,000. The latest population estimate is 429,508.

The people of Kokura have never forgotten how fate spared their city. Japanese speakers adopted the phrase "the Luck of Kokura," meaning avoiding great danger without being aware of it. After the war, Kokura merged with four other municipalities to create the present city of Kitakyushu. Because of this, direct comparisons of the pre- and post-war populations are impossible to make. Kitakyushu is now a city of 961,286. It is known for its green spaces and its cherry blossoms.

Kitakyushu schools give a lesson on the special relationship between their city and Nagasaki and Hiroshima. Together the three cities have called for an end to nuclear proliferation. The former Kokura is a member of the "Nuclear-Free Peace City" initiative.

A monument in Katsuyama Park, near Kitakyushu's City Hall, contains a monument with a plaque that reads: "There was a former army barracks in this area. An American military aircraft carrying an atomic bomb flew over to bomb it, however, they turned around and dropped the atomic bomb on Nagasaki instead as they could not locate the target through the clouds. This memorial plaque symbolizes the sincere prayers for all the losses and casualties suffered due to the bombing."

Chapter

40

London Fog

Fog everywhere. Fog up the river, where it flows among green aits and meadows; fog down the river, where it rolls defiled among the tiers of shipping, and the waterside pollutions of a great (and dirty) city. Fog on the Essex Marshes . . . Fog in the eyes and throats of ancient Greenwich pensioners, wheezing by the fireside of their wards; fog in the stem and bowl of the afternoon pipe of the wrathful skipper, down in his close cabin; fog cruelly pinching the toes and fingers of his shivering little 'prentice boy on deck. Chance people on the bridges peeping over the parapets into a nether sky of fog, with fog all around them, as if they were up in a balloon, and hanging in the misty clouds.[1]

The opening of Charles Dickens's *Bleak House* describes the London of his time. It may sound like literary exaggeration, but it was not. London is synonymous with fog because for many years it was blanketed in a thick haze. These fogs, which at times completely blocked out the sun, frequently hung over the city from the eighteenth century until 1962. The fog was a byproduct of the industrial revolution in the capital city of what was then the largest empire on the planet and was really a smog, a combination of smoke and fog.

Thanks to its temperate maritime climate, London is generally humid. But it was coal dust that gave London its distinctive fog. Between 1800 and 1830 London's population boomed. Homes and factories alike were heated and fueled with coal. The more people that crowded into the city, the more the soot rose from their chimneys. The pollutants had a high sulfur content, which gave the fog a yellow tint.

LONDON FOG

Novelist Edward Frederic Benson described it in his 1905 *Image in the Sand* as "swirls of orange-coloured vapour were momentarily mixed with the black," and "all shades from deepest orange to the pale gray of dawn succeeded one another."[2]

A scientific study published in 1896 put it this way: "Town fog is mist made white by Nature and painted any tint from yellow to black by her children; born of the air of particles of pure and transparent water, it is contaminated by man with every imaginable abomination. That is town fog."[3]

The way light played on the fog was a source of inspiration to impressionist artists such as James McNeill Whistler and Claude Monet. Monet came to the city three times in order to catch different glimpses of the light patterns it created over the river Thames. "Without fog, London would not be beautiful," he said.[4] The result of the visits was a series of thirty paintings, which were exhibited together in 1904.

Novelists from the lowliest pulp fiction writer to renowned figures like Henry James, Robert Louis Stevenson, and Joseph Conrad romanticized the fog in their works. It became such a symbol of the prosperous city that tourists were disappointed if they came to London and saw clear skies.

Artists and tourists might have found it fascinating, but to many Londoners the pollution was deadly. When water droplets mixed with sulfur gas in the air, it created sulfuric acid, which caused bronchitis and lung conditions. It all came to a head in 1952 with an event known as "the Great Smog."

The word "smog" was not new at that time. It had been coined in London in 1905. The first appearance of the term in print was in the Journal of the American Medical Association as reported by Dr. H. A. des Voeux, treasurer of the Coal Smoke Abatement Society:

At a recent health congress in London, a member used a new term to indicate a frequent London condition, the black fog, which is not unknown in other large cities and which has been the cause of a great deal of bad language in the past. The word thus coined is a contraction of smoke fog "smog"—and its introduction was received with applause as being eminently expressive and appropriate. It is not exactly a pretty word, but it fits very well the thing it represents, and it has only to become known to be popular.[5]

November and December 1952 were especially cold and snowy, which meant that people were burning more coal than usual. Matters were made worse when an anticyclone, an area of high pressure, settled over the region. This is the opposite of a cyclone, or low pressure area, and it created an inversion, which is a very stable layer. It is called an inversion because it is an inverse of the normal condition where temperatures decrease as you go higher into the atmosphere. In an inversion, there is warmer air above and cooler, more dense air below trapped in the valley. Since the warmer, lighter air is above and the cooler, denser air is in the valley, there is little air movement in the valley, where the people live, either vertically or horizontally, and so pollutants can build and build until it becomes colder aloft so that air can mix vertically or a significant front goes by to kick up the winds. If neither of those things happen and the inversion persists for a few days, the smoke and pollutants being belched by factories and automobiles and other sources continually increase the density and concentration of harmful chemicals. Thus all the harmful smoke being emitted from the chimneys was trapped and concentrated in a thin layer within a few hundred feet of the ground. There was very little air motion, and winds were very light or calm. So as chimneys continued to belch forth more and more pollution into the air, the concentration of the harmful sulfuric gas and the concentration of particles became greater and greater with increasingly harmful consequences to the residents and animals.

On December 5, the light winds and moist air were just right to create radiation fog. As the temperature dropped, the temperature fell to the dewpoint, causing the water vapor in the air to condense into tiny droplets. This is one of the processes that causes fog. The fog combined with the pollutants to create a smog several hundred feet deep. It took four days for vertical mixing and the wind to clear it out, but by that time the dense smog had done enormous harm. An estimated four thousand people died as a direct result. Tens of thousands more suffered from long-term health effects such as lung disease. A 2016 study compared the incidence of asthma in England in people exposed to the Great Smog and those who were not. They found exposure to the smog in the first year of life increased the likelihood of childhood asthma by 19.87 percent and adult asthma by 9.53 percent. Exposure in utero led to a 7.91 percent increase in the likelihood of childhood asthma. It is likely that this great London smog claimed well over 1 million years of life in total from London residents.

The Great Smog led to the passage of the UK Clean Air Act in 1956. It was phased in so thick fogs and smogs continued to plague the island from time to time until 1962. The fogs that inspired Victorian novelists and impressionists are now a thing of the past in London thanks in part to legislation and in part to the widespread use of central heating, which substantially reduced the use of smog-inducing coal.

London is not the only city to have experienced killing fogs. Donora is an industrial town located on a horseshoe bend in the Monongahela River in western Pennsylvania. It was home to the American Steel & Wire Company, which operated zinc works that employed most of the residents. It had been using the same procedures and billowing smoke from its stacks since 1915. It emitted a combination of carbon monoxide, nitrogen dioxide, sulfur, hydrogen fluoride, and heavy metal particulates. This toxic stew was augmented by the smoke from residential coal furnaces.

Beginning on October 26, 1948, an anticyclone caused a strong inversion trapping the air in a shallow layer near the ground. As is typical of the center of a high pressure area, the winds were very light. Because Donora was in a valley surrounded by hills, the polluted air had no chance of escaping vertically or horizontally. As the yellow haze became thicker and thicker, the zinc works continued to billow smoke. The air was not merely unpleasant—it was literally suffocating. By the time a rainstorm cleared the air five days later, twenty people had died and almost six thousand of the fourteen thousand residents had fallen ill.

In most places in the Northern Hemisphere, October has the highest frequency of this kind of radiation-type fog. The reason is the ground and air are still relatively warm, but the nights are getting longer, allowing for increasing likelihood of the temperature to fall to the dewpoint causing the air to reach saturation. This type of fog can also be enhanced in the fall by nearby rivers, streams, or lakes because the lag of the seasons means that the water temperatures are often higher than the air temperatures at night, causing excessive evaporations compared to other conditions.

In 1961, two biostatisticians at the University of Pittsburgh assessed deaths from cancer and cardiovascular disease in Donora from 1948 to 1957 and found higher than expected deaths from heart disease and cancer in the decade following the incident.

The tragedy sparked the first large-scale environmental health investigation in the United States. Two years later, President Harry Truman cited Donora when he convened the first national air pollution conference. The conference ended with a call for further research, but the stage had been set for the passage of the first US Clean Air Act in 1963.

The positive that came out of these terrible smog events is that significant progress has been made to clean up the air, especially in the more advanced industrialized countries, saving millions of lives and tens of millions of life hours. Not only have these lives been saved, but many people are living healthier lives because of the steps taken to clean up the air. Still, fatalities from polluted air across the world may be as many as four million to twenty million per year, dwarfing deaths from all other weather hazards combined.

If people had driven out of Donora or walked over the hill or mountain, which may have taken an hour or two, they would not have been sick. But unfortunately that information was not available to them seventy years ago.

Chapter

41

More Dallas Rain Might Have Saved President Kennedy

There was an air of glamour and excitement in Dallas on November 22, 1963 as the young and rather charismatic president, John F. Kennedy, got into the presidential limousine alongside his wife Jacqueline, who looked elegant in a pink bouclé suit with a matching pillbox hat. On the seat beside her, she laid a bouquet of red roses that had been given to her earlier that day.

Riding along were Texas Governor John Connally and his wife, Nellie, who looked back at the first couple and enthused, "Mr. President, you can't say Dallas doesn't love you."[1]

It seemed like a charmed day. Even the weather had cooperated. There had been a bit of rain early in the morning, but now it was sunny and beautiful. But all that beautiful sunshine might have been fatal for the president.

The presidential limousine, with the secret service code name SS-100-X , was a modified 1961 Lincoln Continental four-door convertible. Many of the modifications that had been made were for convenience and presentation, not protection. It was equipped with two radio telephones and the rear compartment had been expanded to add another row of seats that could be folded up when they were not occupied by dignitaries. It was given a coat of blue metallic paint that was designed to gleam under the lights and look crisper on black and white television sets. The rear seat allowed the president to be raised up ten inches so he could be better seen by citizens as he passed by. Finally it had a special roof system consisting of removable clear plastic panels that could be stowed in the trunk.

Contrary to popular belief, the so-called "bubble top" was not bullet proof. In fact, there was no protective armor anywhere on the car. The roof "wasn't there for protection or security," explained journalist Jim Lehrer, "it was there for weather. Kennedy was adamant, he didn't want people to think he was something under glass, not to be touched."[2]

Lehrer, who was there to cover the presidential visit, spoke to one of the secret service officers on duty: "He looks up at the sky—I will never forget this. He looks up at the sky and it's clear . . . and he yells down to an agent with a two way radio and he says 'check it downtown. What's it like downtown?'"[3]

When the response came back that it was clear downtown, he ordered his fellow agents to "Lose the bubble top."

Kennedy had arrived in Dallas to deliver a luncheon speech and was only meant to be in the city for a couple of hours. Had it continued to rain, the bubble top would have remained on the limousine. Because the skies were clear it was removed and so the motorcade drove through the crowded streets without any covering. As it turned past the Texas School Book Depository at Dealey Plaza, traveling at about 11 mph/18 kph, shots rang out. Less than an hour later the president was declared dead.

Lehrer saw the same secret service agent later that day. "He comes over to me and he has tears in his eyes and he says, 'Jim, if I just hadn't taken off the bubble top.'"[4]

Could the Plexiglas top have made the difference between life and death? It is possible. Lehrer, who later used this experience as the basis for a novel called *Top Down*, researched the question.

"If it was up, Oswald might not have taken the shot," he said. "He might have thought it was bulletproof. Or the quarter inch Plexiglas might have deflected the bullets. Or the glass could have shattered into shards and killed everybody."[5]

The Warren Commission Report noted the lack of the bubble top as a factor, but never ran any simulations to see if it would have made a difference. The secret service must have thought it was at least a major factor because the presidential limousine was immediately redesigned, giving it a permanent roof and other security features like armor plating, run-flat tires, and an explosion-proof fuel tank. Kennedy's successor, Lyndon Baines Johnson, ordered one more change. The car was repainted from its photogenic midnight blue to a somber black.

Because the Kennedy assassination was such a trauma to the nation, it revolutionized presidential security. Presidents now rarely walk or ride in the open air. The specs for the modern presidential vehicle are classified, but it is known to be basically a stylish tank. And in the wake of the assassination, the US Congress passed legislation to protect former presidents and first families.

Sympathy in the aftermath of the assassination brought President Johnson strong support. This helped him to pass legislation creating programs such as Medicare, Medicaid, Headstart, and the Civil Rights Act of 1964. On the other hand, Kennedy had opposed further escalation of the United States presence in Vietnam, and thus it is likely that he would have avoided any substantial US involvement. Kennedy was more of a student of history and foreign policy than Johnson, whose main expertise was in domestic issues. Johnson relied more heavily on his generals and advisors, who urged massive escalation, while Kennedy, having learned from the Bay of Pigs disaster not to trust military advisors, was more reliant on his instincts, his deep knowledge of history, and the advice of his brother Robert.

The resulting guns and butter combination of the Johnson presidency set the nation on a path of accelerating debt and deficit spending and would set the stage for increasing inflation through the 1970s into the early 1980s.

Kennedy was a Democrat, but also financially conservative. Johnson was a spender and would not cut back on social programs, even though he increased spending on the war. His policies caused interest rates to rise dramatically; mortgages rates spiked at one point to over 20 percent, so many disadvantaged lower income people were not able to buy homes.

Due to Lyndon Johnson's overspending, stagflation (persistent high inflation combined with high unemployment and stagnant demand in a country's economy) continued through the 1970s and into the 1980s. Because of the Vietnam War and these bad economic conditions that followed, the country entered an era of mostly Republican rule. The Republicans won the White House after Johnson from 1969 to 1993, with the one exception of Jimmy Carter, who won election in the aftermath of the Watergate era from 1977 to 1981. Without the scandal and without Nixon's impeachment, it is quite possible that the Republicans would have controlled the White House from 1969 until President Bill Clinton was sworn in in 1993.

If the rain had persisted a few hours longer that Dallas morning, the United States might be a very different country today.

Chapter

42

Heat and Summer Riots

We like to think of ourselves as entirely rational people, but our state of mind can be impacted by external forces like the weather. Bright, warm, sunny days put us in a good mood. Grey, overcast days make us glum, and when things get hot, tempers are more likely to flare.

Research suggests that when the body becomes overheated the same regions of the brain that try to cool it release extra serotonin and adrenaline, two chemicals that are associated with increased aggression. In hot weather, people are more likely to interpret behaviors as signs of hostility, and they are also less likely to condemn violence.

According to a 2013 study published in the journal *Science*, even a 4 percent uptick in summer temperatures can increase the frequency of inter-group conflict by 14 percent until it gets so hot that people become lethargic and avoid social contact all together.[1] The magic number at which people become hot enough under the collar to start a fight and at which they retreat into the shadows or an air conditioned room varies by study. This may be a product of differences in local climate. The people of a tropical region might be comfortable at a warmer range of temperature than someone from a snowy city in the north.

Psychologists Ellen Cohn and James Rotton looked at violent crime over a two-year period in Minneapolis, Minnesota. They concluded that violence rose with the temperature until around 80°F, at which point it started to fall.[2] A study by the National Bureau of Economic Research of crime data for the city of Los Angeles found that on average, overall crime increases by 2.2 percent and violent crime by 5.7 percent on days with maximum daily temperatures above 85° F/29.4°C compared to days with lower temperatures.[3]

Canadian researcher Tony Huiquan Zhang looked specifically at how social movements are affected by weather and when they turn violent. Focusing on data from New York City and Washington, DC, from the years 1960–1995, Zhang found that protests and social movements are more likely to happen on days where there is little rain and the air temperature is moderate.[4] In other words, people are most likely to gather in public places and start protests when the weather is nice. The more uncomfortably hot it gets, the more likely it is that violence will become a part of those protests.

For aggression to morph into actual violence requires a number of factors. Mix anger, distrust, provocation, and the right amount of heat and you have something explosive. All of these were present in the United States in the long, hot summer of 1967. Racial tensions were ignited in more than a hundred cities across the nation, but nowhere did the conflagration do as much damage or cast as long a shadow as it did in the city of Detroit, which was then the fifth largest US city.

Throughout the 1940s, the growing automotive industry attracted a steady stream of laborers for well-paying factory jobs. As Black Americans migrated north, many neighborhoods responded by passing ordinances officially segregating neighborhoods by race. When the Supreme Court finally declared such restrictions illegal, the *Detroit Free Press* reassured its readers with the headline "Migration of Minorities within Detroit Doubted."[5] They were right. Detroit's neighborhoods remained segregated by custom and social pressure if not by law. Things remained that way until the 1950s and '60s when the construction of interstates cut through the Black Bottom neighborhood and forced some of the residents into what had once been all-white neighborhoods. While ordinances could not legally keep Black Americans out, it was still clear that there were some places where they would not be welcome. Working-class Black Americans continued to congregate in illegal bars called "blind pigs." Blind pigs had been necessary in the 1940s when restaurants and bars refused to serve Blacks. Once that prohibition ended, many people still found them more amenable than the legal alternatives.

Saturday, July 23, 1967 was hot and muggy in Detroit with daytime temperatures in the nineties. That night the Detroit police raided a blind pig on 12th Street. The police were overly ambitious that night, but it backfired. Instead of arresting the owner and sending the patrons home, they decided to arrest everyone they found, which was eighty-two people in all. They couldn't bring that many people into the police station themselves, so they held them on the street as they waited for reinforcements. Even at the late hour, the heat and humidity were still oppressive, and years of pent up resentment began to bubble to the surface. The angry voices roused the neighbors, who could hear everything through their open windows—most people in the neighborhood did not have air conditioning. Inside, temperatures were even more stifling because there was no air motion. And the phrase "long, hot summer" began to imply, to some, that there would be riots in the city. People filed out onto the crowded street and the anger was getting as hot as the air around them. When someone threw a rock through a glass window it was the spark that ignited the powder keg. Things quickly got out of control, and what began as a raid on one club spread until looting and fires engulfed fourteen city blocks.

The local police were overwhelmed to the point that the National Guard had to be called in. The violence continued for five days. By the time order was restored, forty-three people had been killed, thirty by police or the military, another seven thousand were arrested, and 2,700 businesses had been damaged or looted. The "white flight" to the suburbs, which had started as a trickle in the 1950s, became a river after the uprising. More than forty thousand whites left the city the following year and twice that number the following year, causing the tax base of the city to decline. As the city's population fell from 1.6 million to 992,000 , tens of thousands of houses were left abandoned.

Chapter 43

Snowstorms End John Lindsay's Promising Political Career and Raise Cory Booker's

In early 1969, John Lindsay, the popular Republican mayor of New York City, was a rising star in his party. There was even talk of him running for president. Something happened in February, however, that completely reversed his fortunes. Not only did he lose the Republican primary, but he was barely able to hold onto his seat as mayor. He lost the mayoral primary the following election cycle and managed to stay in office only by running as an independent.

What explains his dramatic loss of popularity? Snow. Lots of snow. The event that changed his fortunes was dubbed "the Lindsay Snowstorm."

The Lindsay Snowstorm, which occurred February 8–10, 1969, dropped a total of 15.3 in/38.9 cm of snow on New York City. This is substantially more than the average snowstorm of a winter but not close to their record, which at the time was 26.4 in/67.1cm from a storm on December 26–27, 1947— a record since exceeded with 26.9 in/68.3cm in February, 2006 and then by 27.5in/69.9cm in January, 2016. In fact, a 1961 snowstorm had dropped more than 17 in/43 cm on the city.

What made the Lindsay Snowstorm so devastating was not the total amount of snow itself, but that the city was so poorly equipped to deal with it in advance of the storm. The US Weather Bureau had forecasted that there would be a bit of snow but it would not accumulate because the storm was expected to bring mostly rain. But the storm tracked east of its forecast path and the storm brought only snow, as the expected warm air remained to the east and south of the city. Instead the average temperature for the week of February 8–17 was 23.4F/-4.8C (In mid-February, the average overall temperature is about 9 degrees higher, around 32F/0C.) The snow did not melt. (NOTE:

SNOWSTORMS END JOHN LINDSAY'S PROMISING POLITICAL CAREER

The storm occurred in the early years of AccuWeather, and we did not have any clients in the city of Manhattan itself. We did have some clients in northern New Jersey, close by, and for those we did predict heavy snowfall followed by extremely cold temperatures.)

When the storm hit, the city administrator who was in charge of snow removal was out of town and couldn't be reached. To make matters worse, almost 40 percent of the city's snow removal equipment was out for maintenance.

(For an idea of how it looks when snow warnings are successful, in 1978 AccuWeather warned one of our clients in the city of Toledo forty-eight hours in advance that there would be a blizzard with winds approaching hurricane force, and heavy snow creating drifts up to 6 ft/1.8 m. The client rented all the snow plows they could get in a 50 mi/80.5 km radius after the storm. The streets of Toledo were cleaned and opened while most of the other streets in the same county were not.)

When the crisis had passed, forty-two people—half of them in Queens—had died and another 288 were injured.

The borough of Queens was all but ignored in the cleanup. With the roads impassable, transportation ground to a stop for two days. More than six thousand people were stranded at John F. Kennedy International Airport for so long that helicopters had to bring in food and airlift passengers to Manhattan. Another 225 passengers were trapped at the Jamaica Long Island Railroad station, sleeping in heated railroad cars. Doctors and nurses could not reach the hospitals. Trucks could not get in to clear the garbage, allowing an estimated fifty thousand tons to pile up in the streets before the roads became passable again.

As Manhattan was getting back to work, and schools were reopened on February 12, Queens remained buried. Many streets there remained unplowed for a week. Ralph Bunche, United Nations undersecretary, sent the mayor a telegram three days after the storm describing the empty grocery shelves in Queens, concluding, "As a snowbound resident of Kew Gardens, Queens, where I have been a homeowner on Grosvenor Road for 17 years, I urgently appeal to you. In all those years, we have never experienced such neglect in snow removal as now. As far as getting to the United Nations is concerned, I may as well be in the Alps."[1]

When Lindsay tried to take a tour of Queens, his limousine got stuck in the snow. He tried again in a four-wheel-drive truck but even then he found many roads all but impassable. Throughout it all the mayor was booed and shouted at by the residents.

The situation was made even worse, as there had been a lengthy sanitation workers' strike and many plows were not in good repair. Also Lindsay had cut the budget for combating snow and the city was not ready. The Lindsay Snowstorm serves as a cautionary tale for public officials that they will be judged by how they prepare for and appear to respond to natural disasters and crises, a lesson you will see in a later chapter that President George W. Bush was to learn with Hurricane Katrina. Lindsay's career never fully recovered. He switched to the Democratic Party in 1971 and failed in his run for the Democratic presidential nomination.

Lindsay was not the only mayor to see his political future melt after a snowstorm. Michael Bilandic was mayor of Chicago in January 1979. It was a bitterly cold winter, the second coldest the city had experienced with an average temperature of 18.4°F/-7.6°C. (The first coldest was 1903–04, which was only one-tenth of a degree colder.)

On January 13, a massive blizzard hit Chicago, dumping 20.3 in/51.6 cm. The heavy accumulation weighed down and crushed roofs and garages and paralyzed transit at O'Hare International Airport, and on buses and trains. Parked cars buried in snow blocked the roads. On January 19, with most Chicago residents unable to leave their homes, the *Chicago Tribune* reported that one particular subdivision had been completely cleared—the neighborhood where Mayor Bilandic lived.

As pressure mounted on the mayor for his mishandling of the crisis, he adopted a dismissive tone and then announced he was going to order the police to start towing parked cars with "no exceptions" for anyone who was sick, elderly, or unable to get to their vehicles. "If there are such hardship cases, they can tell that to a judge. That's what a judge is for," he said.[2] The mayor's apparent lack of empathy on top of his inability to get the city up and running outraged the voters and paved the way for Chicago to elect its first female mayor.

The *Chicago Tribune* reporting on the election that February wrote, "An avalanche of snow protest votes carried Jane Byrne to the most stunning political upset in Chicago history late Tuesday as the second biggest primary election turnout in 40 years crushed the legendary Democratic political machine and ended Michael Bilandic's two-year reign in City Hall."[3]

As Bilandic's story shows, the way a mayor communicates with the public about a problem can be as important as the response itself in determining his or her political future. Two further cases illustrate this: the careers of Cory Booker and Kasim Reed.

Cory Booker was a popular candidate for president in the 2020 Democratic primary, and Reed, well, unless you live in Atlanta you have probably never heard of him. Reed was the telegenic, young mayor of Atlanta from 2010 to 2018. He was seen as a rising star in Georgia politics and there was talk that he might become the state's first Black American governor. But he had the misfortune to be in charge when a rare 2014 snow storm, which has come to be dubbed locally as the "snowpocalypse," buried the South.

The storm dropped 2.3 in/5.8 cm of snow on the Atlanta metro area. To northern cities, this might not sound like much, but in Atlanta where the average low temperature in January is above freezing, (34.9°F/1.6°C) snow accumulation is rare. AccuWeather not only predicted the snowstorm more accurately than any other sources for Atlanta, but we also warned that the extremely cold temperature preceding the storm would cause snow to accumulate, not melt on the road, and would likely shut down traffic by land and air for twenty-four hours. Not everyone heard or heeded the message, however.

Motorists were stranded in their cars for hours, students were forced to sleep in school gyms, and workers had to camp in shops and offices. Some drivers abandoned their cars on the freeway and walked home, exacerbating the gridlock. The National Guard had to be called in to get Atlanta's freeway system moving again and to get food and water to people. The story received all-day coverage on the news networks and some popular media figures publicly blamed Reed for ignoring forecasts before the storm.

Reed's response only made things worse. The *New York Times* described the image of the mayor that emerged from his press conferences as "more peevish than powerful."[4] Instead of taking a "buck stops here" approach, Reed appeared on MSNBC's *Morning Joe* to point out that most of the stranded commuters who were shown on television were stranded outside Atlanta and beyond his sphere of responsibility. This was true, but did nothing to warm voters to him. The snowstorm took the sheen off Reed's rising political career.

By contrast, Cory Booker's response to a snowstorm when he was the mayor of Newark, New Jersey, in 2010 earned him the title "Blizzard Superhero" in *Time* magazine. When a blizzard blanketed the Northeast on December 26 of that year, Booker used a then-novel means of communicating with his constituents. He fielded requests for help from residents on Twitter. He and his staff responded personally to messages from people who said they were snowed in. Pictures of the mayor shoveling his constituents' driveways made national news and raised the mayor's profile.

As Jelani Cobb pointed out in the *New Yorker*:

His frosty heroics earned Booker adoration far beyond Newark's city limits. And yet, almost by definition, a storm in which the mayor has to take clearing snow into his own hands is one that has been badly mismanaged. As the *New York Times* later reported, at the time of the 2010 storm, the city had no contract for snow removal. Booker's high-profile shoveling gambit diverted attention from a crisis that might not have been fatal to his ambitions for higher office but would certainly have been a stumbling block.[5]

So while Reed saw his fortunes decline after a crisis that was not entirely of his making, Booker was able to leverage his success of handling a storm into a successful Senatorial bid in 2013, and a less successful presidential run in 2020.

Chapter

44

A Cyclone "Creates" Bangladesh

On November 12, 1970, the Bhola cyclone ravaged northeastern India and what was then East Pakistan, creating a storm surge that killed as many as half a million people and set off social unrest that led to the creation of a new country. The World Meteorological Organization, founded in 1873, declared it the deadliest cyclone ever recorded by the organization. (This is in modern times. There were earlier storms that probably killed more people of which we do not have a definitive record.)

The Bay of Bengal is the largest bay in the world and is no stranger to tropical storms and tidal surges. In fact, eight of the ten deadliest tropical cyclones in history hit the Bay of Bengal. Tropical cyclones are common in the Indian Ocean, and, because of this, both the Bay of Bengal and the Arabian Sea experience them. But thanks to its specific geography, the Bay of Bengal has about five times as many as the Arabian Sea, and these are among the most deadly because of its high population. More than five hundred million people (about 1/16th of the world's population) live on the bay's costal rim, which means a storm surge of even moderate intensity can cause devastating losses of lives and property.

But when the landfall location of the tropical cyclone lines up perfectly so the south winds on the east side of the storm combine with the apex of the triangular shape of the coastline, this can drive the water inland many miles. Keep in mind that much of this land contains rice paddies and thus may only be a few feet at best above sea level, many miles and in some cases ten miles or more inland. Add on to the storm surge which could reach ten to twenty feet or even more, along with severe hurricane winds.

A CYCLONE "CREATES" BANGLADESH

Five cyclonic storms had already passed through during the North Indian Ocean season of 1970 when the Bhola cyclone developed. The sixth storm started from a tropical depression in the southern part of the bay. Although the Indian Meteorological Department was tracking it, they could see where the system was moving, but did not have a measurement of its strength.

By November 12, according to the NOAA Hurricane Research Division, ships were reporting winds near 130 mph/205 kph.

Following the cyclone season of 1960, the Pakistani government had established a program to issue storm warnings, but they were ineffective for two reasons. The most vulnerable lived in poor fishing villages without access to radios. Even so, about 90 percent of the people in the region received the warnings but failed to act on them. Today, even though Bangladesh is a poor country with a very low median income, it has a high rate of cell phone ownership.

While meteorologists in Pakistan had the ability to predict cyclones, they were not able to distinguish between cyclones that would produce dangerous storm surges, and less-deadly storms. In the decade between the establishment of the system and the Bhola cyclone, coastal residents were regularly warned of conditions of "Great Danger" (the highest degree of danger) only to find nothing serious had happened. The residents started to view the warnings as the boy who cried wolf and when a real emergency headed toward them they paid them no heed.

Even if they wanted to evacuate, many had nowhere to go, lacking the means to travel to reach a small number of shelters. Importantly, Bangladesh is located on a vast plain. It only rises a few feet above sea level for hundreds of miles. This is an extremely flood prone area, probably the most susceptible to floods, crop damage, and fatalities of anyplace on the planet. Perhaps there were so few ways out, or perhaps it was that the people did not believe the warnings, but apparently only 1 percent of those who did hear the warnings actually fled to safety.

That evening, ahead of the cyclone, a storm surge reaching 35 ft/10.5 m inundated the outlying islands, including Bhola, wiping out entire villages. Those who had survived by clinging to trees walked through corpses they were too weary to bury as their arms and chests were raw and scarred. When the damage could be assessed, it was almost inconceivable. Entire villages were wiped out and more than 85 percent of the homes in the area were destroyed, leaving 130,000 people homeless.

Seven months after the storm the *Bulletin of the American Meteorological Society* issued a dire warning, due to the loss of fishing boats:

> It is estimated that approximately 65% of the total annual fishing capacity of the coastal region of East Pakistan was destroyed by the storm. The full impact

of this loss becomes evident when it is realized that 80% of the total per capita intake of animal protein by East Pakistan's 73,000,000 residents comes from fish. Prior to the November cyclone, the protein consumption was already 10% below what is normally considered minimum adequate requirements to sustain life. Unless immediate emergency measures are taken, the per capita supply of fish will drop by another 35% during the coming months.[1]

Cattle and rice harvests were washed away. Three months after the disaster, 75 percent of the population was dependent on food relief to avoid starvation. The damage was estimated at over $490 million (in 2010 US dollars). East Pakistan at the time had a GDP of $26.4 billion. So that damage estimate seems way underdone. The total damage and economic impact from that storm probably approached 10 percent of the GDP of that nation, placing the real loss in excess of $2 billion in 1970 dollars. This brings up an interesting point—it is often in the interest of governments to underestimate the damage caused by natural disasters so they are not as subject to criticism.

The Pakistani government's response was slow and exacerbated political discord that had existed before the storm. The official response from Pakistan seemed to imply that the East Pakistani political leaders were exaggerating their people's suffering. Initially more supplies and support came in from the international community than from their own government.

The crisis came at just the right moment for everything to be politicized. The first direct democratic election in Pakistan's history was scheduled for that July. (It was eventually postponed to December because of flooding in East Pakistan.) Thousands of protesters took part in anti-government rallies, and the opposition won in a landslide victory in the post-storm elections. The divisions became so pronounced that a civil war broke out on December 16, 1971, a little more than a year after the cyclone, and expanded into a war with India. At the end of the conflict, East Pakistan had become the independent nation of Bangladesh.

Chapter
45

Desert Storm Thwarts Iranian Hostage Rescue

On November 4, 1979, a group of armed students stormed the US Embassy in Tehran and took its occupants hostage. They demanded that Iran's deposed pro-Western autocrat Shah Mohammed Reza, who was in the United States for cancer treatment, be returned to Iran to stand trial. The students initially captured sixty-six embassy workers. They released a few, but fifty-two were still in captivity through April of the next year as President Jimmy Carter tried to negotiate for their release.

As it became clear that talks were going nowhere, an ambitious military rescue named Operation Eagle Claw was set in motion. There were many challenges in extracting the prisoners. Tehran was surrounded by mountains and desert. The military felt that the best option would be a multi-stage helicopter evacuation. The rescue team, in eight helicopters, and a team of support aircraft would stage in an area in Oman, about fifty miles outside Tehran.

The plan was for American intelligence agents, who knew how to get to the hostages, to rendezvous with troopers in Oman and take them to the embassy where they would free the hostages and move them to a nearby soccer stadium where the helicopters could land and fly them out of the city.

Accurate weather forecasting was a major part of the planning, and the Air Force put its best meteorologists to work to help them determine the best day to launch the operation. They predicted that everything would be clear on April 24, with only a few thunderstorms to the west of the flight route.

Haboobs are formed in desert regions when downbursts from a storm throw up sand and particles, creating a fast moving wall of dust and reducing visibility to near zero. In

1979, haboobs were difficult to predict because it was hard to know when a particular storm would create this type of downdraft.

Because of equipment problems, one of the eight helicopters was grounded before the mission even started. So the mission began with only six, and a seventh followed the group about fifteen minutes behind. In order to maintain the necessary stealth for such an operation, the pilots were flying under strict radio silence and had to maintain visual contact. This proved impossible when they flew into a haboob that decreased visibility to one mile. Because they could not see each other, nor communicate by radio, each pilot was now working on their own.

After a time they seemed to emerge from the dust cloud, only to fly into a second haboob. Sand and particles clogged the equipment, causing the altitude indicator on one of the helicopters to fail and forcing the pilot to turn back. That left only six helicopters, which arrived at the rendezvous point not as a group but individually, each about an hour late. At the Oman staging area another helicopter's equipment failed. Five working helicopters would not be enough to safely complete the mission, and it was called off. Tragically, eight soldiers were killed on the retreat, as a helicopter created a blinding dust cloud and collided with a fixed wing aircraft. Their bodies were left behind and were later paraded in front of Iranian television cameras. The failure was a humiliating blow to the Carter administration.

When he heard about the debacle, one of the president's senior political aides, Rick Hernandez, said, "We just lost the election."[1] He was right.

The hostages were still being held prisoner a year later when the election of 1980 rolled around. Reagan ousted Carter with 51 percent of the popular vote. The hostages were finally released on Ronald Reagan's inauguration day, January 20, 1981.

Had the sand storm not happened and the rescue been successful, Carter might have had a second term. Instead, the so-called, "Reagan Revolution," with a philosophy of low taxes and small government, kicked off a period in which Republicans held the highest office for twenty out of twenty-eight years. Reagan worked with Paul Volcker, the Federal Reserve Chairman who had been appointed by President Carter, to combat inflation by reducing the growth in the money supply combined with very high interest rates from back-to-back recessions that squeezed malinvestment out of the economy in the first Reagan term, but set the stage for a prolonged multi-decade period of growth. Taking a hard line with the Soviet Union, his presidency helped lead to the ultimate collapse of the communist nation and changed the international balance of power. One can hypothesize that this series of events is similar to the butterfly effect in which Lorenz postulated that a butterfly flapping its wings in one part of the planet can set off a series of atmospheric factors that ultimately will change the weather somewhere else on the planet days or weeks later. In this case, it is possible that the sandstorm in the desert and the failure to accurately predict it, preventing the successful rescue of the hostages, led to a significant change in the balance of power in America and the world that would influence economics and politics for decades into the future.

Chapter 46

Record Cold in Florida Leads to the *Challenger* Disaster

The loss of the *Challenger* space shuttle shortly after takeoff was a national trauma. It was the first time the United States had lost a launched space vehicle with a crew on board. What made the event hit home was that NASA had arranged for students to watch a special broadcast of thirty-six-year-old Christa McAuliffe, the first teacher in space, making her way into the cosmos where she was to teach classes. McAuliffe had been chosen to represent the people, a non-astronaut that everybody could identify with, and to bring back some of the awe of space travel.

"[The disaster] was even more shocking because Christa McAuliffe was not a professional astronaut," former astronaut Leroy Chiao told Space.com. "If you lose military people during a military operation, it's sad and it's tragic, but they're professionals doing a job, and that's kind of the way I look at professional astronauts. But you're taking someone who's not a professional, and it happened to be that mission that got lost—it added to the shock."[1]

Contrary to popular belief, not many Americans saw the events unfold on live television. The *Challenger* launched at 11:39 a.m. on a Tuesday when most people were at work. CNN existed in those days, but did not have a large audience, and the major networks all cut away when the shuttle broke apart. Unfortunately, the ones who did see it live were mostly the school children who were watching the video feed in their classrooms. That evening, images of McAuliffe's proud parents, decked out in "teacher in space" buttons watching from the viewing area as the shuttle split apart, ran over and over on the nightly news.

The reaction to the tragedy was such that President Ronald Reagan postponed the annual State of the Union address to address the nation about the *Challenger*.

RECORD COLD IN FLORIDA LEADS TO THE *CHALLENGER* DISASTER

Space flights have been taking off from Florida since 1950. The state has clear advantages over the previous launch site at the White Sands Missile Range in New Mexico. First, it is near the ocean, and in the event of any problems, a rocket could be brought down over the ocean instead of crashing down over inhabited land.

Florida is also closer to the equator than most of the continental United States, which allows NASA to take advantage of Earth's natural rotation, giving rockets an extra boost and saving on fuel.

The climate has its advantages and disadvantages. One of the main disadvantages is lightning. Florida has the most thunderstorms of any state in the union. Rockets are essentially giant lightning rods. Not only do their metal skins conduct electricity, but they can actually trigger lightning strikes as they shoot straight up through the rapid changes in the ambient atmospheric electrical field. The long plumes of ionized gases they trail create the perfect conditions for lightning. Had lightning been detected within five miles of the launch pad, NASA safety regulations would have required that the launch be delayed. But lightning was not the problem in January 1986. The problem was cold.

The launch site at Cape Canaveral in Florida is normally temperate in winter with average lows in January falling only to 47°F/8°C. On January 28, 1986, the morning temperatures were 28°F/-2°C. (This was not the lowest temperature ever recorded for Cape Canaveral, however. The coldest weather ever officially recorded there was 19°F/-7.2°C, which had previously been reached twice, January 26, 1905 and January 22, 1985, and would again be reached on December 23, 1989. Melbourne and Orlando, Florida had each reached lows of 26°F/-3.3°C on January 28, 1986, which was a record for that date for each of the cities.) The *Challenger* had been sitting on the launching pad for thirty-eight days prior to launch and it had been rainy. Some of the engineers from Morton Thiokol who manufactured the solid rocket booster were concerned that the combination of moisture and freezing temperatures could cause a rubber motor seal to fail. The O-rings kept hot gases from blowing out of the seals between the sections of the shuttle's solid rocket boosters. During a shuttle launch the previous year, hot gases had breached one of the booster's primary O-rings. Only a secondary ring kept the gas from escaping.

The managers at Morton Thiokol, after listening to the engineer's warnings, recommended that the launch be delayed, but only by two hours. At 11:38 a.m., the temperature had climbed to 36°F/2.2°C, 15°F lower than the previous coldest launch, but still above freezing. The shuttle carrying McAuliffe and her crew mates—Richard Scobee, Michael Smith, Ronald McNari, Judy Resnick, Ellison Onizuka, and Gregory Jarvis—was launched on time.

Just as the engineers had feared, moisture had gotten into the O-rings on a seal in the shuttle's right solid-fuel booster and froze, making it unable to contain the hot gasses.

The ring and its backup failed, causing the tank to fall apart and release a flood of liquid oxygen and hydrogen. From the ground the fireball it created looked like an explosion. The crew cabin remained intact and briefly continued upward. The crew probably survived the initial incident, but could not survive the loss of cabin pressure and oxygen or the impact with the ocean at more than 200 mph. The solid rocket boosters, no longer held together, flew off in various directions until they were destroyed by the Air Force.

In the bleachers where friends had gathered to watch the launch, there was silence and confusion. "Flight controllers here looking very carefully at the situation," came a voice over the speaker. "Obviously a major malfunction."[2]

In the aftermath of the disaster, NASA changed a number of its processes. It redesigned the rocket boosters, installed a new crew escape system, and adopted stricter weather criteria for launches. It was another three years before manned space flight resumed with the launch of *Discovery* on September 29, 1988.

Chapter

47

Could a Hurricane Have Prevented September 11?

Those of us who are old enough to remember the events of September 11, 2001, and who lived on the East Coast near New York, will never forget that morning. The sky was a clear, cloudless blue. It was primary election day in New York City, and the polls were open. Newscasters were reporting on an education bill being debated in the House of Representatives.

Then at 8:46 a.m., American Airlines flight 11 crashed into the North Tower of the World Trade Center. A few minutes later, United Airlines 175 crashed into the South Tower. Seventeen minutes later, another passenger jet dived into the Pentagon, and a fourth crashed in a field in Pennsylvania.

A horrified public across the nation watched, transfixed, as the tallest buildings in New York billowed smoke. As firefighters made their way up the stairs and workers made their way down, some of those above the line of impact were making the unimaginable choice of whether to stay and be consumed by fire or to jump to certain death.

At 9:59 a.m., the South Tower collapsed, unleashing a cloud of dust that darkened the sky and covered everything for blocks. Papers from the offices billowed down the streets as people, who looked as though they had been painted gray, ran for their lives. A half hour later, the North Tower fell.

The loss of life was staggering: 2,753 people were killed at the World Trade Center site, 184 died at the Pentagon, and forty passengers and crew died in United Airlines Flight 93 (the passengers took back the plane, intended for the US Capitol building, and it crashed in a field in Pennsylvania). It would take 3.1 million hours of labor to search and clear the 1.8 million tons of debris at the World Trade Center site alone. As photographs of the missing were posted throughout New York and a shocked nation mourned, a picture gradually began to emerge of what had happened that day.

Under the leadership of Osama bin Laden, a team of Al-Qaeda hijackers had made a plan to attack the United States by using fuel-filled jet planes as bombs. For the greatest psychological effect, they would all strike at once, hitting symbols of American financial and military strength.

As their chosen day of September 11 approached, a major storm, called hurricane Erin, was in the Atlantic bearing down on the Eastern United States. Hurricanes do not often make landfall in New York City, but it is not unheard of. Since the Civil War, nine tropical storms and two hurricanes have tracked within 65 nautical miles/120 km of the city. In more recent times, Hurricane Irene and Superstorm Sandy, in 2011 and 2012, triggered major storm surges in New York, while the remnants of Hurricane Ida brought record rainfall and widespread flooding in 2021.

On the morning of September 10, a cold front swept through the area, bringing rain and thunderstorms with it. The increased westerly winds aloft pushed Erin to the east and then northeast. If the cold front had moved more slowly, and Erin had come closer to New York, could it have interrupted air travel and prevented the attacks?

As with all exercises in alternative history, we can never know, but it is at least possible. Bin Laden's men were, as a famous national security memo once put it, "determined to strike." If the conditions on September 11 had been less than ideal, we might instead be talking about the September 12 or 16 attacks. On the other hand, there is a small chance that a delay of even a few days could have made a difference. On September 10, national security advisers presented George W. Bush with a plan to combat Al-Qaeda, but probably not the hijacking itself. The president was traveling that day and planned to look at it later.

If a storm had thwarted the attack, the world would be a different place today. In the wake of the terrorist attacks, the United States launched a "War on Terror" that has had long-lasting impacts both domestically and internationally. The response included a restructuring of government agencies. The Bush Administration merged twenty-two existing agencies into a new cabinet-level office called the Department of Homeland Security. One of the bureaus was the newly created Transportation Security Administration or TSA, which took over and standardized security protocols that had previously been provided by private companies. Airline travel was changed forever. Before September 11, 2001, it was possible to wait with someone at the gate before they boarded their flight. There were no pat downs or full body scans, sharp objects like scissors, pocket knives, and box cutters were allowed on board flights, and you could arrive a half hour before your international flight and make it on board on time with a large bottle of soda in your hand.

Surveillance and intelligence gathering boomed. In 2013, Edward Snowden leaked details of a massive surveillance program with a $52.6 billion budget that oversaw a controversial network of telephone and internet surveillance within the United States.

The US Immigration and Customs Enforcement (ICE) agency was created out of the Immigration and Naturalization Service and the US Customs Service, which had both been part of the Department of Justice. The number of deportations overseen by ICE has nearly doubled since the attacks of 2001. Deportations hit a record high of nearly four hundred thousand a year in the first two years of the Obama administration.

By far the largest impacts were the two wars that began in response to the attacks. On October 7, 2001, the United States invaded Afghanistan where the Al-Qaeda terrorist group was based under the protection of the Taliban government. The US invasion of Iraq two years later, in March 2003, was not directly linked to the terrorists' attacks, but was part of the larger "War on Terror." The US government suspected Saddam Hussein of producing weapons of mass destruction (none were found) and of supporting terrorism. On April 9, 2003, US troops took control of Baghdad.

Saddam Hussein was captured eight months later. He was turned over to Iraqi authorities and tried for crimes against humanity. He was found guilty and executed on December 30, 2006. The war raged on for another five years. The end of the war was declared at a ceremony in Baghdad on December 15, 2011, yet troops remained

The US war in Afghanistan was the longest military conflict in US history. While formal US combat operations were suspended in late 2014, final troops were not removed until 2021.

The cost of the war in Iraq and Afghanistan exceeded six trillion dollars, equalling 30 percent of the entire national debt, continuing to drag on future economic growth.

Conclusion

Our look back ends here, but the role that weather and climate play in shaping human history does not. Our ability to forecast and understand weather and climate change has grown by leaps and bounds over the past decades, yet we must remain humble. We have become better at modeling and predicting, but no better at controlling the weather. We can tell you the path of the hurricane more accurately than ever, but we cannot stop it. We can warn you of a blizzard, but not keep it off your doorstep.

As I write this in the summer of 2023, we are living with fresh memories of record heatwaves on multiple continents, Canadian wildfires that brought smoky conditions to the United States, and a hurricane bringing flooding rains to California, all of which have been linked to changing climate conditions in those areas. However, we need to keep in mind that the weather, by itself, is quite variable and often extreme in certain places for limited times. The press and politicians should be more careful in labeling every seemingly abnormal event as being due to climate change. While some of the recent records have been extraordinary, the large majority of events that have been called a result of climate change by the press have not been caused by climate change.

In recent years, whole nations were in lockdown thanks to a novel new coronavirus. The exact cause of the outbreak is still under investigation at the time of this writing, and time will give us greater insight into what role weather and climate might have played. And this raises questions about the future. As changing climates put animals into contact with humans in new ways, will another pandemic emerge? We are still in the immediate aftermath of these disasters, and it is too early to know how history will be impacted.

Weather nudges us in ways large and small. We can only imagine how it will continue to alter our best-laid plans and shape our history as we go forward. Yet I remain optimistic in our ability to meet these challenges. Statistician and author Nate Silver has studied the methodology and accuracy of many types of forecasts, including those in politics and economics. In his 2012 essay, "The Weatherman is Not a Moron," he called weather forecasting "the one area in which our predictions are making extraordinary progress."[1]

Weather knowledge that was not even possible a century ago is now at our fingertips. Where our ancestors relied on folklore and slow reports from sailors, today AccuWeather provides forecasts with minute-by-minute accuracy and delivers them right to your mobile device with services like MinuteCast. If it is about to rain on your house, but not on your neighbor's two streets away, we can tell you about it.

Five hundred years ago human knowledge doubled every five hundred years. A century ago it doubled every hundred years. Now human knowledge is doubling every twelve months. In three years, it will double every month. In a decade, human knowledge is slated to double every hour. Think about it—today you will see the least change of any day of your life going forward. Our ingenuity knows no bounds.

This is why I find meteorology to be such a fascinating and meaningful profession. Yes, your meteorologist tells you when to carry an umbrella or wear a jacket, and that's important. But meteorology does so much more. It helps us navigate our moment in time and plan for the future. It helps us to be forewarned and forearmed against threats. In doing so, weather forecasting changes history by saving lives.

Next time you call out to your phone and ask it to tell you what the weather will be like, take a moment to marvel at and to imagine how magical that device would have seemed—what that simple knowledge might have meant—to Napoleon at Waterloo or at the Battle of Salamis. Then pause a moment to wonder at the life-altering inventions yet to come. We can't predict them yet, but history tells us they are coming.

Appendix
How Climate and Weather Affect Archaeology, the Stock Exchange, and the GDP

Climate and Archaeological Discovery

This book owes a debt of gratitude to archaeologists. Much of what we know about the rise and fall of ancient civilizations is due to their painstaking work. Archaeology reveals the role climate change and weather played, and climate and weather also played a role in some great archaeological discoveries.

In 1970, archaeologist Richard Daugherty's study of the Makah tribe took great strides thanks to a storm that washed away a bank near Lake Ozette, Washington. Daugherty had been trying, for years, to confirm an oral history that said the Makah's village had been buried in a giant mud slide. When the bank was washed away, it revealed a treasure trove of artifacts that dated back to the days of Christopher Columbus's arrival on the continent. The Makah Tribal Council created a museum to house the many objects, including a harpoon shaft, a canoe paddle, inlaid boxes, fishhooks, and even a woven hat.

Four years later, the remains of the ancient human who scientists dubbed "Lucy" was discovered in Ethiopia. Thanks to a flash flood, a bone that had been underground for millions of years was brought to the surface where it was, fortunately, spotted by two people who understood its significance, anthropologist Donald Johanson and his graduate student, Tom Gray. Excavating the site for three weeks, the team found several hundred more fragments. The hominid skeleton they assembled was the most complete and the oldest known at the time. Lucy was three million years old, give or take. She was a meter tall and had walked erect. The discovery changed the timeline of when scientists believe humans started walking upright.

"If I had waited another few years," Johanson wrote in his book *Lucy: The Beginnings of Human Kind*, "the next rains might have washed many of her bones down the gully. What was utterly fantastic was that she had come to the surface so recently, probably in the last year or two. Five years earlier, she would still have been buried. Five years later, she would have been gone."[1]

In 1991, Helmut and Erika Simon, a pair of German tourists, were hiking in the Otztal Alps on the Austrian-Italian border. It was a lovely, sunny morning in September 1991. Deciding to take the road less traveled, the pair wandered off the main trail and were shocked to find a dead body in a sheet of melting ice. Believing the body to be the remains of a fellow hiker, the tourists called the police. When the body was chipped out of the ice, however, it became clear that this was a job for an archaeologist.

Further research revealed that the man had died in about 3300 BC. He had fallen into a rock hollow where his body was covered in snow. This kept predators away long enough for the body to be incorporated into a glacier. Thanks to its position in the rocks, it had not been crushed. This unique set of circumstances meant the body was remarkably well-preserved along with his clothing and tools. This gave archaeologists a window into the culture and community from nearly six thousand years ago.

In 2018, a record-breaking heat wave in Britain and Ireland revealed the remains of dozens of previously unknown settlements, which showed up in aerial photography of parched fields. Plants that grow in enough soil to support deep roots are hardier and able to reach more nutrients and water during the dry times than plants with shallow roots. When the heatwave caused the crops and grass to dry out, the ones that were planted on top of an ancient buried wall turned brown first, revealing the outlines of old fortifications and villages.

In Scotland and Wales, photographers spotted the telltale signs of Roman ruins. In Ireland, a drone spotted a previously unknown henge—a stone circle that is believed to be five thousand years old. Once he realized that the heat had created a temporary opportunity, the investigator for the Royal Commission on the Ancient and Historical Monuments of Wales started photographing as many sites from the air as possible to be able to capture the ghost images before the rain washed them away again.

Weather and the Stock Exchange

People often speak of the stock market as having a mood. If markets are nudged by emotions, and emotions are impacted by weather, it begs the question of whether the markets are influenced by the weather.

The weather, of course, can impact the price of specific stocks, such as those of insurance companies, tourism, utilities, energy, and agriculture. Furthermore, the price of commodities from orange juice to cattle, corn, wheat, soybeans, cocoa, coffee, and others can be greatly impacted by major weather events. When major storms such as hurricanes are forecast, there is often a rally in stocks for engineering and home improvement companies and those that produce batteries, electric generators, and water testing, treatment, and delivery. Insurance companies can be hit by major losses when a severe hurricane or a series of severe hurricanes hit the areas that they insure. However, we have seen on a number of occasions the initial selling has been overdone and the insurance stocks bounce back and sometimes wind up even higher than they started before the storm threatened because investors realize that premiums in the areas affected will rise, increasing the potential profit margin of the insurance companies, assuming that weather conditions will return to the historic averages, and in the past this has tended to be the case. Global warming and climate change, however, may change the trajectory of future stock prices.

Savvy weather watchers can also make good money by investing in agricultural or energy futures, where you can buy or sell contracts for crops or oil products for future delivery, and gain or lose money from their price fluctuations.

Frozen orange juice futures were particularly affected by weather until about ten years ago. Now much of the oranges that go into frozen orange juice futures come from Brazil, but up until the 1990s, the orange crop in central Florida played a very important role in the market. From time to time, temperate Florida has freezing weather, and orange trees are highly sensitive to cold. Oranges lose their juice content because of freezing when the air temperature drops below 28 degrees for four hours or more. Extreme cold can actually damage the orange trees themselves. Of course, farming technology has improved a great deal since 1895 when a major freeze on February 8 destroyed 97 percent of the orange crop. Still, a Florida freeze can cause a significant drop in the amount of fruit produced. I have used my forecasting ability to make significant profits in the frozen orange juice futures market, but to do so requires that you be ahead of virtually all other forecasters and traders because once others become aware of the threat of a freeze, either the prices go up and you cannot buy in, or the price immediately adjusts to the threat of the freeze. Sometimes only a few hours can make a big difference. Sometimes the threat of a freeze causes the price to rise, and if you know a damaging freeze will not materialize, even if it is a light freeze you can make money by then shorting the orange juice futures, i.e. selling the futures contracts with the expectation of a profit when the price goes down if a damaging freeze does not materialize. Further, the weather can impact the stock market as a whole by influencing traders' emotions. Economists and behavioral scientists do not always agree on the nature of this impact, but there have been a number of studies that suggest our human reactions to the weather do, indeed, move markets.

In 2002, David Hirschleifer of the University of California, Irvine, correlated weather and stock returns of twenty-six countries in the 1980s and 1990s. He found that in twenty-five out of twenty-six countries, returns were worse on cloudy days.

That same year, Mark Kamstra of the University of Toronto looked at seasonal swings in the markets. He identified big swings in asset prices in the winter, especially in countries like Sweden, Canada, and the United States. Kamstra argues that Seasonal Affective Disorder causes people to be more risk averse in winter.

One year later, William Goetzmann of Yale, using data from surveys of investors, discovered that investors gave more optimistic responses on sunny days.

In 2009, two scholars from National Taiwan University investigated the relationship between wind speed and daily returns in eighteen European countries from 1994 to 2004 and concluded that the effect of wind was "significant and pervasive" and had an even more significant correlation on stock returns than that of sunshine.

Six years later, a Stanford University study found that bad weather created a mild depression that made brokerage analysts become a bit sluggish. On overcast days, analysts reported earnings announcements more slowly and were 9 to 18 percent less likely to issue an annual earnings forecast in bad weather. Later reports mean a smaller window of opportunity for investors.

A study that same year by researchers at Case Western University concluded that on cloudy days investors were more likely to perceive individual stocks as overpriced, which made them more likely to sell.

A researcher at Vilnius University in Lithuania in 2019 looked at historic weather patterns in New York from 1885–1914. He found that stock returns on very hot days were lower than on more comfortable days; that is, until 1903 when an air conditioning system was installed in trading rooms at the New York Stock Exchange. After that, the correlation dropped significantly.

Does Climate Affect a Nation's GDP?

If you were to imagine the best place to live on earth, a sunny beach with palm trees and ample fruit trees might come to mind. When it comes to the economy, however, you might want to choose someplace a bit colder.

APPENDIX

Tropical countries are among the poorest on earth. Why should this be? Scholars have grappled with the question for decades. One theory is that a bit of frost improves health and agriculture enough to tip the scales.

While it may seem counter-intuitive to people from areas where their mothers wrapped them up in layers to avoid "catching their death from cold" a bit of frost makes a population healthier. It forces insects into a dormant state. This makes it easier to eradicate insect-borne diseases like malaria and sleeping sickness.

In the lush environs of the tropics, dead plants do not sit around long before being broken down by insects and microbes. In an area with a bit of frost, the organic material builds up and remains in the soil, making it rich and fertile. Snow and ice that build up over the winter also ensure moist soil for spring planting. A bit of moisture is vital to farming, but too much moisture is deadly. The seasonal rains in the tropics can wash crops away and can leach nutrients out of the soil and make it more difficult to grow certain crops.

Humidity also plays a role. As temperature and humidity increase, so does the diversity and transmission of infectious disease. A 2007 study found that a large percentage of human infectious diseases originate in tropical or temperate regions. When early humans migrated out of Africa to more temperate areas, they left behind most of the major tropical diseases, taking only cholera with them.

Another explanation is that seasonal fluctuations require communities to plan ahead and to develop complex systems to store and trade resources in order to get through fallow periods. When food is readily available year round, there is no need to waste energy with extra activity, yet this type of productivity is what tends to produce economic growth. Tropical civilizations that thrived throughout history, such as the Mayans and Egyptians, tend to have settled in areas where natural phenomenon like the flooding of rivers created periods of feast and famine and the heat at that time was less excessive.

In 2009, a team at MIT decided to compare the GDP/temperature connection within countries rather than between countries. They found that in poor countries, an increase in annual average temperature by one 1 degree corresponded to a 1.1 percent drop in per-capita GDP. The study's lead author, Ben Olken, did not identify a cause but postulated that it might be low crop yields, increased disease, or simply the lethargy that comes with hot, humid weather.

"This stuff is not implausible," Olken said. "If you look back at the US before the advent of air conditioning, there were times when the federal government would shut down. It was too hot out."

The team did not see the same effects in wealthier countries, perhaps due to greater availability of air conditioning.

Of course, today's economy is no longer based on farming, but researchers believe that this history allowed nations with better agriculture to accumulate wealth, which gave them an advantage over time. But climate is not destiny. Tropical Hong Kong and Singapore are centers of trade that built economies that do not depend on local resources. These exceptions to the rule point the way to how tropical nations could thrive in the future.

Chronology

ca. 66.5 Million BC—A comet triggers massive climate disruption that leads to the extinction of the dinosaur.

ca. 5500 BC—The "Black Sea Deluge" leads to the creation of cross-cultural flood narratives, including the story of Noah's Ark.

1549 BC—A tempest helps bring Ahmose to power in Egypt, ushering in Egypt's Eighteenth Dynasty, the height of the empire's power.

1213 BC—A dramatic climate shift creates the conditions for the Ten Plagues of Egypt, a foundational moment in three major world religions.

400 BC—Superior knowledge of the winds allows the ancient Greeks to prevail over Persian attackers.

44 BC—The eruption of a volcano on Umnak Island, Alaska, causes cold and rainy conditions in the Mediterranean, which reduced crop yields and contributed to the political instability that ended with Rome's transformation from a republic to an empire.

200—Severe drought leads to the collapse of the Mayan Empire.

541—Climate disruption caused by an asteroid unleashes the world's first pandemic. The so-called Justinian Plague hastened the fall of the Roman Empire.

1200—A period of favorable climate conditions allows the Mongols to build a huge force of soldiers on horseback and create the second largest empire in the world's history.

1273—Tropical storms thwart Mongol invaders and preserve an independent Japan.

1348—Climate change created the conditions for the spread of the Black Death, which killed about 30 to 50 percent of Europe's population.

1300-1850—The "Little Ice Age" ushered in a period of severe winters and wet, cool summers, leading to widespread famine, social disruption, and witch trials. The great era of European witch trials lasted from 1430-1762.

1562—A hurricane destroyed a French fleet in Florida, allowing Spanish mariners to expel their rivals and colonize the area.

1609—The shipwreck of the *Sea Venture* in an Atlantic hurricane inspires Shakespeare's last play *The Tempest*.

1666—Drought sparked the Great Fire of London.

1666-1684—Antonio Stradivari crafts some of the world's most prized violins with spruce wood that was exceptionally dense due to the growth patterns of the Little Ice Age.

1709—An exceptionally cold winter known in England as "the Great Frost" causes that nation's greatest economic recession. The cold also thwarted Swedish King Charles XII's ambitions in Russia as Swedish soldiers were overcome by the harsh Russian winter. The war marked the end of Sweden's great empire and showed Europe that Peter the Great was a force to be reckoned with.

1776—A heavy fog allows George Washington's badly outnumbered forces to retreat and fight another day after the disastrous Battle of Long Island. The Americans had lost the battle, but would win the war, and with it independence.

1778—Famine caused by heavy storms and hail lead to the social unrest that culminated in the French Revolution.

1803—Dramatic sunsets resulting from the eruption of the Krakatoa volcano inspire works of art, including Edvard Munch's iconic *The Scream*.

1806—Napoleon is forced to abandon his Russian ambitions after his soldiers perish in large numbers in the Russian winter.

1812—A tornado protects Washington, DC, from destruction by British forces during the War of 1812.

1814—Rainy conditions lead to Napoleon's defeat against Wellington at the Battle of Waterloo.

1815—The exceptionally cold "Year without a Summer" has widespread ramifications, including famine and mass migrations.

1819—The Panic of 1819, America's first economic depression, is spurred by disruption caused by the "Year without a Summer."

1862—The disastrous "Mud March" that prevented Union Army Major General Ambrose Burnside from capturing Richmond was one of many weather events during the Civil War that persuaded the US government to take a more active role in weather forecasting.

1871—Dry conditions and meteor showers spark the Chicago Fire and the lesser known, but more deadly, Peshtigo Fire.

1873—A drought in the Rocky Mountains causes an outbreak of locusts that plagued the Midwest and created expectations for how the US government would respond to natural disasters.

1888—Two major blizzards, one in the Midwest and one on the East Coast, trap residents, cause widespread loss of life, and lead to improvements in infrastructure, including the New York subway system and the creation of the US Weather Bureau.

1900—The Galveston hurricane, the deadliest natural disaster in US history. With Galveston largely destroyed, Houston was poised to become one of the largest cities in the United States.

1903—An ill-timed gust of wind caused Samuel Langley's aviation experiment to fail and caused him to lose the race to be the first in flight to the Wright Brothers a few weeks later.

1912—After a series of warm years in the Arctic increased the rate of melt of glaciers in Greenland, an iceberg-filled Atlantic Ocean and unusual weather conditions caused the "Ship of Dreams," the *Titanic*, to sink.

1918—Climate changes in the Pacific created the conditions that allowed the Spanish Flu pandemic to spread.

1935—Extreme drought in the US west led to the "Dustbowl" migrations.

1937—The *Hindenburg* exploded in front of news cameras while docking after its outer surface became charged by storm clouds, bringing the age of the airship to an end.

1940—Cloudy skies and calm seas allowed the British soldiers to retreat safely to England after the disastrous Battle of Dunkirk.

1941—Hitler's Russian ambitions are thwarted when German soldiers become the victims of the cold Russian winter.

1944—Meteorological forecasting played a major role in identifying the right time to launch the D-Day invasion and make it a success.

1945—Cloud cover over the primary target determined that Nagasaki, not Kokura, would be the target of the second nuclear bomb dropped in war.

1948—A suffocating fog blanketed Donora, PA, causing twenty deaths and six thousand illnesses and leading to the passage of the US Clean Air Act.

1952—The "Great Smog" in London led to the deaths of four thousand people and the passage of new clean air laws in England, which changed the character of London fog.

1963—Thanks to sunny skies in Dallas, a bubble top was not used on the convertible car that transported John F. Kennedy on his ride past the book depository, making him an easier target for assassination.

1967—Hot temperatures sparked civil unrest in Detroit, changing the nature of the city.

1969—New York Mayor John Lindsay's political career was stalled by a poor response to a major snowstorm.

1970—The Bhola cyclone killed as many as half a million people and set off social unrest that led to the creation of the country of Bangladesh.

1979—A dust storm in the desert thwarts an attempt to rescue US hostages in Iran. The Carter administration's inability to free the hostages was a major factor in the victory of Ronald Reagan in the next presidential election.

1986—Cold temperatures on the Florida launch pad cause an O-ring in the *Challenger* shuttle to fail, leading to its destruction shortly after takeoff and the deaths of all of the astronauts on board.

2001—Clear skies provided the conditions for hijackers to pilot aircraft into the World Trade Center and Pentagon on September 11, but a hurricane that remained off the coast had the potential to delay the attack long enough for the US president to possibly take action that would have prevented it.

Bibliography

Sources

Books

Ancient History Encyclopedia. https://www.ancient.eu.

Barnard, Bryn. *Dangerous Planet: Natural Disasters that Changed History*. New York: Crown, 2003.

Browning, Andrew H. *The Panic of 1819: The First Great Depression*. Columbia: University of Missouri Press, 2019.

Creasy, Edward Shepherd. *Fifteen Decisive Battles of the World*. 1851.

DeBlieu, Jan. *Wind*. Boston: Houghton Mifflin, 1998.

Diamond, Jared. *Collapse: How Societies Choose to Fail or Succeed*. New York: Viking, 2005.

Diamond, Jared. *Guns, Germs and Steel*. New York: W. W. Norton, 1999.

Dolan, Eric J. *A Furious Sky: A Five Hundred Year History of America's Hurricanes*. New York: W. W. Norton, 2020.

Durschmied, Erik. *The Hinge Factor*. New York: Arcade Publishing, 2000.

Durschmied, Erik. *The Weather Factor*. New York: Arcade Publishing, 2000.

Encyclopedia Britannica. https://www.britannica.com/.

Fagan, Brian. *The Little Ice Age: How Climate Made History 1300-1850*. New York: Basic Books, 2000.

Garrison, Webb. *Lost Pages from American History*. Harrisburg, PA: Stackpole Books, 1976.

Hastings, Max, ed. *The Oxford Book of Military Anecdotes*. New York: Oxford University Press, 1985.

Huler, Scott. *Defining the Wind*. New York: Crown, 2004.

Jankovic, Vladimir. *Reading the Skies: A Cultural History of English Weather, 1650-1820*. Chicago: University of Chicago Press, 2000.

Kieckhefer, Richard. *European Witch Trials: Their Foundations in Popular and Learned Culture, 1300-1500*. London: Routledge, 1976.

Laskin, David. *The Children's Blizzard*. New York: Harper Collins, 2004.

Lee, Laura. *Blame it on the Rain*. New York: Harper Collins, 2006.

Lockwood, Jeffrey A. *Locust: The Devastating Rise and Mysterious Disappearance of the Insect that Shaped the American Frontier*. New York: Basic Books, 2009.

Mitchell, Joseph B and Edward Creasy. *Twenty Decisive Battles of the World*. Old Staybrook, CT: Konecky & Konecky, 1964.

Morton, Jamie. *The Role of the Physical Environment in Ancient Greek Seafaring*. Leiden: Brill, 2001.

Pickerell, John. *Weird Dinosaurs*. New York: Columbia University Press, 2017.

Reynolds, David S. *Waking Giant: America in the Age of Jackson*. New York: Harper Collins, 2009.

Rosen, William, *Justinian's Flea*. New York: Penguin, 2007.

Rosenfeld, Jeffrey. *Eye of the Storm*. New York: Plenum Trade, 1999.

Sheets, Bob and Jack Williams. *Hurricane Watch*. New York: Vintage Books, 2001.

Teague, Kevin Anthony and Nicole Gallicchio. *The Evolution of Meteorology: A Look into the Past, Present, and Future of Weather Forecasting*. Hoboken NJ: John Wiley and Sons, 2017.

Wilson, Derek. *Calamities & Catastrophes: The Ten Absolutely Worst Years in History*. New York: Simon and Schuster, 2012.

Winters, Harold A. *Battling the Elements*. Baltimore, MD: Johns Hopkins University Press, 1998.

Articles and Other Sources

General

Brockell, Gillian, "Weird Weather Saved America Three Times," *Washington Post*, March 20, 2019.

Cappucci, Matthew, "'Gargantuan' Argentine hailstone in 2018 may have surpassed world record," *Washington Post*, May 1, 2018.

"Carbon emissions from volcanic rocks can create global warming," *Science Daily*, December 5, 2019.

"Climate change-driven droughts are getting hotter, study finds," *Science Daily*, August 1, 2018.

Gerber, Nicolas and Alisher Mirzabaev, "Benefits of action and costs of inaction: Drought mitigation and preparedness – a literature review," Integrated Drought Management Programme Working Paper No. 1, World Meteorological Organization. https://library.wmo.int/doc_num.php?explnum_id=3401.

Hays, Brooks, "Scientists say new theory 'solves 2 mysteries about Snowball Earth,'" AccuWeather, December 9, 2019. https://www.AccuWeather.com/en/weather-news/snowball-earth-how-life-survived-when-the-globe-was-covered-in-ice-snow/641131.

"History Blows Hot, Cold," *Sunday News* (Lancaster, Pennsylvania), April 13, 1941.

Sengupta, Somini, "What a Week's Disasters Tell Us About Climate and the Pandemic," *New York Times*, May 23, 2020.

"Ten Deadliest Storms in History," *NBC News,* May 7, 2008. http://www.nbcnews.com/id/24488385/ns/technology_and_science-science/t/deadliest-storms-history/#.XrBuuZl7mCg.

Battle of Salamis

Bothwell, John. "All is at Stake at Salamis." *Naval History*, February, 2005.

Kelly, Thomas. "Persian Propaganda—A Neglected Factor in Xerxes Invasion of Greece and Herodotus." *Iranica Antiqua*, Vol. 38, 2003.

Neumann, J. "The Sea and Land Breezes in the Classical Greek Litarature." *Bulletin of the American Meteorological Society*, January, 1973.

Battle of Waterloo

"Battle of Waterloo," History.com, November 6, 2009. https://www.history.com/topics/british-history/battle-of-waterloo.

John, Tara, "Seven Reasons the Battle of Waterloo is Still Important," *Time*, June 18, 2105.

Lichfield, John. "Waterloo's Significance to the French and British," *The Independent*, November 17, 2004.

Neumann, J. "Great Historical Events that were Significantly Affected by the Weather. Part 11: Meteorological Aspects of the Battle of Waterloo." *Bulletin of the American Meteorological Society*, March, 1993.

Black Death

Barras, Colin, "Black Death Casts a Genetic Shadow Over England," *New Scientist*, August 1, 2007.

Guarino, Ben, "We Were Wrong About Rats Spreading The Black Death Plague," *Washington Post*, January 17, 2018.

Levine, Steve, "How the Black Death Radically Changed the Course of History," *Medium*, April 2, 2020. https://gen.medium.com/how-the-black-death-radically-changed-the-course-of-history-644386f5b803.

Mark, Joshua, "Effects of the Black Death on Europe," *Ancient History Ecyclopedia,* April 16, 2020.

Meacham, Jon, "Pandemics of the Past," *New York Times,* May 7, 2020.

Pamuk, Sevket, "The Black Death and the Origins of the 'Great Divergence' across Europe, 1300-1600." *European Review of Economic History*, vol. 11, no. 3, 2007

Pennisi, Elizabeth, "Black Death Left a Mark on Human Genome," *Science News,* February 3, 2014.

Pruitt, Sarah, "Microbe Behind Black Death Also Caused Devastating Plague 800 Years Earlier," History.com, August 30, 2018. https://www.history.com/news/microbe-behind-black-death-also-caused-devastating-plague-800-years-earlier.

Richard, Katherine Schultz, "The Global Impacts of the Black Death," Thought Co. https://www.thoughtco.com/global-impacts-of-the-black-death-1434480#unexpected-economic-benefit-of-the-black-death.

Schmid, Boris V. et al. "Climate-driven introduction of the Black Death and successive plague reintroductions into Europe." *Proceedings of the National Academy of Sciences of the United States of America* vol. 112, 10 (2015): 3020-5. doi:10.1073/pnas.1412887112.

Bhola Cyclone

Alham, Mabub et al. "Frequency of Bay of Bengal Cyclonic Storms and Depressions Crossing Different Costal Zones." *International Journal of Climatology,* 2003.

Biswas, Soutik, "Amphan: Why Bay of Bengal is the world's hotbed of tropical cyclones," *BBC*, May 19, 2020.

Dolce, Chris and Brian Donegan, "The Deadliest Tropical Cyclone on Record Killed 300,000 People," *Weather Channel*, May 1, 2019. https://weather.com/storms/hurricane/news/2019-05-01-deadliest-tropical-cyclone-bhola-cyclone-bay-of-bengal-bangladesh.

Frank, Neil and S. A. Husein, "The Deadliest Tropical Cyclone in History?" *Bulletin of the American Meteorological Society,* June 1971.

Sen, Nifolier, "Why is the Bay of Bengal So Prone to Cyclones," *Weather Channel*, June 20, 2018. https://weather.com/en-IN/india/science/news/2018-06-20-bay-of-bengal-cyclone

"UN recognises 1970 Bengal Cyclone as Deadliest Weather Event Ever," *Dhaka Tribune*, May 18, 2017.

Whitten, Howard, "From the archive, 18 November 1970: Fight for life as aid reaches stricken isles," *The Guardian*, November 18, 2014.

Challenger

Eberhart, Jonathan. "*Challenger* Disaster: Rooted in History," *Science News*, June 14, 1986.

Eberhart, Jonathan. "Launch score: Nature 3, NASA, 0," *Science News*, June 20, 1987.

Grandy, Monica, "What the *Challenger* disaster meant for the race into space," *BBC*. January 28, 2016.

Howell, Elizabeth, "*Challenger*: The Shuttle Disaster That Changed NASA," Space.com, May 1, 2019.https://www.space.com/18084-space-shuttle-challenger.html.

Mailander, Joseph L., "Climate of the Kennedy Space Center and Vicinity," NASA, June 1990. https://ntrs.nasa.gov/archive/nasa/casi.ntrs.nasa.gov/19900018991.pdf.

Palca, Joe, "Lessons Linger 25 Years After *Challenger* Tragedy," *Morning Edition, NPR*, January 27, 2011.

"Weather and the Space Shuttle *Challenger* Disaster," *News 4 Jacksonville*. https://www.news4jax.com/weather/2013/01/29/weather-and-the-space-shuttle-challenger-disaster/.

Chicago Fire

Abbott, Karen, "What or Who Caused the Great Chicago Fire?" *Smithsonian*, October 4, 2012.

"Chicago Fire of 1871," History.com. https://www.history.com/topics/19th-century/great-chicago-fire.

Schons, Mary, "The Chicago Fire and the Great Rebuilding," *National Geographic*, January 25, 2011.

"Weather Played a Role in the Chicago Fire." AccuWeather. https://www.AccuWeather.com/en/weather-news/weather-played-a-role-in-great-chicago-fire/148277.

"What if the Great Chicago Fire of 1871 Never Happened?" Chicago Architecture.com. http://www.architecture.org/news/happening-caf/what-if-the-great-chicago-fire-of-1871-never-happened/.

Civil War

"10 Facts: Perryville," *American Battlefield Trust*. https://www.battlefields.org/learn/articles/10-facts-perryville.

Noe, Kenneth, "The Drought that Changed the War," *New York Times*, October 12, 2012.

Ouchley, Kelby, and Kathryn Shively Meier, *Journal of the Civil War Era*, vol. 4, no. 4, 2014, pp. 603–606. JSTOR, www.jstor.org/stable/26062211. Accessed 4 May 2020.

Seger, Richard and Celine Herweijer, "Causes and consequences of nineteenth century droughts in North America," Lamont-Doherty Earth Observatory, Columbia University, http://ocp.ldeo.columbia.edu/res/div/ocp/drought/nineteenth.shtml.

Thomas, M. W., "Weathering the Storm: Whitman and the Civil War," *Walt Whitman Quarterly Review* 15 (Fall 1997), 87-109. https://doi.org/10.13008/2153-3695.1522.

D-Day

Conway, Gavin et al, "D-Day: An Expert View of the Weather Forecast That Changed History," *The Weather Channel*, June 6, 2019. https://weather.com/news/news/2019-06-05-d-day-weather-forecast-changed-history

Detroit

Asher, Jeff, "A Rise in Murder? Let's Talk About the Weather," *New York Times*, September 21, 2018.

Crumm, David, "Untold Stories of '67 Riot Divide Our Region, Our Lives." *Knight Ridder*, October, 19, 2004.

Field, Simon, "THE EFFECT OF TEMPERATURE ON CRIME," *The British Journal of Criminology*, vol. 32, no. 3, 1992, pp. 340–351. JSTOR, www.jstor.org/stable/23637533. Accessed 17 Aug. 2020.

Keim, Brandon, "The Hazy Science of Hot Weather and Violence," *Wired*, July 22, 2011.

Zhang, T. H., "Weather Effects on Social Movements: Evidence from Washington, D.C., and New York City, 1960–95." *Wea. Climate Soc.* 8, (2016) 299–311, https://doi.org/10.1175/WCAS-D-15-0072.1.

Dinosaurs

Black, Riley, "What Happened the Day a Giant, Dinosaur-Killing Asteroid Hit the Earth," *Smithsonian*, September 9, 2019.

Botin-Kowacki, "If it weren't for that meteor, would there still be dinosaurs?" *Christian Science Monitor*, July 29, 2014.

Carter, Jamie, "Climate Change Killed The Dinosaurs. 'Drastic Global Winter' After Asteroid Strike, Say Scientists," *Forbes*, June 29, 2020.

"Coal-burning in Siberia after volcanic eruption led to climate change 250 million years ago," *Science Daily*, June 16, 2020.

Crane, Leah, "Asteroid that killed the dinosaurs hit just right for maximum damage," *New Scientist*, May 26, 2020.

Kane, Sean, "The human race once came dangerously close to dying out—here's how it changed us," *Business Insider*, March 18, 2016.

La Page, Michael, "Asteroid that killed the dinosaurs caused massive global warming," *New Scientist*, May 24, 2018.

Pickrell, John, "What if dinosaurs hadn't died out?" *BBC*, September 18, 2017. https://www.bbc.com/future/article/20170918-what-if-the-dinosaurs-hadnt-died-out.

Robock, Alan, Caspar M. Ammann, Luke Oman, Drew Shindell, Samuel Levis, and Georgiy Stenchikov, "Did the Toba volcanic eruption of ~74 ka B.P. produce widespread glaciation?" *Journal of Geophysics Research*, May 27, 2009.

Schweitzer, Mary H., "Dinosaurs Reveal Clues about Adaptation to Climate Change," *Scientific American*, May 2014.

Dustbowl

Bryner, Jeanna, "Why the 1930s Dustbowl Was So Bad," *Live Science*, May 5, 2008. https://www.livescience.com/4915-1930s-dust-bowl-bad.html.

Gutmann, Myron P. et al. "Migration in the 1930s: Beyond the Dust Bowl." *Social science history* vol. 40,4 (2016): 707-470. doi:10.1017/ssh.2016.28.

Klein, Chistopher, "10 Things You May Not Know About the Dust Bowl," History.com, March 21, 2019. https://www.history.com/news/10-things-you-may-not-know-about-the-dust-bowl.

Wartzman, Rick, *Obscene in the Extreme: The Burning and Banning of John Steinbeck's The Grapes of Wrath*, New York: Public Affairs, 2008.

Egyptian Empire

Allen-Chicago, Susan, "World's Oldest Weather Report Could Alter Egyptian History," *Futurity*, April 2, 2014. https://www.futurity.org/bronze-age-weather-report-may-change-middle-east-timeline/.

Benaim, Rachel, "Ancient Egyptians Prepared for Climate Change 3,000 Years Ago, Scientists Find," *Weather Channel*, March 23, 2018. https://weather.com/news/news/2018-03-19-ancient-egyptians-prepped-for-climate-change.

De Chant, Tim, "Climate Change May Have Brought Ancient Egypt to Its Knees," *Nova*, October 22, 2013.

"Egypt's historical sites facing climate threat," *China Daily*, December 24, 2019.

Fortuna, W. Harry, "A study shows how ancient Egypt struggled with drastic changes in the climate," *Quartz*, October 17, 2017.

Hoyt, Alia, "How the Nile River Works," *How Stuff Works*, https://adventure.howstuffworks.com/nile-river2.htm.

Jarus, Owen, "Ancient Egypt: A Brief History," *Live Science,* July 28, 2016.

Manning, J. G., Ludlow, F., Stine, A. R. et al. "Volcanic suppression of Nile summer flooding triggers revolt and constrains interstate conflict in ancient Egypt." *Nat Commun* 8, 900 (2017). https://doi.org/10.1038/s41467-017-00957-y.

"Tempest Stela of Ahmose: World's Oldest Weather Report," *Sci News*, April 3, 2014.

Tyldesley, Joyce, "Ancient Egypt and the Modern World," BBC, February 17, 2011. http://www.bbc.co.uk/history/ancient/egyptians/egypt_importance_01.shtml.

Florida Settlement

Bransford, Margaret, "A Hurricane That Made History," *The French Review*, vol. 23, no. 3, 1950, pp. 223–226. *JSTOR*, www.jstor.org/stable/381883. Accessed 30 Apr. 2020.

Harris, Sherwood, "The Tragic Dream of Jean Ribaut," *American Heritage*, October 1963.

Robertson, William, *The History of America: Including the United States, Volume 2.* New York: Blakeman and Mason, 1859.

Flu Pandemic

Anice C. Lowen, John Steel, "Roles of Humidity and Temperature in Shaping Influenza Seasonality," *Journal of Virology*, June, 2014.

"Flu virus' best friend: Low humidity," *Science News Daily*, May 13, 2019.

Huntington, Ellsworth. "Influenza and the Weather in the United States in 1918." *The Scientific Monthly*, vol. 17, no. 5, 1923, pp. 462–471. *JSTOR*, www.jstor.org/stable/3693043. Accessed 4 May 2020.

"New Look at 1918/1919 El Niño Suggests Link to Flu Pandemic," National Oceanic and Atmospheric Administration. https://www.pmel.noaa.gov/elnino/1918-1919-Flu-Pandemic.

Shamblovsky, Suzanne, "Nearly a century after it killed millions, a journalist reflects on how the Spanish flu changed the world," *Science,* September 18, 2017.

Spanish Flu, History.com. https://www.history.com/topics/world-war-i/1918-flu-pandemic

Spinney, Laura, "How the 1918 Flu Pandemic Revolutionized Public Health," *Smithsonian*, September 27, 2017.

Spinney, Laura, "The World Changed Its Approach to Health After the 1918 Flu. Will It After The COVID-19 Outbreak?," *Time*, March 7, 2020.

French Revolution

Doyle, William, "The Execution of Louis XVI and the End of the French Monarchy," *History Review*, 2000.

BIBLIOGRAPHY

Knowles, Lilian, "New Light on the Economic Causes of the French Revolution." *The Economic Journal*, vol. 29, no. 113, 1919.

Neumann, J., "Great Historical Events that Were Significantly Affected by the Weather: 2, The Year Leading to the Revolution of 1789 in France," *Bulletin of the American Meteorological Society*, February, 1977.

Prein, Andreas and Greg Holland, "Global estimates of damaging hail hazard." *Weather and Climate Extremes*. Volume 22, December 2018.

Galveston

Burnett, John, "The Tempest At Galveston: 'We Knew There Was A Storm Coming, But We Had No Idea," *NPR*, November 30, 2017. https://www.npr.org /2017/11/30/566950355/the-tempest-at-galveston-we-knew-there-was-a-storm -coming-but-we-had-no-idea.

Fletcher, Abner, "What If The 1900 Galveston Hurricane Had Never Happened?" *Houston Public Radio*, April 11, 2019. https://www.houstonpublicmedia.org/articles /shows/houston-matters/2019/04/11/328825/what-if-the-1900-galveston -hurricane-had-never-happened/.

George Washington

Adams, Charles Francis, "The Battle of Long Island," *The American Historical Review*, vol. 1, no. 4, 1896, pp. 650–670. *JSTOR*, www.jstor.org/stable/1833753. Accessed 4 May 2020.

Hopkins, Mark, "America's Dunkirk," *Independent,* August 26, 2017.

Myers, J. Jay, "George Washington: Defeated at the Battle of Long Island," History.Net, https://www.historynet.com/george-washington-defeated-at-the-battle-of-long -island.htm.

"Silent Retreat," Museum of the American Revolution, July 30, 2013. https://www .amrevmuseum.org/read-the-revolution/history/silent-retreat.

Great Chicago Fire

Abbott, Karen, "Who or What Caused the Great Chicago Fire," *Smithsonian*, October 4, 2012.

"The Great Chicago Fire of 1871," *Chicago Architecture Center*, http://www.architecture. org/learn/resources/architecture-dictionary/entry/the-great-chicago-fire-of-1871/

Schons, Mary, "The Chicago Fire of 1871 and the 'Great Rebuilding'," *National Geographic,* January 25, 2011.

"Weather Played a Role in the Great Chicago Fire," AccuWeather, https://www.AccuWeather.com/en/weather-news/weather-played-a-role-in-great-chicago-fire/148277

Great Fire of London

"10 Things You (Probably) Didn't Know About the Great Fire of London," History Extra, www.historyextra.com.

"The Great Fire of London Was Blamed on Religious Terrorism," *Smithsonian,* September 2, 2016.

Heathcote, Edwin, "How the Great Fire of 1666 Shaped Modern-Day London," *Financial Times,* September 2, 2016.

Museum of London, https://www.museumoflondon.org.uk/application/files/6514/5511/5493/what-happened-great-fire-london.pdf.

Nayeri, Farah, "The Fire that Shaped London," *New York Times*, August 10, 2016.

Squires, Mike, "The 100 Hour Snowtorm of 1969," *Climate.gov*, February 22, 2016. https://www.climate.gov/news-features/blogs/beyond-data/100-hour-snowstorm-february-1969.

Great Frost of 1709

Anderson, Jennifer L., "Nature's Currency: The Atlantic Mahogany Trade and the Commodification of Nature in the Eighteenth Century," *Early American Studies*, vol. 2, no. 1, 2004.

Inman, Philip, "War and the weather: what caused the huge economic slump of 1706?" *The Guardian*, May 7, 2020.

Kahn, Eve, "Beyond the Luster of Mahogany," *New York Times*, August 23, 2012.

Pain, Stephanie, "1709: The year that Europe froze," *New Scientist*, February 4, 2009.

Great Northern War

Egorov, Boris, "5 facts about the war that turned Russia into a great power," *Russia Beyond,* August 17, 2018.

Valenta, Jiri and Leni Friedman Valenta, "Russia's Strategic Advantage in the Baltics: A Challenge to NATO?" *The Began-Sedat Center for Stragetic Studies*, January 2018. https://besacenter.org/wp-content/uploads/2018/01/143-Monograph-Russias-Strategic-Advantage-in-the-Baltics-Valenta-WEB.pdf.

Great White Hurricane

"Blizzard brings tragedy to Northwest Plains," History.com. https://www.history.com/this-day-in-history/blizzard-brings-tragedy-to-northwest-plains.

Epstein, David,"50 Years Ago, It Snowed For 4 Days Straight. Just Think Of The Hype If That Happened Now," WBUR Boston, Feburary 22, 2019. https://www.wbur.org/news/2019/02/22/100-hour-storm-social-media-storm-effect.

Evans, Mike, "Remembering a Snowstorm that Paralyzed the City," *New York Times*, February 10, 2009.

Ford, Alyssa, "125 years ago, deadly 'Children's Blizzard' blasted Minnesota," *MinnPost*, January 11, 2013.

Friedman, Jackie, "The Storm that Swallowed Gotham," *The Week*, https://theweek.com/captured/669025/macabre-life-russias-arctic-reindeer-herders.

"Great Blizzard of '88 hits East Coast," History.com, March 10, 2020. https://www.history.com/this-day-in-history/great-blizzard-of-88-hits-east-coast.

Hendee, David, "Blizzard of 1888 ravaged the Plains with hurricane-like winds, deadly cold," *Omaha Herald*, January 13, 2018.

Moore, Tom, "Great Northeast Blizzard of 1888," *Weather Concierge,* March 15, 2019. https://www.weatherconcierge.com/the-great-northeast-blizzard-of-1888-the-great-white-hurricane/.

Valle, Dan, "The Blizzards of 1888," *National Weather Service Heritage.* https://vlab.ncep.noaa.gov/web/nws-heritage/-/the-children-s-blizzard.

Waldman, Benjamin, "The Great White Hurricane of 1888: The Storm That Put NYC's Wires Underground," *Untapped New York*, November 1, 2012. https://untappedcities.com/2012/11/01/the-great-white-hurricane-of-1888-the-storm-that-put-nycs-wires-underground/.

"Weather, or not: Without any warning, Blizzard of 1888 threw a knockout punch," *Keene Sentinel*, March 16, 2019.

Hindenburg

Artist Sam Shere. International Center for Photography. https://www.icp.org/browse/archive/constituents/sam-shere?all/all/all/all/0.

Benson, Clare, "The legacy of the *Hindenburg* disaster," *Chemistry World*, May 5, 2017.

Blakemore, Erin, "How a Navy Dirigible Became the World's Deadliest Airship," History.com. https://www.history.com/news/how-a-navy-dirigible-became-the-worlds-deadliest-airship.

Burgan, Michael., *The Hindenburg in Flames,* North Mankato, MN: Compas Point Books, 2017.

Dick, Joseph A., "Helium Hokum: Why Airships Will Never Be Part of Our Transportation Infrastructure," *Scientific American*, May 27, 2011.

"Forgotten airship disaster recalled 80 years later," *USA Today*, March 13, 2013.

Ling, Justin, "The Age of the Airship May Be Dawning Again," *Foreign Policy*, February 29, 2020.

Szalay, Jesse, "*Hindenburg* Crash: The End of Airship Travel," *Live Science,* May 4, 2017.

Taylor, Alan, "75 Years Since the *Hindenburg*," *The Atlantic*, May 8, 2012.

"U.S.S. Akron (ZRS-4) and U.S.S. Macon (ZRS-5)," Airships.net. https://www.airships .net/us-navy-rigid-airships/uss-akron-macon/.

Webster, Donovan, "What Really Felled the *Hindenburg*?" *Smithsonian*, May 4, 2017.

Zhang, Benjamin, "These amazing color photos of the *Hindenburg* Zeppelin show what luxury flying was like 80 years ago," *Business Insider*, March 1, 2018.

Hiroshima

"After Nagasaki: Examining the Cultural Fallout," *Talk of the Nation*, NPR, August 9, 2005.

Ahmed, Samira, "How The Bomb changed everything," BBC, July 2, 2015. https: //www.bbc.com/culture/article/20150702-how-the-bomb-changed-everything.

Allen, Thomas B. and Norman Polar, "The Radio Broadcast That Ended World War II," *The Atlantic,* August 7, 2015.

Alperovitz, Gar., "Hiroshima: Historians Reassess," *Foreign Policy*, June 22, 1995.

Highnett, Katherine, "The Devastation of Nagasaki and the Luck of Kokura: A Tale of Two Cities," *Newsweek,* August 9, 2018.

Kokura, Richard Lloyd Perry, "City remembers day it escaped the bomb," *The Independent*, August 9, 1995.

Kristoff, Nicholas D., "Kokura, Japan: Bypassed by A-Bomb," *New York Times*, August 7, 1995.

"Nagasaki Rebuilds Without Fanfare Accorded Hiroshima," *Bend Bulletin*, October 17, 1955.

Nossal, Frederick, "Huge Shipbuilding Industries Give New Life to Port City of Nagasaki," *Oakland Tribune*, November 2, 1969.

Pearson, Drew, "Army Did not Intend Originally to Drop Atom Bomb on Nagasaki," *Corpus Christi Caller Times*, December 15, 1947.

Richarz, Allan, "The City the A-Bomb Missed," *Bloomburg Citylab*, August 9, 2019.

Wallerstein, Alex, "Nagasaki: The Last Bomb," *The New Yorker*, August 7, 2019.

Hostage Crisis

Fong, Chua Lu., "Operation Eagle Claw, 1980: A Case Study in Crisis Management and Military Planning," *Journal of the Singapore Armed Forces*, April-June, 2002.

Justinian Plague

Harper, Kyle, "How Climate Change and Plague Helped Bring Down the Roman Empire," *Smithsonian*, December 19, 2017.

Rigby, Emma et al, "A comet impact in AD 536?" *Astronomy & Geophysics*, Volume 45, Issue 1, February 2004, Pages 1.23–1.26, https://doi.org/10.1046/j.1468-4004.2003.45123.x.

Than, Ker, "Two of History's Deadliest Plagues Were Linked, With Implications for Another Outbreak," *National Geographic*, January 31, 2014.

Zielenski, Sarah, "Sixth Century Mystery Tied to Not One But Two Volcanic Eruptions," *Smithsonian*, July 8, 2015.

Kennedy Assassination

Brands, H. W. "Book review: 'If Kennedy Lived: An Alternate History' by Jeff Greenfield," *Washington Post*, October 25, 2013.

Levenson, Eric, "History's Favorite Guessing Game: What If JFK Had Lived?" *The Atlantic,* November 21, 2013.

Oskin, Becky, "If JFK Lived: 5 Ways History Would Change," *Live Science,* November 21, 2013.

Porter, Tom, "How the Kennedy assassination totally transformed presidential cars, from an open-top Lincoln Continental to the heavily-armored 'Beast' used by Trump and Obama," *Business Insider*, November 12, 2019.

Rossoll, Nicki, "Five Ways Kennedy's Assassination Changed Presidential Security Forever," ABC News, November 22, 2013. https://abcnews.go.com/Politics/ways-kennedys-assassination-changed-presidential-security-forever/story?id=20776254.

Little Ice Age

Collins, Jeffrey, "'Nature's Mutiny' Review: Tracking History's Turbulence," *Wall Street Journal*, March 1, 2019.

Lanchester, John, "How the Little Ice Age Changed History," *The New Yorker*, March 25, 2019.

Rafferty, John P. et al, "Little Ice Age Geochronology," *Encyclopedia Britannica*, March 18, 2016. https://www.britannica.com/science/Little-Ice-Age.

Lindsay Snowstorm

Benzkofer, Stephan, "1979 blizzard was debacle," *Chicago Tribune*, January 5, 2014.

Chan, Sewell and Liz Robbins, "Mayors Grow Attuned to the Politics of Snow Removal," *New York Times*, February 10, 2010.

Cobb, Jelani, "How Snowfall Stopped a Rising Political Star," *New Yorker,* February 4, 2014.

Donovan, Doug, "Plowing politics can be as treacherous as the snow in Maryland," *Baltimore Sun*, January 25, 2016.

Gregory, Sean, "Cory Booker: The Mayor of Twitter and Blizzard Superhero," *Time Magazine*, December 29, 2010.

Khan, Huma and Devin Dwyer, "Do Mayors' Political Fates Hang in the Outcome of Snowstorms?" February 11, 2010. ABC News. https://abcnews.go.com/Politics /politics-snow-washington-dc-mayor-adrian-fenty-spotlight/story?id=9809564.

Moritz, Owen, "How a blizzard became a political storm for New York City Mayor John Lindsay," *New York Daily News*, August 14, 2017.

Moritz, Owen, "Winter of Discontent: Lindsay's Snowstorm, 1969," *New York Daily News*, October 22, 1998.

Moster, Whet, "Snowpocalypse Then: How the Blizzard of 1979 Cost the Election for Michael Bilandic," *Chicago Magazine*, February 2, 2011.

Phillips, Amber, "7 politicians whose careers were broken—or made—by massive storms," *Washington Post*, August 29, 2017.

Severson, Kim, "Questions Fly in Storm That Stopped Atlanta," *New York Times*, January 30, 2014.

Sperling, Jonathan, "51 years ago today, a blizzard paralyzed Queens," *Queens Daily Eagle*, February 10, 2020.

Squires, Mike, "The 100-Hour Snowstorm of February 1969," NOAA, February 16, 2016. https://www.climate.gov/news-features/blogs/beyond-data/100-hour -snowstorm-february-1969.

Locust Outbreak of 1874

Cartwright, R. L. "Winged menace: The Minnesota grasshopper plagues of 1873-1877," *Minnesota Post*, June 11, 2013.

Fraser, Caroline, "Laura Ingalls Wilder and One of The Greatest Natural Disasters in American History," LitHub, December 5, 2017. https://lithub.com/laura -ingalls-wilder-and-the-greatest-natural-disaster-in-american-history/.

Lyons, Chuck, "1874: The Year of the Locust," History.net, https://www.historynet .com/1874-the-year-of-the-locust.htm.

Wagner, Alexandra M, "Grasshoppered: America's Response to the 1874 Rocky Mountain Locust Invasion," *Nebraska History* 89 (2008): 154-167.

London Fog

Bharadwaj, Prashant et al. "Early-Life Exposure to the Great Smog of 1952 and the Development of Asthma." *American journal of respiratory and critical care medicine* vol. 194, 12 (2016): 1475-1482. doi:10.1164/rccm.201603-0451OC.

Brown, Paul, "Monet's Obsession with London Fog," *The Guardian*, February 19, 2017.

Corton, Christine, "Have We Learned the Lessons From the History of the London Fog?" *The Guardian*, January 28, 2017.

Jacobs, Elizabeth T. et al., "The Donora Smog Revisited: 70 Years After the Event That Inspired the Clean Air Act," *American journal of public health* vol. 108,S2 (2018): S85-S88. doi:10.2105/AJPH.2017.304219.

Kiester, Edwin, "A Darkness in Donora," *Smithsonian Magazine*, November, 1999.

Leser, Simon, "The Reason London is Renowned for Being Foggy," *Culture Trip*, November 24, 2016.

Quinn, Anthony, "London Fog Review—A City in the Thick of It," *The Guardian*, December 13, 2015.

Mayan Civilization

"Ancient and Living Maya in the 19th and 20th Centuries: Archaeological Discovery, Literary Voice, and Political Struggle" is an enhanced electronic version of a physical exhibition of the same name that took place at Wilson Library at UNC-Chapel Hill from October 8, 2012 to January 27, 2013. https://exhibits.lib.unc.edu/exhibits/show/maya/intro.

Gabriele, Matthew, "How Massive Drought Ended The Classic Mayan Civilization (And Why We Already Knew That)," *Forbes,* August 20, 2018.

"Mayans Sacrifices Were Boys," *Globe and Mail*, January 23, 2008.

Urioste, Jose, "The Caste War of Yucatan," *Yucatan Times*, August 2, 2019.

Wu, Brian, "Blue Hole of Belize May Explain What Happened to the Mayans," *Science Times*, May 4, 2020.

Wylie, Robin, "Severe Droughts Explain the Mysterious Fall of the Maya," *BBC*, February 22, 2016. http://www.bbc.com/earth/story/20160222-severe-droughts-explain-the-mysterious-fall-of-the-maya.

Mongol Empire

Cartwright, Mark, "The Mongol Invasions of Japan, 1274 & 1281 CE," *Ancient History Encyclopedia*, July 2, 2019.

Courtros, Peter, "When Did Horses Transform Mongolians' Way of Life?" *Sapiens,* January 24, 2018.

Inglis-Arkell, Esther, "The Mongols built an empire with one technological break-through," *Ars Technica*, May 9, 2017.

Kramer, Sarah, "Scientists Finally Know What Stopped the Mongol Hordes from Conquering Europe," *Science Alert*, May 28, 2016. https://www.sciencealert.com/scientists-finally-know-what-stopped-mongol-hordes-from-conquering-europe Accessed February 24, 2020.

"Mongol Empire Rode Wave of Mild Climate, Says Study," *Earth Institute,* Columbia University.

Neumann, J. "Great Historical Events that Were Significantly Affected by the Weather: I. The Mongol Invastions of Japan." *Bulletin of the American Meteorological Society*, November, 1975.

Nuwer, Rachel, "Typhoons Saved 13th Century Japan From Invasion," *Smithsonian*, December 10, 2014.

Walsh, Bryan, "How Climate Change Drove the Rise of Genghis Khan," *Time*, March 10, 2014.

Napoleon in Russia

Greenspan, Jesse, "Why Napoleon's Invasion of Russia Was the Beginning of the End," History.com, https://www.history.com/news/napoleons-disastrous-invasion-of-russia-200-years-ago.

Tarm, Michael, "This Europe: Mass Grave Shows How Hunger and Cold Devastated Napoleon's Army on Retreat from Moscow," *The Independent* (UK), September 3, 2002.

Zamoyski, Adam, *Moscow 1812: Napoleon's Fatal March*, London: HarperCollins, 2004.

Noah's Flood

Ballard, Robert D., "Deep Black Sea," *National Geographic*, May, 2001.

Hecht, Jeff. "Black Sea Bore the Brunt of Two Gushing Neighbours," *New Scientist*, July 26, 2003.

"How Literally Should we take the Story of Noah and the Flood?" *Kansas City Star*, December 3, 2003.

Spotts, Peter, N., "Black Sea Find May Explain Noah's Flood," *Christian Science Monitor*, September, 15, 2000.

Steinberg, Avi, "Myth and Realism in Noah's Ark," *New Yorker*, April 21, 2014.

Trefil, James, "Evidence for a Flood," *Smithsonian*, April 1, 2000.

BIBLIOGRAPHY

Roman Empire

Carlson, Cody, "This week in history: Mark Antony has Cicero assassinated," *Deseret News*, December 4, 2013.

Deininger, Jürgen, "Explaining the Change from Republic to Principle in Rome." *Comparative Civilizations Review*, 1980. Vol. 4 : No. 4.

Fleming, Thomas, "George Washington's Favorite Play," *Journal of the American Revolution*, December 11, 2013.

Goldsworthy, Adrian, "The Bloody Rise of Augustus," *History Extra*, August 17, 2018.

Hunt, Katie, "Scientists identify Alaskan volcano that may have helped the rise of the Roman Empire," CNN, June 22, 2020. https://www.cnn.com/2020/06/22/world /volcano-ancient-rome-scn/index.html.

Lund, Graham, "Democracy vs. Grandeur: Was Augustus Good or Bad for Rome?" *History Hit*, July 30, 2018. https://www.historyhit.com/democracy-vs-grandeur -was-augustus-good-or-bad-for-rome/.

Machemer, Theresa, "How an Alaskan Volcano Is Linked to the Decline of the Roman Republic," *Smithsonian*, June 29, 2020.

Meany, Paul, "Rome's Heroes and America's Founding Fathers," *Journal of the American Revolution*, October 23, 2018.

"Rome's Transition from Republic to Empire," *National Geographic*, July 6, 2018. https://www.nationalgeographic.org/article/romes-transition-republic-empire/.

Schultz, Isaac, "Did an Alaskan Volcano Help Change the Face of the Mediterranean World?" *Atlas Obscura*, June 23, 2020. https://www.atlasobscura.com/articles /alaskan-volcano-mediterranean-climate.

Sidebottom, Harry, "Jury is still out on Julius Caesar's killing," *Irish Times*, March 15, 2018.

Sterner, Eric, "Joseph Addison's Cato: Liberty on the Stage," *Journal of the American Revolution*, November 2, 2016.

Voosen, Pal, "Alaskan megaeruption may have helped end the Roman Republic," *Science*, January 22, 2020.

The Scream

"10 Things You May Not Know About The Scream," The British Museum. https://blog .britishmuseum.org/10-things-you-may-not-know-about-the-scream/.

"Disaster, Screams and Sunsets, Krakatoa's Legacy Recalled by Asian Tsunami." *Agence France Presse*, January 4, 2005.

Lubow, Arthur, "Edvard Munch: Beyond The Scream," *Smithsonian*, March 2006.

Witze, Alexandra. "Scientist Links Famous 'Scream' Painting to Devastating Volcano." *Dallas Morning News*, December 9, 2003.

September 11

Green, Matthew, "How 9/11 Changed America: Four Major Lasting Impacts," KQED, September 8, 2017. https://www.kqed.org/lowdown/14066/13-years-later-four-major-lasting-impacts-of-911.

"September 11 Warnings Fast Facts," CNN.com, August 23, 2019. https://www.cnn.com/2013/07/27/us/september-11th-warning-signs-fast-facts/index.html.

"This Day in History: December 15," History.com, https://www.history.com/this-day-in-history/united-states-declares-end-to-iraq-war.

Spanish Armada

Cartwright, Mark, "Spanish Armada," *Ancient History Encyclopedia*, May 28, 2020.

Fernandez-Armesto, "What if the Armada had Landed..." *New Statesman*, December 20, 1999.

Flanagan, Laurence, "Wrecks of the Spanish Armada," *Natural History*, September, 1988.

Hutchinson, Robert, "How the Spanish Armada Was Really Defeated," *The History Reader*, May 30, 2014.

Lamb, H. H., "The Weather of 1588 and the Spanish Armada," *Weather*, November 1, 1988.

"Spanish Armada Defeated," History.com, https://www.history.com/this-day-in-history/spanish-armada-defeated.

Stradivarius

"Cool Weather May Be Stradivarius' Secret," CNN, December 8, 2003.

Pickerell, John, "Did Little Ice Age Creat Stradivarius Violins' Famous Tone?" *National Geographic News*, January 7, 2004.

The Tempest

Doherty, Kieran, *Sea Venture: Shipwreck, Survival, and the Salvation of Jamestown*, New York: St. Martin's Press, 2007.

Moniz, Jessie, "Eye of the storm: Our Tempest Connection," *Royal Gazette,* October 16, 2014.

"The Sea Venture," Bermuda 100. http://bermuda100.ucsd.edu/sea-venture/index.php.

"The Wreck of the Sea Venture. The Untold Story," *The Bermudian*, April 23, 2019.

Ten Plagues of Egypt

Ehrenkranz, N. Joel and Deborah A. Sampson, "Origin of the old testament plagues: explications and implications," The Yale journal of biology and medicine vol. 81,1 (2008): 31-42.

Hebblethwaite, Cordelia, "Eating locusts: The crunchy, kosher snack taking Israel by swarm," *BBC*, March 21, 2013.

Joffre, Tizvi, "The Bible Coming to Life? Locusts 'Plague' Middle East, Asia," *Jerusalem Post*, February 20, 2020.

Leon, Benjamin, "The Ten Plagues of Egypt Happened," *The Standard* (Zimbabwe), April 9, 2017.

Milliman, Jenna and Ralph Avellino, "Did the Exodus of Moses and His People Really Happen?" ABC News, December, 26, 2012. https://abcnews.go.com/International /exodus-moses-people-happen/story?id=18068905.

Mortlock, Stephen, "The Ten Plagues of Egypt," *Biomedical Scientist*, January 7, 2019.

Raver, Anne, "Biblical Plagues: A Novel Theory," *New York Times,* April 4, 1996.

Waxman, Olivia, "Did the Ten Plagues of Egypt Really Happen?" *Time*, April 18, 2019.

Titanic

Bitette, Nicole, "Titanic: Three ways the disaster changed laws and safety on the seas," *New York Daily News*, September 1, 2015.

Bressan, David, "The Climate Science Behind The Sinking Of The Titanic," *Forbes*, April 12, 2017.

Cox, Stephen D., "Why the Titanic fascinates more than other disasters," CNN, April 9, 2012.

Dotinga, Rod, "What Sank the Titanic," *Christian Science Monitor,* April 13, 2012.

Floyd, Charles, "Did the Titanic Sink Because of an Optical Illusion?" *Smithsonian,* March 1, 2012.

Lipman, Don, "The weather during the Titanic disaster: looking back 100 years," *Washington Post,* April 11, 2012.

Navarro, Andrea, "Cold front that made Fenway Park's first game chilly also impacted the sinking of the Titanic," AccuWeather, April 17, 2020. https://www.AccuWeather .com/en/weather-news/cold-front-that-made-fenway-parks-first-game-chilly-also -impacted-the-sinking-of-the-titanic/721675.

Ravilious, Kate, "Weatherwatch: Did warm weather cause the Titanic disaster?" *The Guardian*, April 27, 2014.

"Titanic sank due to 'mirage' caused by freak weather," *Telegraph*, March 12, 2012.

Wilson, Andrew, "Why the Titanic Still Fascinates Us," *Smithsonian*, March 2012.
Wright, Pam, "Letter Penned by Doomed Titanic Passenger Sells at Auction For Record $166,000," Weather Channel, October 23, 2017. https://weather.com/en -CA/canada/news/news/2017-10-23-letter-titanic-sold-auction

War of 1812

Klein, Christopher, "10 Things You May Not Know About the War of 1812," History.com. August 29, 2018. https://www.history.com/news/10-things-you-may-not-know-about -the-war-of-1812.

Washington, DC Tornado

"The tornado that stopped the burning of Washington," Constitution Center, April 25, 2015. https://constitutioncenter.org/blog/the-tornado-that-stopped-the-burning -of-washington/.

Weather and Economic Growth

Balls, Andrew, "Why Tropical Countries Are Underdeveloped," National Bureau of Economic Research, https://www.nber.org/digest/jun01/w8119.html.

Barber, Nigel, "Does Weather Effect Economic Growth?" *Psychology Today*, August 30, 2016.

Jones, Benjamin et al, "Does Climate Change Effect Economic Growth?" *VOX CEPR Policy Portal*, June 6, 2009.

Kestenbaum, David, "Hot Climates May Create Sluggish Economies," *Morning Edition, NPR*, July 17, 2009.

Khwar, Miriam, "Tropical Climate And Economic Development; Further Evidence," *Council on African Security and Economic Development*, February 24, 2017.

Lambert, L. Don, "The Role of Climate in the Economic Development of Nations," *Land Economics*, vol. 47, no. 4, 1971, pp. 339–344. *JSTOR*, www.jstor.org/stable /3145070. Accessed 4 May 2020.

Roser, Max and Esteban Ortiz-Ospina. "Global Extreme Poverty." Published online at OurWorldInData.org. Retrieved from: 'https://ourworldindata.org/extreme-pov-erty' [Online Resource]

Tally, Steve, "Wealth of Nations Depends on Jack Frost, Study Finds," *Perdue News*, https://www.purdue.edu/uns/html4ever/010917.Masters.frost.html.

Weather and Stock Market

Chediak, Mark, "There's One Stock That Always Rallies When a Big Storm Hits," *Bloomberg*, September 14, 2017.

"In the Mood to Trade?" *Science Daily*, January 15, 2015. https://www.sciencedaily .com/releases/2015/01/150115141651.htm.

O'Mahoney, Proinsias, "Is Bad Weather Bad for Stock Markets?" *Irish Times*, July 31, 2018.

Palmieri, Barclay, "8 Stocks that Benefit from Severe Weather Events," *Investopedia*, February 18, 2019.

Ross, Sean, "Does Weather Affect the Stock Market?" *Investopedia,* December 6, 2019. https://www.investopedia.com/articles/markets/111015/does-weather-affect -stock-market.asp.

Wells, Charlie, "How Bad Weather Could Affect Stock Prices," *Wall Street Journal*, November 8, 2015.

Witch Trials

Bressan, David, "Medieval Witch Hunts Influenced by Climate Change," *Scientific American*, November 3, 2014.

Oster, Emily, "Witchcraft, Weather and Economic Growth in Renaissance Europe," *Journal of Economic Perspectives*, Winter, 2004.

Pfister, C. and R. Brázdil, "Climatic Variability in Sixteenth-Century Europe and its Social Dimension: A Synthesis," *Climatic Change* 43, 5–53 (1999). https://doi .org/10.1023/A:1005585931899.

Roll, Richard, "Orange Juice and Weather," *The American Economic Review*, vol. 74, no. 5, 1984, pp. 861–880. *JSTOR*, www.jstor.org/stable/549. Accessed 7 Aug. 2020.

Wolchover, Natalie, "Did Cold Weather Cause the Salem Witch Trials?" Live Science, April 20, 2012. https://www.livescience.com/19820-salem-witch-trials.html.

World War II

Glantz, David M. and Jonathan House, *When Titans Clashed: How the Red Army Stopped Hitler*. Lawrence, KS: University Press of Kansas, 1995.

Neumann, J. and H. Flohn, "Great Historical Events That Were Significantly Affected by the Weather: Part 8, Germany's War on the Soviet Union, 1941–45. I. Long-range Weather Forecasts for 1941–42 and Climatological Studies," *Bulletin of the American Meteorological Society,* Volume 68 No. 6, June 1987.

Neumann, J. and H. Flohn, "Great Historical Events that were Significantly Affected by the Weather: Part 8, Germany's War on the Soviet Union, 1941-45. II. Some Important Weather Forecasts, 1942-45," *Bulletin of the American Meteorological Society*, July, 1988.

Poroskov, Nikolai, "Stalingrad: The Battle that Broke Hitler's Back," *Russian Life*, November-December, 2002.

Wright Brothers

Garloch, Karen, "Brazil's claims to be 'First in Flight' strike Tar Heels as 'hot air'," *Charlotte Observer*, August 6, 2016.

"How the Wright Brothers Blew It," *Forbes*, November 19, 2003.

Kidder, Chris, "Wright Brothers Were Little Known in Flying Community," *Virginian Pilot*, November 18, 2001.

McCartney, Scott, "Wright Brothers' Patent Battle Proved Costly in Aviation Race," *Wall Street Journal*, December 17, 2003.

Year without a Summer

Ashton, Curtis, "Early Struggle of the Smith Family," *Church of Jesus Christ of Latter Day Saints*, March 1, 2019. https://history.churchofjesuschrist.org/content/historic-sites-palmyra-vermont-new-york.

Belleville, Peter K., "Year Without a Summer," *Church of Jesus Christ of Latter Day Saints*, https://www.churchofjesuschrist.org/study/ensign/1983/01/a-year-without-a-summer?lang=eng.

Bressan, David, "How Volcanoes And Climate Triggered Migration To America," *Forbes*, November 21, 2017.

Kirschbaum, Erik, "Whatever Happened to German America?" *New York Times*, September 23, 2015.

"May 28, 1830 CE: Indian Removal Act," *National Geographic*. https://www.nationalgeographic.org/thisday/may28/indian-removal-act/.

Remini, Robert, "Texas Must Be Ours," *American Heritage*, February/March 1986.

Townsend, Chris, "Year Without a Summer," *Paris Review*, October 25, 2016.

Wood, Gillen D'Arcy, "The Volcano That Changed the Course of History," *Slate*, April 9, 2014.

Endnotes

Chapter 1

1   According to Penn State scientists, it appears that about 50 percent or more of significant plant species were lost. Plants, of course, outweigh all animals combined by more than two hundred fold. Dinosaurs were many times less diverse and abundant than plants, thus it was much easier to kill off nearly all major categories of them—only birds survived. Interestingly, this extinction ushered in the rise and true dominance of flowering plants and helped establish the planet's tropical rainforests that hold most of its biodiversity.

Monica Carvalho, an assistant professor at the University of Michigan and co-author of the study said, "There is a transformative effect on ecosystems—what they are made of, how they operate. Fossils show that post-extinction tropical rainforests were profoundly different from their predecessors in composition, structure, and ecology." (Matthew Carroll, "Fossils show widespread plant extinctions after asteroid wiped out dinosaurs," Penn State, Earth and Mineral Sciences, September 26, 2023, https://www.psu.edu/news/earth-and-mineral-sciences/story/fossils-show-widespread-plant-extinctions-after-asteroid-wiped-out/?utm_audience=Combined&utm_source=newswire&utm_medium=email&utm_campaign=Research%20headlines%20issue&utm_content=10-05-2023-10-18&utm_term=Stories%20-%202)

2   John Pickrell, "What if the Dinosaurs Hadn't Died out," BBC, September 18, 2017, https://www.bbc.com/future/article/20170918-what-if-the-dinosaurs-hadnt-died-out.

Chapter 2

1   David R. Montgomery, "The Real Landscapes of the Great Flood Myths," *Nautlius*, June 4, 2015.

2   Ishaan Tharoor, "Before Noah: Myths of the Flood Are Far Older Than the Bible," *Time*, April 1, 2014.

3   Avi Steinberg, "Myth and Realism in Noah's Ark," *New Yorker*, April 21, 2014.

Chapter 3

1   Robert K. Ritner and Nadine Mueller, "The Ahmose 'Tempest Stela', Thera and Comparative Chronology," *Journal of Near Eastern Studies* 73, no. 2 (April 2014); "Tempest Stela of Ahmose: World's Oldest Weather Report," *Sci News*, April 3, 2014.

2   J. G. Manning, F. Ludlow, A. R. Stine, et al. "Volcanic suppression of Nile summer flooding triggers revolt and constrains interstate conflict in ancient Egypt," *Nat Commun* **8**, 900 (2017). https://doi.org/10.1038/s41467–017-00957-y.

Chapter 4

1   Sanjay Gupta, "A Doctor's Take on the Plagues," CNN, April 9, 2007; J. S. Marr and C. D. Malloy, "An epidemiologic analysis of the ten plagues of Egypt," *Caduceus* 12, no. 1 (Spring 1996): 7–24. PMID: 8673614; Olivia Waxman, "Did the Ten Plagues of Egypt Really Happen? Here are 3 theories," *Time*, April 18, 2019.

Chapter 5

1   Plutarch, *Plutarch's Lives*, Volume 2 (New York: William Heinmann, 1914).

Chapter 6

1   Issam Ahmed, "Alaskan Volcano Eruption Linked To Fall Of Roman Republic: Study," *Agence France Press News*, June 22, 2020; Kate Hunt, "Scientists identify Alaskan volcano that may have helped the rise of the Roman Empire," CNN, June 22, 2020; Theresa Machemer, "How an Alaskan Volcano Is Linked to the Decline of the Roman Republic," *Smithsonian Magazine*, June 29, 2020; Joseph R. McConnell et al., "Extreme climate after massive eruption of Alaska's Okmok volcano in 43 BCE and effects on the late Roman Republic and Ptolemaic Kingdom," *Earth, Atmospheric and Planetary Sciences*, June 22, 2020; "Period of Extreme Cold in Ancient Rome Linked to Eruption of Alaska's Okmok Volcano," *Sci Tech Daily*, June 22, 2020.

2   Ibid.

3   Ibid.

4   Ibid.

5   "Rome's Transition from Republic to Empire," *National Geographic*, https://education.nationalgeographic.org/resource/romes-transition-republic-empire/.

6   Jurgen Deininger, "Explaining the Change from Republic to Principle in Rome," *Comparative Civilisations Review*, April 1, 1980.

7   Paul Meany, "Rome's Heroes and America's Founding Fathers," *Journal of the American Revolution*, October 23, 2018; Paul Meany, "Why the Founding Fathers Loved Ancient Rome," *Medium*, October 30, 2018; John Miller, "On Life, Liberty and Other Quotable Matters," *Wall Street Journal*, July 2, 2011; Charles Mullett, "Classical Influences on the American Revolution," *The Classical Journal*, November 1939.

8   Eric Sterner, "Joseph Addison's Cato: Liberty on the Stage," *Journal of the American Revolution*, November 2, 2016.

9   Ibid.

Chapter 7

1   Elizabeth Kolbert, "Pandemics and the Shape of Human History," *New Yorker*, March 30, 2020.

2   Emma Rigby, Melissa Symonds, and Derek Ward-Thompson, "A comet impact in AD 536?" *Astronomy & Geophysics* 45, no. 1 (February 2004): 1.23–1.26, https://doi.org/10.1046/j.1468–4004.2003.45123.x.

3 Kolbert, "Pandemics."
4 Ibid.
5 William Rosen, *Justinian's Flea* (New York: Penguin Books, 2008).

Chapter 8

1 "Mayans' sacrifices were boys," *Globe and Mail*, January 22, 2008.
2 Douglas J. Kennett et al., "Drought-Induced Civil Conflict Among the Ancient Maya," *Nature Communications*, July 19, 2022.

Chapter 9

1 "Climate of Genghis Khan's ancient time extends long shadow over Asia of today," National Science Foundation News Release 14–032; Nethaniel Massey, "Rise of Genghis Khan Linked to Unusual Rains in Mongolia," *Scientific American*, March 12, 2014; Neil Pedersen et al., "Pluvials, droughts, the Mongol Empire, and modern Mongolia," *Earth, Atmospheric and Planetary Sciences*, March 10, 2014; Roff Smith, "Genghis Khan's Secret Weapon Was Rain," *National Geographic,* March 12, 2014; Bryan Walsh, "How Climate Change Drove the Rise of Genghis Khan," *Time*, March 10, 2014.
2 Smith, "Genghis Khan's Secret Weapon Was Rain."

Chapter 11

1 John Donne, "The Flea," in *The Norton Anthology of Poetry*, ed. Margaret W. Ferguson, Mary Jo Salter, and Jon Stallworthy (W. W. Norton, 1996), 4th edition, https://www.poetryfoundation.org/poems/46467/the-flea.
2 William Stubbs, *The Constitutional History of England in Its Origin and Development Vol. II* (Oxford: Clarendon Press, 1887).
3 Steve Levine, "How the Black Death Radically Changed the Course of History," *Medium*, April 20, 2020.
4 Şevket Pamuk, "The Black Death and the Origins of the 'Great Divergence' across Europe, 1300–1600," *European Review of Economic History*, 11, no. 3 (2007): 289–317. *JSTOR*, http://www.jstor.org/stable/41378468.
5 Francis Aidan Gasquet, *The Great Pestilence* (London: Simpkin, Marshall, Hamilton, Kent & Co, 1893).
6 Şevket Pamuk, "The Black Death."

Chapter 12

1 Alan Burke, "Did climate change cause witch hysteria?" *Salem News*, April 19, 2012; Natalie Wolchover, "Did Cold Weather Cause the Salem Witch Trials?" *NBC News*, April 11, 2012.
2 David Bressan, "Medieval Witch Hunts Influenced by Climate Change," *Scientific American*, November 3, 2014.

Chapter 13

1 Sherwood Harris, "The Tragic Dream Of Jean Ribaut," *American Heritage*, October 1963.

Chapter 14

1   Dale Brumfield, "Three colonial Virginia hurricanes, including one that inspired Shakespeare's *Tempest*," *Medium*, October 23, 2018.
2   William Strachey, "A true reportory of the wracke, and redemption of Sir Thomas Gates Knight; upon, and from the lands of the Bermudas . . . July 15. 1610 in Purchas his Pilgrimes," Vol. 4, Chap. VI," 1625. You can find a photo reproduction on the web site of the British Library: https://www.bl.uk/collection-items/stracheys-a-true-reportory-of-the-wreck-in-bermuda.
3   Ibid.

Chapter 15

1   Ian Irvine, "'What an unbuttoning!' The best historical accounts of long, hot summers," *The Prospect*, July 20, 2017; The Diary of Samuel Peyps. June 7, 1655, https://www.pepysdiary .com/diary/1665/06/07/.
2   "Your guide to the Great Fire of London, plus 10 surprising facts," History Extra. https: //www.historyextra.com/period/stuart/great-fire-london-facts-guide/.
3   Donna Herwick Rice, *You Are There! London 1666*, Teacher Created Materials, 2017.

Chapter 16

1   Tai Hwan-Ching et al., "Chemical distinctions between Stradivari's maple and modern tone-wood," *Chemistry,* December 19, 2016.
2   Steph Yin, "The Brilliance of a Stradivari Violin Might Rest Within Its Wood," *New York Times*, December 20, 2016.

Chapter 17

1   Stephanie Pain, "1709: The year that Europe froze," *New Scientist*, February 4, 2009.
2   Frank Ried Diffenderffer, *The German exodus to England in 1709* (Pennsylvania German Society, 1897).
3   Derek Wilson, *Calamities and Catastrophes: The Ten Absolutely Worst Years in History* (Short Books, 2011).

Chapter 18

1   Fernand Braudel, *A History of Civilizations* (Penguin, 1995).
2   Boris Egorov, "5 facts about the war that turned Russia into a great power," *Russia Beyond*, August 17, 2018.
3   Henry Kissinger, *World Order* (Penguin, 2015).

Chapter 19

1   Joseph J. Ellis, *Revolutionary Summer* (New York: Vintage Books, 2013).
2   Ibid.

Chapter 20

1   Oscar Browning, *Despatches from Paris 1784–1790* (London: Offices of the Society, 1910).
2   Lilian Knowles, "New Light on the Economic Causes of the French Revolution," *Economic Journal*, March 1919.

3   Ibid.

Chapter 21

1   Jesse Greenspan, "Why Napoleon's Invasion of Russia Was the Beginning of the End," History.com, https://www.history.com/news/napoleons-disastrous-invasion-of-russia.

Chapter 22

1   J. A. MacDonnell, *Sketches Illustrating the Early Settlement and History of Glengarry in Canada* (Montreal: W. M. Foster, Brown & Co, 1893).

Chapter 23

1   Alexander McAdie, *War Weather Vignettes* (New York: MacMillian, 1925).

Chapter 24

1   Bernice de Jong Boers, "Mount Tambora in 1815: A Volcanic Eruption in Indonesia and Its Aftermath," Indonesia, October 1995; Charles Daubeny, *A description of active and extinct volcanos, of earthquakes, and of thermal springs : with remarks on the causes of these phænomena, the character of their respective products, and their influence on the past and present condition of the globe* (London: Richard & John E. Taylor, 1848).

2   Ibid.

3   Charles Townsend, "A Year Without a Summer," *Paris Review*, October 25, 2016; David Bressan, "April 10, 1815: The Eruption that Shook the World," *Scientific American*, April 10, 2012.

4   Paul Simons, "Lake Geneva storms inspired Frankenstein," *The Times* (London), August 12, 2020.

5   Michael Ruane, "Even after 200 years, Mary Shelley's famous 'Frankenstein' still lives on," *Daily Herald*, August 24, 2016.

6   Lord Byron, "Darkness," https://www.poetryfoundation.org/poems/43825/darkness-56d222aeeee1b.

7   Curtis Ashton, "Early Struggles of the Smith Family," The Church of Jesus Christ of Latter Day Saints, https://history.churchofjesuschrist.org/content/historic-sites-palmyra-vermont-new-york?lang=eng.

8   Andrew Browning, *The Panic of 1819* (University of Missouri Press, 2019).

9   Murray N. Rothbard, *The Panic Of 1819 Reactions And Policies* (Auburn, AL: Ludwig von Mises Institute, 2007).

10 This quotation comes from the words of Daniel Webster and those of John Marshall in the Supreme Court case, *McCulloch v. Maryland*. Webster, in arguing the case, said: "An unlimited power to tax involves, necessarily, a power to destroy," 17 U.S. 327 (1819).

     In his decision, Chief Justice Marshall said: "That the power of taxing it [the bank] by the States may be exercised so as to destroy it, is too obvious to be denied" (p. 427), and "That the power to tax involves the power to destroy . . . [is] not to be denied" (p. 431).

11 Trail of Tears, History.com, https://www.history.com/topics/native-american-history/trail-of-tears.

Chapter 25

1   Walt Whitman, "News from Washington," *Walt Whitman Quarterly Review* 2 (Winter 1984).
2   Kenneth Noe, "The Drought that Changed the War," *New York Times*, October 12, 2012.
3   David Ludlum, *The Weather Factor*, American Meteorological Society, 1984.
4   "Weather in War," *The Atlantic*, May 1862.
5   T. Harry Williams, *Lincoln and His Generals* (Vintage, 2011).
6   Denise Gess and William Lutz, *Firestorm at Peshtigo: A Town, Its People, and the Deadliest Fire in American History* (Holt Paperbacks, 2003).

Chapter 26

1   Karen Abbott, "What (or Who) Caused the Great Chicago Fire?" *Smithsonian*, October 4, 2012.
2   Chicago Clergyman, *The great fires in Chicago and the West; history and incidents, losses and sufferings, benevolence of the natives, etc.* (University of Toronto, 1871).
3   The Great Chicago Fire of 1871: https://www.architecture.org/learn/resources/architecture-dictionary/entry/the-great-chicago-fire-of-1871/.

Chapter 27

1   Chuck Lyons, "1874: The Year of the Locust," History.net, February 5, 2012.
2   A. W. Johnson and Isabella Johnson to Robert S. Wickizer. March 24, 1875. Kansas Historical Society, Topeka, Kansas. Kansas Memory. Web. June 29, 2010.
3   Solomon D. S. D. Butcher, *Butcher's pioneer history of Custer County : and short sketches of early days in Nebraska* (Broken Bow, NE: Merchant's Publishing Co, 1901).
4   Jeffrey A. Lockwood, *Locust,* (Basic Books, 2005).
5   Charles Riley et al., *Second Report of the United States Entomological Commission for the years 1878 and 1879 relating to the Rocky Mountain Locust, and the Western Cricket* (Washington, DC: Government Printing Office, 1880).
6   Blake Layton, "Bug's Eye View," *American Bird Locust* 6, no. 15 (June 17, 2020).
7   Caroline Fraser, "Laura Ingalls Wilder and One of The Greatest Natural Disasters in American History," *Literary Hub*, December 5, 2017.
8   Lockwood, *Locust.*

Chapter 28

1   Mia Fineman, "Existential Superstar Another look at Edvard Munch's The Scream," *Slate*, November 22, 2005.

Chapter 29

1   Andrew Glass, "Great Blizzard strikes New York City, March 12, 1888," *Politico*, March 12, 2018.
2   Alyssa Ford, "125 years ago, deadly 'Children's Blizzard' blasted Minnesota," *Minnesota Post*, January 11, 2013.

Chapter 30

1 https://quotes.pub/q/no-sir-dunwoody-snapped-it-cannot-be-no-cyclone-ever-can-mov -209226.
2 Eric Dolin, *Furious Sky* (Liverlight, 2020).

Chapter 31

1 Karen Garloch, "Brazil's claims to be 'First in Flight' strike Tar Heels as 'hot air,'" *Charlotte Observer*, August 7, 2016.
2 Ibid.

Chapter 32

1 Andrew Wilson, "Why the Titanic Still Fascinates Us," *Smithsonian*, March 2012.
2 Stephen D. Cox, *The Titanic Story: Hard Choices, Dangerous Decisions* (Open Court, 1999).
3 "Letter found on Titanic victim's drowned body is sold at auction," *Columbus Dispatch*, October 22, 2017.
4 Randy Dotinga, "What sank the Titanic?" *Christian Science Monitor*, April 13, 2012.
5 "Did the Titanic Sink Because of an Optical Illusion?" *Smithsonian*, March 1, 2012.
6 "Titanic sank due to 'mirage' caused by freak weather," *Telegraph*, March 21, 2012.

Chapter 33

1 Centers for Disease Control and Prevention, "History of 1918 Flu Pandemic," https://www .cdc.gov/flu/pandemic-resources/1918-commemoration/1918-pandemic-history.htm.

Chapter 34

1 Lynn Neary, "'Grapes Of Wrath' And The Politics of Book Burning," *NPR*, September 30, 2008.

Chapter 35

1 Kyle Almond, "What makes an image unforgettable?" *CNN*, September 4, 2013.
2 Claire Benson, "The legacy of the Hindenburg disaster," *Chemistry World*, May 5, 2017, https://www.chemistryworld.com/news/the-legacy-of-the-hindenburg-disaster/3007067. article.

Chapter 36

1 Harold Winters, *Battling the Elements: Weather and Terrain in the Conduct of War* (Johns Hopkins University Press, 2001).
2 Ibid.
3 Ibid.
4 Hugh Sebag-Montefore, "Dunkirk's darkest day: when the evacuation came close to disaster," *The Guardian*, July 16, 2017.
5 "The Beaches of Dunkirk," *The Atlantic*, August 1940.
6 Ian Kershaw, "Disaster at Dunkirk: A Nightmare Fantasy," *Lampham's Quarterly*, https: //www.laphamsquarterly.org/about-money/disaster-dunkirk-nightmare-fantasy,
7 Ibid.

Chapter 39

1   Richard Lloyd Parry, "City remembers day it escaped the bomb," *The Independent,* August 8, 1995.
2   Thomas B Allan and Norman Polmar, "The Radio Broadcast That Ended World War II," *The Atlantic*, August 7, 2015.
3   Al Kaff, "Nagasaki Quietly Rebuilding Bombed City with Fanfare Given to Sister Hiroshima," *Cincinnati Enquirer,* October 9, 1955.

Chapter 40

1   Charles Dickens, *Bleak House* (London: Bradbury and Evans, 1853).
2   E. F. Benson, *Image in the Sand* (J. B. Lippincott, 1905).
3   Christine Corton, *London Fog: The Biography* (Belknap Press, 2015).
4   Paul Brown, "Monet's obsession with London fog," *The Guardian*, February 19, 2017.
5   *Texas State Journal of Medicine*, November 1905.

Chapter 41

1   "Politics Called Kennedy to Dallas and His Death," *Daily News*, September 28, 1964.
2   Eleanor Clift, "Would It Have Saved JFK? Jim Lehrer on the Mystery of the Bubble Top," *Daily Beast*, July 11, 2017.
3   Ibid.
4   Ibid.
5   Ibid.

Chapter 42

1   Solomon M. Hsiang , Marshall Burke, and Edward Miguel, "Quantifying the influence of climate on human conflict," *Science* 341, no. 6151 (September 2013) doi: 10.1126/science .1235367. Epub 2013 Aug 1. PMID: 24031020.
2   Ellen Cohn and James Rotton, "Assault as a function of time and temperature: A moderator-variable time-series analysis," *Journal of Personality and Social Psychology* 72, no. 6 (1997): 1322–1334, https://doi.org/10.1037/0022–3514.72.6.1322.
3   Ujala Sehgal, "How Severe is the Link Between Hot Weather and Violence?," *The Atlantic*, July 23, 2011.
4   Tony Huiquan Zhang, "Weather Effects on Social Movements," *Weather, Climate and Society*, July 2016.
5   *Detroit Free Press*, May 4, 1948.

Chapter 43

1   Sewell Chan, "Remembering a Snowstorm That Paralyzed the City," *New York Times*, February 10, 2009.
2   "City Botches Plowing of School Parking Lots," *Chicago Tribune*, January 18, 1979.
3   F. Richard Ciccone, "Historic Upset in Big Turnout," *Chicago Tribune*, February 28, 1979.
4   Wally Northway, "Winter Woes," *Mississippi Business Journal*, February 7, 2014.
5   Jelani Cobb, "How Snowfall Stopped a Rising Political Star," *New Yorker*, February 4, 2014, https://www.newyorker.com/news/news-desk/how-snowfall-stopped-a-rising-political-star.

ENDNOTES

Chapter 44

1 *Bulletin of the American Meteorological Society* 52, no. 6 (June 1971).

Chapter 45

1 Suzanne Maloney, *The Iranian Revolution at 40* (Brookings Institution Press, 2020).

Chapter 46

1 Mike Wall, "Challenger Disaster 30 Years Ago Shocked the World, Changed NASA," *Yahoo News*, January 28, 2016.
2 "Lethal Flash Ends Historic Mission," *Miami Herald*, January 29, 1986.

Conclusion

1 Nate Silver, "The Weatherman is Not a Moron," *New York Times*, September 7, 2012.

Appendix

1 Donald Johnson, *Lucy: The Beginnings of Human Kind* (Simon & Schuster, 1981).

Index

INDEX

Acknowledgments

I would like to thank Laura Lee, my contributor, and Mike Steinberg for their help with the writing and researching of this book. Also thanks to my brother, Evan Myers, and my son-in-law Peter Johnson for their candid comments and improvements offered on many sections. My appreciation to my assistant, Gabrielle Robinson, for her help in bringing this project to completion.

I would like to thank my Penn State professors, especially Dr. Al Blackadar and Dr. Charles Hosler, who mentored and guided me through my formative years at Penn State University and to my friend John Cahir who always had creative ideas.

Also, my gratitude to my beloved wife, Mariya, who is always very supportive, and to my eight children for also being a very important part of my life.

NOTES

NOTES

NOTES

NOTES

NOTES